Poverty, Battered Women, and Work in U.S. Public Policy

INTERPERSONAL*VIOLENCE*

SERIES EDITORS

Claire Renzetti, Ph.D.
Jeffrey L. Edleson, Ph.D.

Parenting by Men Who Batter: New Directions for Assessment and Intervention
Edited by Jeffrey L. Edleson and Oliver J. Williams

Coercive Control: How Men Entrap Women in Personal Life
Evan Stark

Childhood Victimization: Violence, Crime, and Abuse in the Lives of Young People
David Finkelhor

Restorative Justice and Violence Against Women
Edited by James Ptacek

Familicidal Hearts: The Emotional Styles of 211 Killers
Neil Websdale

Violence in Context: Current Evidence on Risk, Protection, and Prevention
Edited by Todd I. Herrenkohl, Eugene Aisenberg,
James Herbert Williams, and Jeffrey M. Jenson

Child Victims and Restorative Justice: A Needs-Rights Model
Tali Gal

Poverty, Battered Women, and Work in U.S. Public Policy
Lisa D. Brush

Poverty, Battered Women, and Work in U.S. Public Policy

LISA D. BRUSH

OXFORD
UNIVERSITY PRESS

Published in the United States of America by Oxford University Press, Inc.,
198 Madison Avenue, New York, NY, 10016
United States of America

Oxford University Press, Inc. publishes works that further Oxford University's objective
of excellence in research, scholarship, and education

Oxford is a registered trade mark of Oxford University Press in the UK and in certain other countries

Library of Congress Cataloging-in-Publication Data

Brush, Lisa Diane.
    Poverty, battered women, and work in U.S. public policy / Lisa D. Brush.
        p. cm. — (Interpersonal violence)
    Includes bibliographical references and index.
    ISBN 978-0-19-539850-2 (hardcover : alk. paper)
    1. Abused women—United States. 2. Man-woman relationships—United States.
3. Welfare recipients—Employment—United States. I. Title.
    HV6626.2.B78 2011
    362.82'925610973—dc22   2011012597

3 5 7 9 10 8 6 4 2

Typeset in Arno Pro Regular
Printed on acid-free paper
Printed in the United States of America

ACKNOWLEDGMENTS

Support for this project came from the usual suspects as well as some unlikely sources. The interviews and community literacy project were supported by Grant No. 2000-WT-VX-0009 awarded by the National Institute of Justice, Office of Justice Programs, U.S. Department of Justice. Points of view in this book are those of the author and do not necessarily represent the official position or policies of the U.S. Department of Justice. The Pennsylvania Department of Public Welfare's Bureau of Program Evaluation authorized site access and release of findings. All research projects included in this book received expedited review and approval from the University of Pittsburgh Institutional Review Board (IRB #001097 and #0806004).

This project would have been impossible without the enthusiastic support of Bob Reynolds of the Pennsylvania Department of Public Welfare and Paula Hustwit of RTC. Danielle Ficco and Lisa H. Ruchti served as research assistants on the interview project. Jason Seiler elegantly programmed data collection and data management on the interview project. Lorraine Higgins organized and implemented the community literacy project and recruited and trained the volunteer writing mentors who worked with the community literacy project participants. Her skills, labor, and insights made possible both the community literacy project and what has become Chapter 5 of this book. Others who helped make the community literacy project happen include Joyce Baskins and Wayne Peck of the Community House, who provided facilities, and Jean Sieper, Chris Weber, and Mike Schneider, who mentored the writers. Eileen Kopchik performed awesome feats of programming and data matching with the administrative data from the Department of Public Welfare, the Bureau of Unemployment Compensation and Benefits Administration, and the Allegheny County Prothonotary (whose office records petitions for protective orders), without which the analysis in the last section of Chapter 4 would never have happened. The intrepid Melanie Hughes proved the perfect collaborator in the analyses of the administrative data, and her work on this project was indispensable, especially to the data analysis in Chapter 4 and the revision of the Methodological Appendix. Sarah Deren copyedited the entire manuscript on a very tight schedule and did her best to eliminate my most egregious abuses of standard written English. I was unbelievably happy to discover she had this valuable skill and am grateful she had the time to help me. I wish her luck with the new Great Dane puppy. Thanks to all of them.

The main sites of intellectual production for this manuscript were my office in the building formerly known as Forbes Quad at the University of Pittsburgh, the newly renovated East Liberty and Squirrel Hill branches of the Carnegie Public Library of Pittsburgh, Jitters Café & Ice Cream and the Oh Yeah! Café and Ice Cream in Shadyside, Commonplace Coffee Company in Squirrel Hill, Coffee Tree Roasters in Squirrel Hill and Shadyside, Jess's Shadyside Starbuck's (especially when she opened at 5:30 a.m. for the Early Riser Writing Sessions), Crazy Mocha Coffee Company's various locations, the patios of the 61C Café and Té Café in Squirrel Hill (weather permitting), and Enrico's Tazza D'Oro in beautiful Highland Park. I spent three precious days in Versailles during October 2010 with my friends Dahlia Mani and Gangadhar Sulkunte (and my favorite little dude, Neel Mani-Sulkunte), working on revisions, preparing a conference presentation, and diligently practicing my horn. These options complemented the hours I spent in my lonely writer's garret (much warmer since my father generously helped me to insulate my attic crawlspace!) and brought important sociability to my labor. Thank you to all of the *baristas* who take such good care of the writers, scholars, and rabble-rousers of the modern world. I overheard someone somewhere say that coffee shops are the middle-class person's methadone clinic. True.

Thanks for comments and inspiration to Kathleen Blee, Amy Elman, Chloé Hogg, Myra Marx Ferree, Jody Raphael, Claire Renzetti, Pat Ulbrich, Sylvia Walby, and Kathrin Zippel. Lynne Haney organized a fabulous thematic session at the 2010 American Sociological Association meetings in Atlanta, where I presented what became key parts of the introduction and conclusion of the revised manuscript, and I thank Lynne, the other panel participants (especially Ellen Reese), and the audience members for their stimulating questions and exciting research on gender and citizenship. Thanks also to Kathrin, who arranged an invitation for a well-timed speaking engagement in Paris, and to my comrades at the Equality Now! conference sponsored by the Foundation for European Progressive Studies. My conversations with Sonya Michel and Kim Gandy were especially helpful when I was in the final throes of drawing conclusions, and they encouraged me enormously (and shared a hair-raising cab ride to Charles de Gaulle airport). Strong norms of constructive critique and reciprocity are the lifeblood of the feminist intellectual community, and my mentors (especially Myra and Amy) and *compañeras* embody these norms.

My dear buds from my virtual writing group (Kirsten Christensen, Katie Hogan, Linh Hua, Anita McChesney, Sara "Sally" Poor, and Maggie Rehm) offered sociability and opportunities for reflection for which I am deeply grateful. Special thanks to Katie, who introduced me to two practices that transformed my life: Boice's Brief Daily Sessions writing method and Iyengar yoga. Let's hear it for the writer's journey toward comfort and fluency, and for the yogi's cultivating stability, vitality, clarity, wisdom, and bliss!

I am delighted to be able to acknowledge Judy Postmus (Rutgers), Fran Danis (UT Arlington), and an anonymous reviewer for Oxford University Press, who provided encouraging, critical comments on the book proposal. They pushed me to broaden and strengthen my argument and renewed my commitment to figuring out what I have to say and saying it clearly to the widest possible audience. I also humbly acknowledge the thorough, constructive reviews of the manuscript from three anonymous scholars whose sharp minds, hard work, and generosity exemplify the peer review process. Thank you, whoever you are. Many thanks also to Series Editors Claire Renzetti and Jeff Edelson, and to Senior Editor Maura Roessner (ably assisted by the speedy and steady Nicholas Liu—good luck with the flute lessons, dude!). My success in this as in several concurrent endeavors (including guest editing a special issue of the journal she so ably edits, *Violence Against Women*) is due in no small part to Claire's benevolence, practical advice, and spirited engagement with this work. Claire is my kind of feminist. She trains in kick-boxing. She drinks her bourbon neat. She collects and wears *über*-cool eyeglasses leashes. She laughs at my jokes. Who could ask for anything more?!

Mohammed Bamyeh and Randy Halle, Malke and Ivan Frank, Jessica Garrity, David Goldstein and the whole Tikkun Chant Circle (who keep reminding me that my container is bigger than I think), Amelia Haviland (statistician, policy analyst, and friend extraordinaire), Adam and Alex (and Falco and Tia, their goofy greyhounds), Jamie Phillips, Maggie Rehm (and Sadie the Rag Dog), Lyle Seaman (and Junior Seamen Becca and Caleb), and fabulous singer-songwriters Brad Yoder and Eve Goodman offered nurturing friendship, intellectual stimulation, and opportunities to get out and have a little fun every once in a while. Erika Luckett, Awesome Priestess of At/One/Ment, once again came through with tunes and lyrics that started my day by getting me to Pay Attention in the morning and sent me off to dreamland happily at night. Special thanks to Amelia and Amy for sponsoring the erratically scheduled but unfailingly nourishing Lesbian Pasta Nites, and for the fabulous Superbowl parties featuring the unforgettable vision of that statue of the BVM draped in a Terrible Towel.

I am also happy to thank the people who enriched my life and helped me carry on during the long and sometimes arduous process of researching and writing this book: Dr. Robin S. Barack—may she live long and prosper; Laura Carter, David Lesondak, Mary Pat Mengato, and Stephanie Ulmer, extraordinary body/energy workers; my fellow congregants at Dor Hadash, feminist friends at the Jewish Women's Center, women in solidarity with the Women of the Wall, and the High Holy Day Havurah; Scott Bohannon, my patient and gifted horn instructor, and Zachary Koopmans, with a big horn case to fill; Maestro Federico Garcia of the East Liberty Community Engagement Orchestra, who literally and figuratively orchestrated my learning to play with others; my joyful full-service *rebbe*, Rabbi Yaakov Rosenstein of Torah One-on-One; and my teachers (Christina, Diane, Justin, Sara, Stephanie, and Taya) and fellow *sādhaka*s at Yoga on Centre, especially Maureen and Rebecca, who made weekend morning postyoga grocery shopping so easy and fun; Margie, who gave me rides home after class and only once ran out of gas; Molly Youngling, who laughed along with me and reminded me that revising a book manuscript could be an enjoyable creative process;

and Linda Metropolous, who makes me think growing up might not be so bad after all.

The Faculty of Arts and Sciences at the University of Pittsburgh supported a semester of sabbatical leave during which I prepared the proposal for this manuscript and furnished me with those means of intellectual production that were outside of my own head. My new colleague, Waverly Duck, shared some amazingly productive intellectual/political conversations in his Volvo, for which I am humbly grateful. John Markoff and Kathleen Blee, my department chairs while I worked on this manuscript, commented on early versions of several chapters, arranged my leave, never failed to deliver encouraging words, and enrolled me in the Federal Sabbatical Protection Program: *You don't see me. You don't know me. I'm not here.*

Thanks also to Sage Publications for permission to publish the material in Chapters 2 and 4 and the Methodological Appendix that appeared in different form in the journals *Violence Against Women* and *Gender & Society*.

A quick guide to style, usage, and notation: Texts in *italics* signal emphasis, introduce a concept, are in a language other than English (as in *sādhaka*s), or mark the title of a book (Stark's *Coercive Control*). Double quotation marks ("...") enclose text directly quoted from another text or speaker. Materials in quotation marks include responses to open-ended questions from the interviews and field notes recorded during and immediately after interview and community literacy project sessions. Edits for clarity or to preserve anonymity within quoted material are in [square brackets]. Single quotation marks ('...') distinguish the enclosed text as everyday speech or technical terms in expert discourse.

Finally, for all of the work parties and date nights, for generating both heat and light, for helping me do my best work, for reading aloud, for sharing everything from Mahler's Second Symphony to Shania Twain, for forgiveness and daring, for appreciating both brains and brawn, and so much more: Loving thanks to Dr. Chloé Hogg. You made this a very special time.

Lisa D. Brush

Pittsburgh, PA

November 1, 2010

(Happy 10th Birthday, Jack!!)

CONTENTS

Poverty, Battered Women, and

Work in U.S. Public Policy

Introduction

In the summer of 2001, Alice[1] was 35, the divorced mother of two teenagers. Although employed off and on throughout her adult life and in spite of having worked 36 weeks of the previous year, she depended on public assistance to make ends meet and especially to provide health benefits to help her manage her diabetes.

Alice had outlasted relationships with two abusive men. The father of her older child was so determined to register his outrage over having to provide child support that he showed up one time while she was at work and, as Alice put it, "made an idiot out of himself while I cried." She felt that he was "jealous and scared that I'd find someone else" at work, which she deduced from his snide comments while she prepared for work. He implied that she was preparing to meet other men, when she was just getting ready to go to work by putting on "different makeup or getting dressed up, [wearing a] different pair of shoes." Of the father of her younger child, Alice noted: "When I was at home, I was raising *his* daughter, and he could control me. But [when I was working] out in the real world, he got even more possessive. He would leave his job to check up on me." He used to show up almost daily and would "call 20 times in an hour" when Alice was at work. He told her that "if it weren't for me, nobody else would want you." In what Alice considered the most severe incident of physical abuse that she had experienced, which occurred about four years before the interview, the father of her younger child (by whom she was at that point again pregnant) "beat me so bad I lost the pregnancy. Just pounded on me. I think he wanted to kill me." She said he was "possessive, abusive, and didn't want me to work."

Alice self-identified as White and had been on welfare twice for a total of 31 months. She was one of 40 Allegheny County women enrolled in May–June 2001 in a job search or "work-first" program. Enrollment in this program was part of maintaining their eligibility for welfare after Congress rescinded federal entitlements to income support for poor mothers and their children with the Personal Responsibility Act (PRA) of 1996.[2] The summer of 2001 was an opportune time to listen to Alice and the other members of her cohort[3] in order to learn about their experiences with relationships, welfare, and work in the context of dramatic shifts in the rules and rhetoric, practices, and policies of income support for poor mothers and their children. Political firefights about whether and how to abolish welfare had shifted into what turned out to be a heated four-year debate over reauthorizing the PRA. Under President George W. Bush, reauthorization ultimately incorporated stricter work requirements and an even greater emphasis on marriage, abstinence, and other elements of what political scientist Anna Marie Smith calls the "sexual regulation" of poor women.[4] By the middle of 2001, the time limits, work requirements, paternity establishment and child support enforcement provisions, and other elements of the repeal of entitlements set in place in early 1997 had become routine. The initial plunge in the number of welfare enrollees had ended, partly due to the weakening of the economy; the country was slipping into a recession after the relatively high-growth period of the 1990s. Nationwide, welfare caseloads had declined from 5 million families receiving Aid to Families with Dependent Children (AFDC) in 1994 to 4.4 million in 1996, when entitlements were repealed, and then plummeted to 2.1 million in March 2001.[5] Yet welfare caseloads had increased significantly (averaging over 10 percent among the 34 states showing an increase) in two thirds of 49 states and the District of Columbia between March 2000 and March 2001. By the summer of 2001, when I met Alice, the steady and steep decline in the welfare rolls was over.[6]

Locally, enrollments had stabilized in the work-first program, where Alice engaged in the work-related activities that maintained her eligibility for cash support. Some program participants were there because 24 months had passed since the time limit "clock" started ticking and work requirements were kicking in. Others were there because welfare office caseworkers were sending even new applicants with very young children to job preparation and job search programs. Through the process known as "diversion," case managers and other low-level bureaucrats charged with determining eligibility for welfare were shifting welfare applicants from public assistance to work programs (or directly into the labor market).[7] Either way, Alice and the other members of her cohort were grappling with the consequences of Bill Clinton's (first as a candidate and then as president) pledge to "end welfare as we know it."[8] Their experiences and voices speak to the specifics of an especially interesting time and place, to the realities of poor women in Allegheny County in the summer of 2001 and the 12 to 18 months that followed, when my research team conducted follow-up interviews. These women's lives also speak to a central question on the minds of advocates, researchers, and administrators alike, the question that motivates this book: How do we understand battering—that is, the physical violence and control men perpetrate on their current and former wives and girlfriends[9]—as a factor in women's poverty, in women's compliance with welfare eligibility requirements, and in women's progress toward safety and solvency through waged work?

Georgia, one of the 33 self-identified Black women enrolled in the program along with Alice and with whom we spoke in the summer of 2001, was also 35 and a mother of two. Both of her children were diagnosed with attention deficit hyperactivity disorder (ADHD). One child had received Social Security disability benefits for a while but had been, as Georgia put it, "cut off" when disability eligibility criteria were also tightened to encourage work rather than welfare, even for mothers caring for children with physical and mental health problems. Georgia had held 10 different jobs as a working adult and had not worked at all in the past year. Three times, for a cumulative total of more than 16 years, Georgia and her children had been on welfare. She, too, was dealing with health problems of her own: Georgia was recovering from open-heart surgery.

Georgia had been involved with what she called "a very abusive man" from whom she had separated by the time of her interview in 2001. He was trained as a boxer; was, as she put it, "involved with drugs"; and was extremely controlling. For example, Georgia said, "He wouldn't let me close a door in the house," even to use the toilet, a tactic that undermined her privacy and dignity and extended her partner's surveillance and control to her bodily functions.[10] Georgia's partner also tried to enforce her domesticity and extend his control over her by interfering with her employment. He was so jealous that he "didn't want me to work or meet people outside the home," Georgia explained. "He would call or come to the job or be there when I got off. He would demand that I come over, would call and threaten the boss when I worked at [a fast food chain]. He stole a VCR from the [discount retailer] where I was working." Her partner's actions had consequences both for him (her employer threatened to have him arrested) and for Georgia (she was fired because of his behavior).

ALICE AND GEORGIA IN CONTEXT

Alice and Georgia were not alone in their experiences of poverty and abuse. Three quarters of the 40 welfare recipients who started in the mandatory work-first program along with Georgia and Alice—all of whom we interviewed[11]—said their former or current husband or boyfriend seemed jealous about the possibility of their meeting someone new at work or job training. Their partners' fears about women's sexual betrayal, their ideas about proper femininity, and their actions to enforce women's domesticity and sexual fidelity joined a long list of reasons why many of these women had trouble using waged work to establish and maintain safety and solvency in their lives. Spotty work histories, low wages, unstable housing, very young children, poor physical and mental health, sole responsibility for housekeeping and childrearing, and low educational attainment were typical of the women we interviewed, as they are for welfare recipients across the United States.[12] The pseudonyms and some basic characteristics of all 40 women are arrayed in Table 1.1.

Table 1.1 provides a bird's-eye view of the women who are at the heart of Chapter 3, all of whom started in the work-first program with Georgia and Alice. For example, the age distribution of women enrolled with Alice and Georgia is *bimodal*. That is, instead of calculating just one average age for these 40 women, it is more revealing to observe that there are two main age groups: women in the 18-to-21 range (relatively new mothers) and women in the 30-to-35 range (Alice and Georgia among them). In fact, almost two thirds of the women enrolled in this program were older than 30 in the summer of 2001. The relatively high average age suggests that a significant proportion of the caseload is longer-term welfare recipients, which is not surprising given the general decline in welfare caseloads since the 1996 reforms. That is, those who remain on welfare at this point, and especially those who, like the women in the study, recently entered a work-first program, are either relatively new mothers or older women who face significant barriers to employment.[13] Table 1.1 also provides some context for

Table 1.1 INTERVIEW PARTICIPANTS (N = 40)

	Race-ethnicity	Marital status at interview	Age <20 at first birth	Age at interview (years)	Weeks worked past year	Hourly wage @ initial interview	Hourly wage @ last interview	Abused at work	Ever filed for PFA*
Alice	White	Divorced	Yes	35	36	$7.25	$6.25	Yes	Yes
Angela	Black	Never married	No	34	0	$7.25	$7.50	No	No
Barbara	Black	Never married	Yes	39	44	$9.50	$10.00	Yes	Yes
Brenda	Black	Never married	Yes	19	20	$6.25	—	No	No
Cecilia	Black	Never married	No	32	0	$0	$7.00	No	No
Clarice	Black	Divorced	No	40	12	$5.15	$9.00	No	No
Dee	Black	Never married	Yes	19	8	$5.15	$5.45	No	No
Donna	White	Never married	Yes	22	24	$6.50	—	Yes	No
Edna	Black	Never married	Yes	22	40	$6.00	$0	Yes	Yes
Evelyn	Black	Never married	Yes	21	8	$7.00	$5.15	No	No
Frankie	Black	Never married	No	42	0	$5.15	$0	No	No
Georgia	Black	Separated	No	35	0	$6.50	$9.00	Yes	Yes
Gina	Black	Never married	Yes	30	16	$10.00	—	Yes	No
Harriet	Black	Never married	No	30	0	$5.40	$5.15	Yes	Yes
Hera	Black	Never married	Yes	30	16	$8.20	—	No	Yes

India	Black	Never married	No	21	10	$9.00	$8.00	No	No
Irene	Black	Never married	Yes	19	36	$5.35	$8.50	No	No
Janice	Black	Never married	Yes	30	36	$8.00	$9.00	No	No
Josie	Black	Never married	Yes	45	40	$7.00	$6.00	No	No
Karen	White	Never married	Yes	18	36	$5.15	$0	No	No
Keshauna	Black	Never married	No	22	0	$0	$0	No	No
Kiesha	Black	Never married	Yes	28	52	$8.00	$8.59	No	No
Larnice	Black	Never married	No	22	4	$9.00	—	Yes	Yes
Lashauna	Black	Never married	Yes	21	8	$6.10	$7.25	No	Yes
Latoya	Black	Never married	No	33	48	$8.25	—	No	No
Marketta	Black	Never married	Yes	37	0	$7.25	—	No	No
Mary	White	Divorced	Yes	41	43	$7.50	$8.25	No	No
Mattie	Black	Never married	Yes	19	14	$6.50	$6.00	No	No
Nancy	White	Divorced	Yes	43	24	$8.65	—	No	Yes
Noa	Black	Never married	Yes	21	20	$6.00	$7.00	No	No
Odelle	Black	Divorced	Yes	35	26	$13.00	$10.50	No	No
Pat	Black	Never married	Yes	20	24	$5.15	$5.15	Yes	Yes
Philippa	Black	Never married	No	29	16	$10.25	—	No	No
Reena	Black	Divorced	No	37	36	$11.60	$6.25	Yes	Yes

(continued)

Table 1.1 INTERVIEW PARTICIPANTS (N = 40) (CONTINUED)

	Race-ethnicity	Marital status at interview	Age <20 at first birth	Age at interview (years)	Weeks worked past year	Hourly wage @ initial interview	Hourly wage @ last interview	Abused at work	Ever filed for PFA*
Ruth	Black	Never married	No	36	24	$10.51	$10.51	No	No
Sally	White/Native American	Separated	No	44	0	$6.00	$6.00	No	Yes
Serena	Black	Divorced	Yes	39	0	$9.13	$12.06	No	No
Tonya	Black/Irish/Indian	Divorced	Yes	41	24	$6.50	$8.00	No	No
Tyronda	Black	Separated	No	33	20	$7.50	$5.15	No	Yes
Virginia	Black	Separated	No	43	35	$6.00	$0	Yes	Yes

*In Allegheny County, the courts call a civil restraining order against an abusive partner an order of Protection From Abuse (PFA).

understanding the obstacles to work that Alice, Georgia, and the other women enrolled in this work-first program face.

Limited work histories: At the time of the retrospective interviews, three quarters of the women enrolled in this mandatory work-first program had worked at least one week during the previous calendar year. However, in addition to the one in five who did not work at all during the previous year, one in four worked fewer than four months of the year. Thus, a significant proportion of these work-first program participants have limited work histories.

Limited occupations: Most work-first enrollees had been employed most recently doing "women's work" in the service sector. That is, they worked in retail sales, clerical work, data entry, food preparation and service, nonprofessional health service, cleaning, or personal services.

Low pay: Virtually all of the women we interviewed earned the low wages typically associated with "women's work." In the retrospective interviews, the mean hourly wage was $7.55 for the most recent job. Although significantly above the minimum wage, the value of this level of earnings was below the "living wage" standard being debated at the time in Allegheny County. These earnings are unlikely to lift single mothers above the poverty line or enable them to leave either welfare or abusive intimates, especially if they are unable to work full time.

Unstable employment: Employment for Alice, Georgia, and many of the women we interviewed has been highly unstable. At the time of the retrospective interviews, they averaged four jobs since age 16, and more than one third had held six or seven jobs since they turned 16 (a large number both for those who had not been in the labor force long because they are young mothers and for those who had only entered the labor force relatively recently). The rate at which the regional economy generates job openings in largely low-wage occupations with little upward mobility outstrips the rate at which it generates jobs in higher-paid, full-time, stable occupations with direct connections to internal labor markets or job ladders. As a result, most welfare recipients cycle off and on welfare and in and out of work and remain poor either way, subject to the "churn" at the bottom of the labor market.

Household composition and support: Three quarters of the women we interviewed along with Alice and Georgia live alone with their children. Women who live alone cannot depend even theoretically on a coresident adult for consistent help with housekeeping and childcare responsibilities. The remaining women live with one or two other adults, most frequently a grown child, an intimate partner, or their own mother.

Relationships: Two thirds of the women enrolled with Georgia and Alice had never been married.[14] None of the remaining third were legally married or involved in a common-law relationship; all were divorced or separated. Women reported a variety of reasons why their relationships ended. The reasons for the breakups (including breakups with the fathers of their children as well as other significant relationships) sometimes included violence and control. The single most common reason was the partner's infidelity, which was the reason for breakup in nearly one in three instances.[15]

Lack of child support and paternal responsibility: Over half of the 37 women no longer with the father of their first child received no cash or gifts for their children from the children's fathers. Twenty-eight of the 40 mothers received no formal child support payments. The majority of fathers who do not pay child support are unemployed, incarcerated, or missing altogether. Nearly one fourth of respondents who gave a reason for not having formal child support said they had no support order. Forty-one percent of the women reported that the child support order was not enforced. *One program participant said explicitly that she was trying to avoid contact with an abusive former intimate.*

Teen childbearing: Six in 10 of the current respondents reported becoming mothers for the first time when they were teenagers, that is, by age 20. The average age at first birth in this group was 19 years old. Half were between 16 and 19, and only four were very young (15 or younger). About a third postponed their first birth until they were 21 or older.

Young children: Twenty-three percent of the women had an infant younger than 1 year old at the time of the retrospective interview. Nearly two thirds had either an infant or a preschool-age child at home. A sizable minority (43 percent) have children by more than one man. Of those, two thirds (65 percent) were teenagers when they gave birth to their first child. The relatively high rates of recent job experience in this study are even more remarkable given the large proportion of respondents who have preschool-age children.

Table 1.1 also shows that 35 percent of the women in the program with Georgia and Alice reported having filed a civil order of protection against their partner in at least one relationship. Four of the 20 women who were in relationships at the time of the retrospective interviews had filed a restraining order in the course of that current relationship. All told, *13 percent of the women enrolled in work-first programs at this site in May–June 2001 were currently in relationships with men against whom they had at one point or another filed restraining orders.*[16]

Understanding the lives and specifically the work histories of Alice, Georgia, and other welfare recipients is complicated because many of the factors that contribute to poverty and constitute hurdles in a woman's transition from welfare to work are also associated with abuse. There are complex feedback loops and convoluted cause–effect patterns between abuse and the factors that often lead women to resort to welfare. Abuse is associated with early childbearing, *and* early childbearing can make women vulnerable to both poverty and abuse. Truncated education, limited work, low wages, and the resulting economic dependency contribute to abuse, *and* (as I show in this book) abusers often interrupt women's learning, earning, and complying with the work requirements instituted by Congress in the 1996 legislation. Women's gendered caring responsibilities—for themselves, their households, and dependent others—make them vulnerable to poverty and abuse, *and* abusers make women's conformity to gendered notions of feminine domesticity and dependency the central terrain in their coercive campaigns for control. Drug addiction and alcohol dependence can aggravate abuse and poverty, *and* some women turn to street drugs, prescription drugs, and alcohol to help them cope with the pain of abuse and injuries.[17]

Moreover, the 33 Black women in the work-first program cohort, such as Georgia, also faced racially specific structural barriers to employment. The racial distribution of welfare recipients and work-first program enrollees—in which Black women are work-first program enrollees far beyond their proportion of the county population—begs explanation. Only 26 percent of county residents are Black. Only 45 percent of the over 133,000 county residents who were eligible for cash and medical assistance from the Department of Public Welfare in May and June of 1998 were Black.[18] The racial imbalance in program enrollment seems to be at least partially explained by the fact that Black women make up about 65 percent of the women heading households in the county and by the racial gap in poverty rates for families headed by women (which is exceptionally wide in the county).[19] In addition, after 1996, "white families left welfare faster than blacks"[20] and urban caseloads, like the one that included Alice and Georgia, increasingly were disproportionately made up of Black women. Black adults and children are vastly overrepresented among those receiving cash assistance in the county; 66 percent of recipients are Black.[21] Pittsburgh residential neighborhoods are racially homogeneous—in this case, either mostly Black or mostly White[22]—and occupations in Allegheny County are profoundly segregated by both sex and race. The Black/White employment and wage gaps in Allegheny County and the city of Pittsburgh are large, and the poverty rate of households headed by Black women—56 percent—is more than twice the poverty rate of households headed by non-Hispanic White women.[23]

Several other factors may also have contributed to the overrepresentation of Black mothers in the cohort of program enrollees. Department of Public Welfare workers who referred enrollees to the program may have consciously or unconsciously harbored prejudices about welfare recipients. For instance, they may have viewed Black women as less domestic and more "work ready" and therefore less likely to benefit from referrals to longer-term training or education programs (had they in fact been available). Racist stereotypes caricaturing Black welfare recipients as sexually promiscuous, addicted to drugs, and lazy may have induced welfare workers to see and treat them as more in need of the moralistic incentives provided by work requirements.[24] Such racist practices by front-line welfare workers could account for some of the overrepresentation of Black women in work-first programs.[25] Finally, Black and White women may have been *referred* to the program at proportionate rates, but White women may have been disproportionately unlikely to *enroll* in the program, perhaps because they perceived alternatives to welfare and its increasingly onerous eligibility requirements, were more easily "diverted" from welfare, or felt less threatened by sanctions for noncompliance.[26]

Thus, to put Alice and Georgia in context, this book moves between individual stories and statistical analyses to examine complicated questions about how poverty, battering, work, and welfare connect. I am especially concerned to describe, explain, and question the ways commentators, advocates, researchers, pundits, and citizens tend to pose *waged work* as the solution to both *battering* and *poverty*. For at least the past 100 years, U.S. experts, reformers, and taxpayers have acted on the assumption that both poverty and battering result exclusively from individual-level factors, such as work ethic and effort, physical and mental health, or personal choices about sexuality, fertility, and education. According to this taken-for-granted understanding, if the state is going to intervene in battering, it should exhort, admonish, and "empower" the victim to stand up for herself in order to stop the abuse or leave.[27] Similarly, if the state is going to intervene in poverty, it should exercise tough love in the service of personal responsibility through benefit cuts, time limits, work requirements, family caps, and other such provisions.[28] Welfare may provide transitional support, but in the long run, the argument goes, public assistance keeps women trapped in poverty and therefore abuse. Moreover, because economic dependence obviously keeps women trapped in abusive relationships, *work* must be the best way to escape the mutually reinforcing traps of poverty and battering. In this view, welfare is a disincentive to employment, marriage, and personal responsibility, and therefore undermines women's safety and solvency.

There are numerous problems with this taken-for-granted account of the causes and cures of poverty and battering; I explore them at length in the next chapter. For now, briefly: If work were the universal solution to the problems of battering and poverty, surely those problems would be solved by now. Research from before and after the restructuring of welfare in the United States in 1996 shows that poor people in general and welfare recipients in particular often have extensive work histories; the problem is less their work ethic or commitment to employment and more the low pay and lack of benefits that plague many jobs in the U.S. economy.[29] Since the eighteenth century, public officials in the industrializing countries of the North Atlantic have increasingly put work ethic and wage discipline at the center of antipoverty policy and practice, without eradicating poverty.[30] Successful antipoverty efforts, such as the clear reduction in poverty rates for the elderly in the United States, have in fact involved redistributive programs of relatively generous, non–means-tested payments through the politically popular programs of Social Security and have not relied exclusively on employment or work ethic.[31]

In addition to structural barriers to full employment, the dearth of jobs that pay a living wage, and other large-scale factors in poverty, people are often poor because they face multiple obstacles or barriers to work.[32] Moreover, above and beyond the shared barriers to getting and keeping living-wage jobs that keep women poor, some women—Georgia and Alice among them—enrolled in this work-first program faced issues related to their abusive current and former boyfriends and husbands. Table 1.1 shows that, as had a dozen of the 40 welfare recipients enrolled with them, Alice and Georgia had filed for a civil restraining order as one strategy to protect themselves and their children from their current or former partners. Fourteen women in addition to Georgia and Alice reported that their current or former boyfriend or husband had sabotaged or tried to prevent their employment.

Finally, as had nine other women in this cohort, Georgia and Alice reported that their partners had harassed, stalked, or even physically assaulted them while they were at work.

For Alice, Georgia, and other welfare recipients enrolled in the work-first program with them, what sociologists and economists call work/family conflict[33]—that is, contradictory expectations, time squeeze, spillover of tasks and feelings from home to work or vice versa, and other tensions between work demands and familial obligations—sometimes took the literal form of their partners' extending invasive surveillance and physical intrusions and violence from the domestic realm of home and family into the parking lots, lobbies, retail aisles, checkout lines, and cubicles where they worked. Their partners subjected them to abuse—in particular, what I call work-related control, harassment, and sabotage[34]—that shaped these women's experiences of both employment and welfare. Some women, like Georgia, were fired because of the actions of their abusive boyfriends or husbands. Others had to ask their employers to change their work phone or pager numbers or had to file incidents with workplace security. Some said that the abuse they experienced at home had nothing to do with their going to work or job training, and some observed that their partners benefited from and therefore supported their labor force participation. But others said that they thought their efforts to finish school or job training, find a job, and earn a living aggravated or even precipitated controlling, coercive, or violent reactions in the fathers of their children.[35]

The interviews we conducted with Georgia, Alice, and the 38 other women enrolled with them in a mandatory work-first program show that abuse and abusers sometimes follow women to work, thus extending what criminologist Evan Stark calls "coercive control"[36] to a new site: the decidedly nondomestic workplace. The administrative data I gathered on women's earnings, welfare status, and filing for civil orders of protection similarly expand what we know and how we think about an individual woman's experiences in the context of broader social problems of poverty and battering and the public debates over how to address them. The experiences and analyses of the current and former welfare recipients who participated in a community literacy project that I ran with Lorraine Higgins help researchers to question the central place of work in both widespread popular and more expert accounts of poverty and battering. All of these sources of evidence show how men's economic control and exploitation of their current and former wives and girlfriends extend to employment and welfare. Moreover, the incidents in these women's lives point to the ways that welfare surveillance reproduces the coercive, controlling dynamics of abuse. The interview, administrative, and literacy project data sources contradict, or at the very least complicate, the taken-for-granted approach to both poverty and welfare that promotes women's employment as the solution to both social problems. They also help to interpret a key finding of cross-sectional research on poverty and abuse: At least in the long run, women with a history of physical violence in their relationships actually work just as much as women who do not report having been battered.

Having introduced Alice, Georgia, and the other women we interviewed; put their experiences with poverty, welfare, work, and abuse in context; and set out the broad outline of my project of using interview excerpts, statistical analyses of administrative data, and materials from a community literacy project to deepen our understanding of the role of work in poverty, battering, and public policy, I turn next to reviewing briefly what researchers know about the connections among poverty, battering, and work, especially in the lives of welfare recipients.

WHAT WE KNOW

The clearest empirical picture of the connections between battering and poverty and the role of work in mitigating poverty and battering emerges from findings on two phenomena: abuse in the lives of welfare recipients and welfare use by battered women. Researchers interested in the causes, prevalence, frequency, severity, and consequences of battering—and whether welfare and employment mitigate or aggravate the ways poverty and abuse trap women—have tracked these two phenomena by studying women on welfare caseloads, in poor neighborhoods, in shelters for the homeless and for battered women, and in the courts where women file for restraining orders. Surveys of welfare caseloads and interviews with clients at welfare-to-work and employment training programs at locations around the country suggest that for a significant number of poor women, welfare does not provide independence from or even leverage against abusive men.[37] In addition, abuse can trap women in poverty as well as in dangerous relationships. Partner-perpetrated physical violence and other abuse can disrupt education and work and prevent women from accumulating the life experiences, social network connections, confidence, and personal resources that are necessary to live a safe, solvent life.

Battering potentially obstructs women's employment, and therefore their efforts to use a transition from welfare to work to escape from poverty, in at least three ways. First, battering creates immediate safety and health crises. Disfiguring or disabling injuries or court appearances to seek a restraining order against an abusive current or former boyfriend or husband, for example, may prevent battered women from attending work or training programs. Advocates have accumulated strikingly similar stories of abuse, such as the following, from studies of women in employment training programs.

- The night before an entrance exam or job interview, men engage their partners in night-long quarrels, leaving the women sleep-deprived and unable to perform well.
- Men promise to provide critical childcare or transportation, only to disappear or become inebriated when needed. Others hide women's clothing and winter coats so they cannot go out.
- Men batter their partners in highly visible places, so that the women become too embarrassed or too injured to expose their black eyes, bruises, and cigarette burn marks to the outside world.[38]

Second, in the intermediate term, batterers sabotage women's aspirations and achievements. Abusive men can easily derail women's progress in education, job training; and consistent labor force participation, prerequisites for family-supporting employment.[39] Abusers may try to get women expelled from job training programs or fired from their jobs by undermining their childcare, threatening or harassing them on-site, or combining low-level or spectacular physical violence, emotional abuse, coercion, and practical obstructions.[40]

Third, the long-term consequences of battering can include debilitating injuries, disrupted education, and cognitive and emotional barriers to learning and education and to training and work performance. Injuries and disruptions can impair women's ability to prepare for, obtain, and maintain family-supporting employment. In particular, some battered women may need time and supportive services to recover from physical injuries and mental health problems that can linger long after the abuse has stopped. Battering and its consequences may make it difficult for currently or formerly battered women to attend to specific job tasks, plan for the future, contain anxiety, interact in high-pressure settings, respond appropriately to criticism, avoid depression, and conform to the professional culture of training programs and employment.[41] When you are being battered, it is hard to be the prompt, friendly, eager-to-serve, ready-for-work employee that supervisors expect in the contemporary competitive job market.

There are no national statistics available on the rates of battering in the population of women on the welfare rolls. However, local surveys of welfare recipients and women in low-income neighborhoods and public housing projects during the period since 1996, when Congress rescinded federal welfare entitlements, have reported a range of prevalence rates for partner-perpetrated physical violence.[42] A study of the Massachusetts statewide welfare caseload estimated that 13 percent reported current or recent physical abuse and estimated the lifetime prevalence of physical abuse in the caseload to be 57 percent. In-person interviews in welfare offices by the same team in Massachusetts found 19 to 26 percent of welfare recipients experienced current or recent physical abuse, and found a 64 to 70 percent lifetime abuse prevalence rate, depending on the instrument used in the interviews.[43] In a study of welfare-to-work program participants in Passaic County, New Jersey, the reported rate of physical abuse in the current relationship was 14 percent and the lifetime prevalence rate was 57 percent.[44] In a study of randomly selected residents in a low-income neighborhood in Chicago, 31 percent reported experiencing physical aggression ever in their lifetime; 19 percent of women reported severe physical abuse in their current relationship.[45] A sample of low-income women in Worcester, Massachusetts, reported severe physical abuse prevalence rates of 32 percent in the current relationship and 58 percent lifetime for housed respondents, and 32 percent in the current relationship and 63 percent lifetime for homeless respondents.[46] A study conducted through Colorado welfare offices reported prevalence rates of 26 percent for the current relationship and 40 percent lifetime.[47] In the Michigan Women's Employment Study (a sample of welfare recipients and low-income women), one in seven respondents reported what the researchers classified as "recent severe domestic violence."[48]

When it comes to moving beyond estimating the prevalence of battering in low-income populations, the connections between poverty and partner-perpetrated abuse—and the roles of welfare and work in helping women to escape from

either—turn out to be complicated. Cash benefits, food stamps, and housing assistance can provide vital resources to women fleeing abusive partners and have
become important sources of financial support for battered women's shelters.[49]
However, in order to avoid sanctions or benefit cuts, some women stay with abusive
men or feel compelled to renew contact with them.[50] In 1996, Congress converted
federal entitlements for income support for poor women and their children into
block grants and instituted performance- and outcomes-based accounting and
funding systems for welfare. The policy shift forced local welfare and other service
organizations and administrators to "privatize"—that is, turn over to nonprofit
organizations or even for-profit companies—many of the work supports for poor
mothers that had been provided, organized, or subsidized by welfare offices since at
least the Family Support Act of 1988.[51] Privatization shifted the burden of arrangements for childcare, transportation, housing, and job training to the market or
family members instead of the welfare state. As a consequence, some women find
themselves relying on men who have abused them or their children in the past for
practical help in meeting work requirements.[52]

Other factors are in play, too. Teen mothers and their children are especially
vulnerable to physical and sexual abuse, often perpetrated by the men (their fathers
and stepfathers, for example) with whom the "lean and mean" and "pro-family"
welfare system requires them to live in order to be eligible for benefits.[53] Women's
conformity to "family values" may put them at risk, as their commitments to domesticity, maternity, and heterosexual relationships can aggravate their financial and
emotional dependence on the fathers of their children.[54] The provisions for
sexual regulation of poor women in the 1996 legislation—the focus on paternity
establishment, child support enforcement, abstinence education, and family caps
on benefits that render babies born to women already receiving welfare ineligible
if their mothers are not married—reinforce women's vulnerability to surveillance
and control by caseworkers, employers, and other bureaucratic authorities as well as
current or former husbands and boyfriends.[55]

In sum, cross-sectional studies—that is, research that looks at associations
between factors at one point in time—of poor women's labor force participation
consistently find that, contrary to the expectation that battering obstructs work, a
history of battering makes no significant difference in women's average employment
rates, compared to women without such a history.[56] Longitudinal studies—that is,
research that follows individuals over time and makes repeated observations of
the same measures over months or years—of the effects of recent and past battering
on employment find that recent abuse is one of several factors that contribute
to battered women's relative lack of employment stability.[57] The combination of
these results belies the taken-for-granted assumption that work is a convenient
silver-bullet solution to the dual traps of poverty and abuse.

The central contradiction here, and the issue driving the research in this book,
involves the problems that arise from casting women's work as the main solution to
poverty and battering. On the one hand, there are the familiar issues of low-wage
work and the time bind facing women with dual responsibilities for earning and
caring. Less familiar is the fact that controlling and coercive men make women's
work a source of conflict, an excuse for abuse, and a site of surveillance, sabotage,

and violence. At the same time, the welfare recipients who shared their experiences and assessments of their own and others' situations resolutely put employment, career options, education, and job training at the forefront of their visions of a world that would make them less vulnerable to both poverty and abuse. In this book, I distinguish among the questions researchers ask. I bring some new data to bear on the question of the connections among battering, work, poverty, and welfare. I show the ways that women's analyses of their experiences and the rhetoric, judgments, and obstacles they face help to put in perspective two big dynamics behind the contradictory and inconsistent findings of past research: the ways that work might be a route out of poverty and away from abusers, and the ways that battering can be both an obstacle and an incentive to work.

THE SETTING OF THIS RESEARCH

In 1996, when Congress rescinded the federal entitlement to public assistance for poor mothers and their children, each state legislature had to pass its own program that conformed to the strictures of the Personal Responsibility Act (PRA). Senators Patty Murray (D-Washington) and Paul Wellstone (D-Minnesota) spearheaded the congressional response to advocates' arguments about both the potential means of escape that welfare represents for some battered women and the ways that partner-perpetrated abuse can obstruct women's attempts to leave welfare through waged work. The Murray-Wellstone provision of the PRA gives state and county welfare benefits administrators and caseworkers some flexibility about applying work requirements, paternity establishment, and child support enforcement measures as well as time limits on welfare benefits to battered women.[58]

In an astute political and logistical move, the framers of the Murray-Wellstone provision made certain that it allows states that adopt it to address the needs of battered women without counting them against the sharply limited "hardship" or "good cause" exemptions for "hard to serve" welfare recipients that states can use to stay within federal block grant performance guidelines. As researchers Sandra Danziger and Kristin Seefeldt note,

> What barriers could make welfare recipients "hard to serve?"... These problems could be employment-related—low basic skills and learning disabilities, lack of recent work experience, lack of "work readiness" or "soft skills," experiences with employer discrimination. They might be related to physical disabilities, health limitations, substance abuse, or mental health problems of parents or children. They might include family breakdown or instability: domestic violence, involvement with the child welfare system, housing instability. Child care and transportation problems, limited English proficiency, and prior felony convictions might also impede employment.[59]

The political savvy of battered women's advocates involved making sure that adopting Murray-Wellstone would allow state politicians and welfare administrators to comply with the PRA requirements that they reduce the number of welfare recipients, increase poor mothers' employment, and lower the number of children born out of wedlock without adding to the number of abortions, all without pitting battered women against other poor people who face obstacles to employment (such as people with disabilities).

Pennsylvania legislators took advantage of Murray-Wellstone and adopted the Family Violence Option (FVO), implemented in the commonwealth through what are known as the Time-Out provisions. Under Time-Out, Pennsylvania welfare recipients identified as victims of "domestic violence" can stop the clock on the 60-month lifetime limit on welfare receipt for an initial six-month period and may be granted an additional six-month extension. Training materials on Time-Out issued in the summer of 2001 (when the research team conducted the initial retrospective interviews with the cohort that included Alice and Georgia) specify "compliance with service plan" as the criterion for receiving the temporary exemption.[60] The politicians and bureaucrats who created the Time-Out provisions considered partner-perpetrated abuse to be a barrier to employment and included a service plan to promote battered women's safety to be one of the "barrier removal activities" through which women could both maintain eligibility for welfare (by fulfilling the requirement for work-related activity) and extend their benefits beyond the five-year limit.

Practically speaking, the situation for battered women on welfare in Allegheny County was not so straightforward. By the summer of 2001, when we first interviewed Alice and Georgia and the other participants as they started their work-first job search/job readiness program, welfare restructuring had been under way for several years in Allegheny County. Yet those same training materials that describe the Time-Out provisions do not describe a procedure for identifying women who might need abuse-related exemptions or services. That omission probably helps to explain why not one of the 40 women in this cohort—including Georgia and Alice—said she had been screened for partner-perpetrated abuse or offered an exemption. In fact, as of May 2001, the month in which the interviews started, the Pennsylvania Department of Public Welfare website had classified only 30 Allegheny County families receiving Temporary Assistance to Needy Families (TANF) as "domestic violence-related" cases. This represented just four tenths of a percent of the 7,000-family TANF caseload in Allegheny County that month.[61]

Unaware of the possibility of temporary exemptions from work requirements and extensions of time-limited benefits, some of the women in the cohort of interviewees voiced added concerns about their ability to comply with work requirements because partner-perpetrated abuse might cause disabling injuries or require court appearances. For example, Tonya, a divorced 41-year-old mother of two who self-identified as Black, Irish, and Indian, showed up on a Monday morning for an interview, saying, "Work *was* going well. I hope I will be able to continue [working] ... . I was in the hospital and have to wear a neck brace because my ex injured me this weekend." Tonya had worked 24 weeks in the previous year. Tonya worried realistically that the effects of her ex-husband's violence and her injuries would spill over from home to work. She could only hope that the pain and restricted range of motion from her neck brace would not derail her transition from welfare to work or jeopardize her welfare benefits by complicating or even preventing her compliance with the program's requirements.

Tonya realized that her efforts to obtain a restraining order against her ex-husband—which required her to spend the morning in family court, several blocks away from the site where she was simultaneously scheduled to fulfill her mandatory job search obligations—would make it impossible for her to meet the attendance requirement through which she maintained her welfare eligibility and avoided a cut in her benefits or other sanction. Her worries about this irresolvable dilemma—how to be in two places at once—were aggravated in part by the fact that no one from the welfare office, the job training program, or the criminal justice or victim advocacy systems had told her about the possibility of an exemption under the FVO.[62] Anxiety about safety, solvency, and sanctions contributed to Tonya's stress about work and welfare. None of it helped her to cope with what she characterized as a "rocky relationship" with her current partner, let alone the physical abuse she still endured from her ex-husband.

DATA SOURCES AND ORGANIZATION OF THE BOOK

This book is rooted in the experiences of Alice, Georgia, Tonya, and other women living at the intersection of poverty and battering, especially since Congress rescinded federal income support entitlements for poor mothers and their children in 1996. I investigate how the rules, rhetoric, and realities of work, welfare, and partner-perpetrated abuse shape their lives. I use three distinct sources of data to examine the relationships among abuse, poverty, welfare, and work, all rooted in the context of Allegheny County, Pennsylvania.[63]

One source is a set of retrospective and prospective interviews that I along with two graduate student research assistants, Danielle Ficco and Lisa H. Ruchti, conducted with Alice, Georgia, and a total of 40 welfare recipients who entered a work-first program together in the early summer of 2001—their cohort of program participants. The profiles of Alice and Georgia that open this and other chapters come from these interviews. Quotes from these interviews help me to catalogue and illustrate the specific types of abuse women like Georgia, Tonya, and Alice experience and reveal how welfare recipients understand conflicts *over work* in their relationships, abuse that *interferes* with their working, and what happens when abusive men *follow* women to the parking lots or buildings where they go to work. This material is the empirical heart of Chapter 3.

A second source is longitudinal administrative data about household characteristics, time on welfare, earnings, and civil restraining order petitions for all welfare recipients in Allegheny County from 1995 to 2000. These data record repeated observations that allow me to compare women's trajectories through this five-year period that included the passage and implementation of welfare rescission in 1996–1997. I complement the interview data with descriptions of the relative timing of petitioning for a protective order and receiving welfare, and with estimates of how petitioning for a protective order changes the earnings growth of a welfare recipient. I link administrative records on women's petitions for civil restraining orders against abusive partners, their applications for welfare assistance, and their earnings. Administrative records help me to document variation in the timing of women's appeals to the welfare state and the law-and-order state for relief from battering and poverty, to track the effects of women's petitioning for a restraining order on changes in the earnings of welfare recipients, and to assess the effect of welfare rescission on welfare recipients who do and welfare recipients who do not petition for protection from abuse. These data provide the empirical material for answering the questions about the costs of taking a beating that I develop in Chapter 4.

The third data source is texts and field notes from a community literacy project that I co-led (with rhetoric and literacy expert Lorraine Higgins) in the spring of 2002. Eight current and former welfare recipients participated. I present narratives about crucial life incidents and analytical commentary about poverty, abuse, and encounters with welfare services and police written by the women who participated in this community literacy project. These narratives and analyses allow readers to listen to what welfare recipients say when they have an opportunity to tell their stories, "talk back" to the stereotypes and stigma they encounter in welfare offices and the media, and present their visions of what would decrease poverty and abuse and increase safety and solvency in their lives. These data are the empirical focus of Chapter 5, and also provide some of the material in Chapter 6.

These data fill gaps in the knowledge produced by previous researchers in several ways. First, in the interviews, we asked substantive questions about work-related control, abuse, and sabotage, and specific questions about occasions on which abusive partners harassed or followed women when they were on the job. That means I can present women's first-hand accounts of these incidents and what happens when abuse spills over into work. Second, rather than cross-sectional, longitudinal "wave," or simple "before and after" data, I have *time-series* data; using both interview and administrative data, I can track individuals at different intervals over a period of up to five years. Consequently, I can compare the earnings trajectories of women who do and women who do not petition for a Protection From Abuse (PFA) order and then assess the effects of major policy shifts, for instance, by observing group differences in the earnings trajectories of welfare recipients who do and welfare recipients who do not petition for a PFA before and after Congress rescinded federal welfare entitlements.

Third, for part of my analysis, I have *administrative* data; rather than relying exclusively on respondent recall or problematic instruments for measuring men's physical violence against and other abuse of their current and former wives and girlfriends,[64] one set of data comes from administrative welfare, wage, and court records. Fourth, my interview data come from a *cohort* of program participants and my administrative data constitute *population* data, not a sample; the Department of Public Welfare provided data on *all* welfare recipients in the cash program for mothers with dependent children (formerly known as Aid to Families with Dependent Children or AFDC, and known since 1996 as Temporary Assistance for Needy Families or TANF) and the family court provided data on *all* protective order filings during the five-year study period. Although these data *do not* include the population of either poor or battered women in the county, they *do* include the populations of women who petitioned for protective orders, received welfare benefits, or both. Fifth, the community literacy project prompted current and former welfare recipients to provide their own descriptions and analyses of the circumstances with which they cope, to identify and respond to familiar expert and popular narratives of their situations and the social problems they have come to represent, and to develop and express their ideas about how to support them and their families in their struggles for safety and solvency.

Finally, the data come from a key setting: a racially mixed, economically postindustrial, gender-traditional county in the rustbelt of the Ohio River Valley where welfare administrators care about the dynamics of battering, work, and welfare in the lives of poor mothers. Moreover, the administrative data cover a key point in *historical* time—before and after the restructuring of welfare—while the interview data start and continue from a key point in *cohort* time—at the beginning of 40 women's participation in a mandatory job search program. I contribute to knowledge about battering, poverty, and public policy by putting interview, administrative, and literacy project data in dialogue. By combining these data sources, I provide a picture of battered women, work, and welfare that is both rooted in everyday experiences and framed by broader realities of possibility and constraint. Throughout, I focus on what we learn from listening to the ways poor people and battered women are "taking a beating."

Conventional Wisdom and
Its Discontents

On the face of it, it does not take much of a conceptual apparatus to understand Alice, Georgia, Tonya, and the situations they face. They face all of the obstacles to obtaining and maintaining stable, living-wage employment that plague many poor mothers: lack of affordable childcare and reliable transportation; brief and interrupted or truncated education and work experience; limited opportunities and unequal rewards in segregated labor markets; and physical and mental health problems such as diabetes, depression, heart disease, and addiction. In addition, the abuse that the fathers of their children and their current or former boyfriends or husbands visit on them presents yet another barrier to employment.

The basic argument goes like this: One of the main reasons why women stay with abusive men is economic dependence. Pro-work features of the 1996 welfare legislation—for instance, job preparation, job search, and work support provisions such as childcare subsidies and extended health care benefits—make it easier for poor mothers to find and keep a job. The Earned Income Tax Credit (EITC) redistributes millions of dollars to low-wage workers, bridges the gap between the minimum wage and the poverty line, and, as policy analyst and Clinton administration Department of Health and Human Services official David Ellwood put it, helps "make work pay."[1] These welfare programs and work provisions reduce women's economic dependence on public assistance and, eventually, on men. Reducing women's economic dependence contributes significantly to reducing women's vulnerability to physical violence and abuse from their current and former boyfriends and husbands.

The argument continues: In addition to the ways work supports and work-contingent redistribution programs such as the EITC decrease women's vulnerability to poverty and abuse, the changes Congress brought about with the 1996 welfare legislation enacted other important shifts. The threat of sanctions (in the form of benefit cuts or expulsion from public housing) for women who do not conform to work requirements, who refuse to cooperate with paternity establishment and child support enforcement efforts, or who participate in or tolerate drug trafficking encourages personal responsibility in terms of both work and family. As I will show later in this chapter, according to this basic argument, personal responsibility is as central to responding to battering as it is to reducing poverty. Welfare changes that promote personal responsibility at home and at work therefore have the presumed virtue of striking at the heart of both problems at once. In addition, making welfare eligibility conditional on employment gives men incentives to support rather than undermine women's education, job training, and employment. Earnings, experience, self-esteem, and social networks from employment—and everything that women learn at work about time management, efficiency, incentives, communication, cooperation, and the rewards to discipline—increase both battered women's resources and leverage *within* relationships and their ability to *leave* an abuser. In short, waged work, especially the virtues and resources that employed women cultivate in themselves and model and provide for their children, is the best route to women's safety and solvency; welfare programs that encourage work remedy both poverty and battering by alleviating economic dependence and promoting personal responsibility.

For better or worse, as even the very brief introductions in the previous chapter show, this conventional wisdom regarding the connections between battering and poverty through personal responsibilities for work and family fails to accommodate the complex situations of Alice, Tonya, and Georgia. When battering is an obstacle to work, it is also potentially an obstacle to fulfilling work requirements and can jeopardize women's eligibility for welfare, giving an abusive man an additional source of leverage in his campaign of coercion and control. Moreover, the review of the cross-sectional and longitudinal research in the Introduction highlights the apparently contradictory findings about the effects of physical violence and other abuse men perpetrate against their current and former wives and girlfriends on women's employment and earnings, and therefore their economic dependence on abusive men. One way to think about these contradictions is to attend to variations in the ways that battering can be *both* a *barrier* to women's employment stability *as well as* an *incentive* to women's seeking, finding, and maintaining paid labor. One goal of this book is to show the variations in the ways poverty and partner-perpetrated abuse shape some women's lives. The evidence I analyze calls into question the notion that waged work is always every woman's best route to safety and solvency. In addition, not all abuse has the same implications for a woman's employment, earnings, and welfare eligibility. Therefore, another goal of this book is to explore specifically work-related control, abuse, and sabotage as a factor in women's transitions from welfare to work and to understand what happens when abusive and controlling men follow women into the workplace—a phenomenon beyond the comprehension of the conventional wisdom that poses work as the solution to poverty and battering. In addition, conventional wisdom is institutionalized—in sometimes contradictory ways—in policies such as the Personal Responsibility Act (PRA) of 1996 and the Violence Against Women Act (VAWA) of 1994 and in the practices of welfare and law enforcement bureaucracies. The final goal of this book is to show what the varied experiences of poor women tell us about these policies and practices.

To provide the intellectual scaffolding for meeting those goals, this chapter reviews the explanatory frameworks that together constitute the conventional wisdom about poverty, battering, and the central role of women's work in addressing them. I then present an alternative approach (drawn from feminist structural challenges to conventional wisdom) and conclude the chapter with a critical description of the contradictory dynamics of the institutionalization of conventional wisdom in U.S. policies on poverty and battering.

CONVENTIONAL WISDOM AS HEGEMONIC EXPLANATION

Conventional wisdom draws on shared experiences and taken-for-granted assumptions of ordinary people. When conventional wisdom allows experts and professionals to define and organize the entire debate over a social problem (such as *What causes poverty?* or *What should we do to stop battering?*), conventional wisdom can be an important element in what Italian neo-Marxist Antonio Gramsci calls "hegemony."[2] Hegemony is a mode of power that imposes the interests and perspectives of one group over another—indeed, over the entire social order—without the use of physical force. Conventional wisdom is hegemonic to the extent that its proponents set the terms of debate. In particular, conventional wisdom emphasizes particular questions and legitimates certain answers while rendering other questions and answers at best trivial and easily dismissed, and at worst simply inconceivable. Hegemonic explanations generally remain below the threshold of critical or even conscious rationality, and so appear intuitive, obvious, natural, and unquestionably normal—thus, conventional wisdom. Moreover, hegemonic explanations are all the more robust and difficult to perceive because they incorporate key aspects of people's everyday experiences and understandings, both their hopes and longings for justice (*You get what you deserve. What goes around comes around. The squeaky wheel gets the grease. Work hard and play by the rules and you'll come out ahead. There's power in numbers.*) and their fears (*You can't fight City Hall. The rich get richer and the poor get children. Justice follows the Golden Rule: Those who have the gold make the rules.*).

Hegemonic explanations are hard to perceive, let alone critique, because there is a high degree of "correspondence between... social structures and mental structures," between the objective structuring principles of society and the structured dispositions and subjective viewpoints of individuals.[3] The high degree of correspondence between people's mental maps of the social world and the interactions and institutions they encounter makes the otherwise arbitrary and political character of social organization appear natural and inevitable. Appearances notwithstanding, hegemonic explanations are not neutral. Rather, conventional wisdom is socially constructed, highly structured, and indelibly stamped with the power relations that characterize the broader society in which it arises.[4] The seeming naturalness and inevitability of the conventional wisdom about poverty, battering, and work is why, appearances aside, I invoke a critical conceptual apparatus for understanding Georgia, Alice, Tonya, and the social world they inhabit.

In the next section of this chapter, I explore the conventional wisdom about poverty, battering, and the connections between them, including the hegemonic posing of employment and personal responsibility as the solutions to women's problems with poverty and battering. For example, what sociologist Nancy Berns calls "victim empowerment folklore" organizes media discussions of battering, such as the women's magazine stories and talk show segments that exhort women to take action on their own behalf and make the batterer stop by refusing to "take it" any more.[5] The emphasis on women's taking action to stop being battered is of a piece with the emphasis on personal responsibility in the work and family provisions of the 1996 welfare legislation. For another instance, conventional wisdom or law-and-order logic about crime, policing, private relationships, and justice, along with criminological expertise, organizes law enforcement and court practices and policies about battering around protection for victims and accountability for perpetrators. Protection and accountability may be what the law-and-order arm of government is prepared to concede to the feminist social movements that have demanded an end to violence against women. However, protection and accountability alone fail to fulfill the vision and demands of feminist antiviolence activists and advocates.[6] Finally, what policy analyst Frank Ridzi calls "'work-first' common sense"[7]—that is, the idea that all poor people need are strict eligibility requirements and, where those fail, punitive sanctions that will motivate them to move from welfare to work—complements the "politics of disgust," or the stigma and condemnation of poor people that organize popular and news media and congressional discussions of welfare.[8]

CONVENTIONAL WISDOM ON POVERTY, BATTERING, AND WORK

Many social movements strive to direct public awareness and resources to understanding and eliminating (or at least ameliorating) what they cast as social problems. Not surprisingly, this applies to both poverty and battering. Social movement actors, elected and appointed public officials, state and nonprofit bureaucrats, advocates, researchers, and others endeavor to focus attention on what they see as the problem, to grasp its causes and its harms, and to support their preferred or recommended solutions.[9] They also frequently do their utmost to assign blame, designate "victims" and "perpetrators," and establish themselves as legitimate authorities on the issue. Social problems entrepreneurs and others inside and outside of government institutions and the nongovernmental organizations that seek to lobby and hold public officials accountable have practical and political agendas designed to mobilize support for social change. Because they are dedicated to "making things happen," they root their strategies for raising awareness and allocating resources in causal theories and explanations.[10]

The Venn diagram in Figure 2.1 presents poverty and battering as distinct but partially overlapping social problems. This figure shows the area of overlap—the connection between poverty and battering—as a realm of mutually reinforcing dependency, vulnerability, and exploitation. It also highlights a mechanism of coercive control that directly involves both poverty and battering: work-related control, abuse, and sabotage. I engage conceptually and empirically with the area of overlap between battering and poverty highlighted in Figure 2.1 in Chapter 3.

Figure 2.1 also maps government responses to poverty and battering as distinct but with an important nexus of overlap; it distinguishes government responses to battering and poverty through different institutions and policies. In the case of

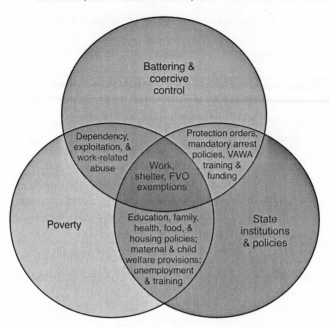

Figure 2.1. Battering, poverty, and the state.

battering and coercive control, these are tools available through the *law-and-order state*. Those tools include mandatory arrest policies; the legislative and evidentiary rules, training programs, and funding priorities of the Violence Against Women Act (VAWA); and the civil restraining or Protection From Abuse (PFA) orders that VAWA guarantees through its "full faith and credit" provisions.[11] Some VAWA provisions are intended to deter and punish criminals by increasing local and interstate law enforcement, prosecution, and penalties. Others are intended to encourage victims to seek help, report abuse, and pursue justice by creating and funding services such as the National Domestic Violence Hotline and by mandating and supporting training for police, prosecutors, and judges.

In the case of poverty, these tools are policies and programs available through the remnants of the *welfare state*. They include provisions for maternal and child health and nutrition; basic and vocational education and training; unemployment, health, housing, and childcare benefits; marriage promotion and parenting training; and child protection services. At their inception, mostly during the Depression and the New Deal era, politicians and reformers designed welfare policies and programs to ease civil unrest and support economic recovery,[12] to protect families against the risks of loss of a breadwinning man,[13] and to reinforce gender, race, and class hierarchies.[14] Since the reforms of 1988[15] and the rescission of entitlements in 1996,[16] welfare is supposed to provide a minimal safety net for the poor without practical or even rhetorical support for full employment (that is, a commitment to federal, state, or local government as employer of last resort).[17] A limited few of the remaining programs are intended to provide direct material support for people suffering "hard times." The majority of programs since 1996 are designed to change the incentives and options poor people confront, increase the resources they bring to work and family, and thus direct their behavior and discipline them to the demands of "personal responsibility and work opportunity."[18]

At the intersection of poverty and battering, Figure 2.1 highlights the content of, and connections and contradictions between, government programs and policies designed to address simultaneously these two social problems and their potentially synergistic combination.[19] These include conditional support and shelter for battered women with limited resources, and mandatory arrest, no-drop prosecution, protective order, and antistalking provisions designed to increase women's willingness and ability to call on the law-and-order state while discouraging women's dependency on the welfare state.[20] In the last section of this chapter, and in the conclusion of the book, I focus on these connections and contradictions.

Figure 2.1 also sets the stage for cataloging the conventional wisdom that constitutes the explanations of poverty, battering, and the connections between them that are hegemonic in the United States today. In the remainder of this section, I set out the causes and source(s) of harm each model identifies, who or what each model places at the center of its analytical focus, the remedies each model recommends, and specifically the role of women's employment in each model's approach to poverty, battering, or their intersection.

"Victim Empowerment Folklore"

Sociologist Nancy Berns researched stereotypical images (in popular media) and dominant public understandings (in "everyday discourse") of "domestic violence" and found what she calls "victim empowerment folklore."[21] Folklore—culturally specific stories that reflect and constitute people's everyday beliefs and values— is "part 'true story,' part myth, part hope, part politics."[22] The most common "domestic violence narratives,"[23] Berns observes,

> have a lot in common with fairy tales. The characters are introduced: a victim and a villain. The plot is propelled forward, often with acts of violence. The plots I examine have a twist on the usual formula: the victim has to become the heroine and rescue herself. To do this, she must become "empowered." Then she lives happily ever after.[24]

According to victim empowerment folklore, Berns finds, the cause of battering is the fact that the victim "takes" or "puts up with" abuse. Authors of women's magazine articles, talk show hosts, and others who purvey victim empowerment folklore encourage and sometimes berate battered women so that they "wake up" and realize "that something needs to change and that this will only happen if she takes control of the situation. She needs to take back the power."[25] Of course, as Berns notes in her critique of victim empowerment folklore, arguing that what causes battering is a woman's "letting him do this to you" is a classic example of blaming the victim.[26]

The source of the harm of battering, according to victim empowerment folklore, is the victim's attitude and her unwillingness or inability to take action. As Berns points out, these representations of battering are numerically dominant in popular media, but their ubiquity is not the only reason they are pernicious. Victim empowerment folklore is culturally hegemonic. That is, as noted above, its stories incorporate everyday understandings, generate consent of the governed, constitute and reproduce an entire set of hierarchical social relations, and organize how people think about the issue.[27] In the process, the stories of victim empowerment folklore "frame" the victim and make the perpetrator and gender inequality disappear.[28] "Framing the victim," in Berns's formulation, refers to the way victim empowerment folklore sets up a woman to be blamed for her plight, in the police entrapment[29] or murder mystery sense of "framed." It also refers to how stereotypical media representations and everyday ways of talking about battering focus the debate and the attention of social problems entrepreneurs and the public on the victim rather than the perpetrator or broader social inequalities between women and men in the sociological discursive sense of "framing."[30]

Proponents of victim empowerment folklore offer several remedies for the harms of battering, including exhorting, admonishing, and "empowering" the victim to stand up for herself in order to stop the abuse or leave. According to the victim-blaming folklore of empowerment, women have to stop letting men "get away" with the abuse. Logically, this makes sense; if the cause of battering is women's attitudes and behaviors, then the solution to the social problem must principally involve women's changing their attitudes and behaviors. The focus on empowerment also directs women's attention to the one aspect of their lives over which they self-evidently have control: their own behaviors and attitudes.[31] Finally, victim empowerment folklore offers waged work as the material and emotional basis of "empowerment" and safety for battered women. When battered women stand up on their own behalf and establish themselves independently in the workforce, the victim empowerment folklore asserts, they can support themselves and their children and live happily ever after.

Criminological Expertise and Law-and-Order Logic

Proponents of criminological expertise and law-and-order logic focus primarily on safety and access to justice for victims and on accountability (and sometimes punishment and deterrence) for perpetrators. The cause of battering, the argument goes, is a combination of women's vulnerability, men's violence, and lack of deterrents. According to hegemonic explanations in criminology, men's violence against their current and former wives and girlfriends is "natural," or at the very least the expected product of notions of masculinity that construct violence as a normal part of masculinity.[32] Men learn to use violence against women to get what they want (instrumental violence), to blow off steam (expressive violence), or to displace anger or frustration that they cannot legitimately perpetrate in other settings (compensatory violence). Without informal social controls, peer pressure, community integration, and serious police and justice system responses, men reason they can, indeed, "get away with it." Men's abusive behavior is rational in part because they reckon they can bolster masculine privilege by using physical force to intimidate a woman into compliance and in part because they may believe the victim empowerment folklore in which they are unknowingly immersed. In addition, battering is rational according to conventional criminological wisdom because abusive men face few social constraints, negative sanctions, or serious consequences for their violence against women.[33]

The source of the harm of battering, as understood by criminological expertise and law-and-order logic, has three elements. One is the breakdown of moral and social control mechanisms in neighborhoods and communities, so that men face few constraints and a general culture of disrespect and violence prevails. Another is women's reluctance to report battering and to press charges, testify, and otherwise cooperate with prosecutors. The lack of deterrents and women's reluctance to report spring from a common third source: ignorance, stereotypes, and lack of accountability for law enforcement and court personnel. Criminal justice logic expands the victim empowerment folklore frame. On the one hand, law-and-order logic "frames" or focuses beyond the victim–perpetrator dyad and brings into view the community and criminal justice system responses to battering. Advocates draw attention to the power dynamics and systematic problems (including racism, lack of responsible community policing, and vulnerabilities and concerns due to limited English proficiency or immigrant status) that discourage women (especially women of color) from reporting and pressing charges.[34] Moreover, unlike the way victim empowerment folklore "frames" the victim and generally excludes men, male power, and masculine privilege from the picture, hegemonic criminology and law-and-order logic focus steadily on deterrents and accountability to stop and punish pathological (instrumental or expressive) male violence.

Given this framing and analysis of the causes and harms of battering, criminologists recommend a variety of remedies. One is to change incentives for women to report battering. A second is to bolster community policing and integrated community response and services. A third is to restrict the rights and access to some means of violence for batterers, using mechanisms such as firearms confiscation and background checks. Another is to mandate arrest and prosecution policies and practices that do not require the cooperation of a potentially intimidated woman in the state's case against a man on whom she may depend even when he abuses her. Yet another is the various provisions of VAWA noted later in this chapter: civil restraining orders and the full faith and credit provisions for enforcing them across jurisdictions, antistalking provisions and other measures that criminalize ostensibly private behavior, and federal resources and mandates for training law enforcement and court personnel. The role of work and employers in law-and-order logic is straightforward if somewhat limited (and mostly implicit), viewing employers as a constituency to mobilize for workplace security, support and safety for victims, and accountability for perpetrators.

The "Politics of Disgust" and "Work-First Common Sense"

Just as the victim empowerment folklore puts responsibility for stopping battering squarely on the shoulders of battered women, so the proponents of the "politics of disgust"[35] blame the poor for their plight. In the rhetoric of U.S. politicians and in the U.S. news media, political scientist Ange-Marie Hancock finds the endlessly reviled figure of the "welfare queen," who defrauds the state and taxpayers and (mis)uses her welfare check to support her Cadillac-and-lobster lifestyle.[36] Washington politicians, state and local government officials and administrators, and news reporters alike see the cause of poverty as individual failings and misfortunes reinforced by perverse incentives. The source of harm is dependence, a culture of poverty, and a lack of work ethic and sexual restraint, reinforced by a "nanny state"[37] that coddles the poor instead of enforcing personal responsibility and family values. In the same way that victim empowerment folklore about battering frames the victim and makes the perpetrator and the social, economic, and cultural institutions and practices that support him disappear, the politics of disgust frame and blame dependent women and bleeding-heart liberals, making economic stratification, capitalism, the right-wing backlash against New Deal and Great Society programs, and racism, sexism, and the politics of class all vanish from the analysis.[38]

What policy analyst Frank Ridzi calls "work-first common sense"[39] complements the politics of disgust. Just as law-and-order logic emphasizes the deterrent power of credible threats of punishment and mechanisms of accountability for perpetrators, adherents of work-first common sense insist that the way to end poverty is to use the powers of the state to monitor and enforce the work, family, and sexual ethics of mainstream middle-class moralism.[40] According to work-first common sense, the remedy for poverty is a version of "tough love"—harsh discipline intended to be beneficial in the long run. Tough love rhetoric is a descendent of the love-the-sinner-hate-the-sin moralism of nineteenth-century approaches to poverty and public assistance. Tough love requires the privileged and powerful to stand firm against pleas for special treatment and indulgence by the poor and powerless and insists that the route out of poverty is the old-fashioned duo of hard work and sexual restraint. Tough love calls for intrusive surveillance and other state and professional powers to enforce strict compliance with high expectations of deferred gratification, discipline, ambition, and competition, even in the face of few rewards (for the poor) for conforming to or espousing these bourgeois virtues. The politics of disgust and work-first common sense thus undergird the underdevelopment, moralism, and individual orientation of education, labor, and housing policies in the United States. They also yield the innovations of the 1996 welfare legislation: rescission of federal entitlements to cash relief for the poor and benefit cuts, time limits, family caps, and other sanctions and provisions designed to express taxpayer outrage at—and to adjust by any punitive means at the disposal of the workfare state—the behavior and attitudes of the poor. Work-first common sense places maternal employment at the heart of welfare, casting work as the moral basis of entitlement, the material basis of self-sufficiency, and the prerequisite for personhood.

****

The conventional wisdom about poverty, battering, employment, and welfare matters in part because it produces and reproduces public identities, such as the notion of the "welfare queen" invoked by Ronald Reagan[41] or the "worthy victim" who is the protagonist in U.S. women's magazine stories about battering.[42] Hegemonic explanations obscure the political, contingent, historical character of the present. They obscure the fact that the current situation is the result of iterative, cumulative struggles, the outcomes of which are heavily weighted toward the status quo but are changeable nevertheless. Conventional wisdom also restricts opportunities for political participation and democratic deliberation; victim empowerment folklore notwithstanding, hegemonic explanations undermine the ability of poor people and battered women to present themselves as authoritative agents of their own lives, with the judgment and capacity to give reasons and grapple with rival views.[43] Conventional wisdom helps its purveyors to regulate labor, sexuality, and fertility, especially for poor women of color, whose work ethic, sexual morals, and suitability for motherhood these self-appointed administrators of the moral order regularly impugn.[44]

Hegemonic explanations require a critical conceptual apparatus to generate counterhegemonic analyses. Having set out the conventional wisdom on poverty, battering, and work, I next set out an important alternative: a feminist structural account.

TRAPPED BY POVERTY, TRAPPED BY ABUSE

Feminist structural analyses present a critical alternative to work-first common sense, victim empowerment folklore, and the other aspects of conventional wisdom explored above. Feminist structuralists argue that what causes poverty and battering are the ways in which gender, race, and class hierarchies systematically organize individual identity, couple and group interaction, and broader social institutions.[45] Structures, institutions, practices, discourses, and interactions that enforce privilege, discrimination, and dominance are the sources of harm in unequal societies. This model views conservative antipoverty strategies themselves as a source of harm, to the extent that they sustain race and gender double standards and push women into the labor market and marriage, settings that often stunt the aspirations and accomplishments and threaten the health and safety of women and girls in general and poor girls and women in particular. Similarly, researchers and theorists using a feminist structuralist approach emphasize the extent to which victim empowerment folklore blames the victim and lets men off the hook. They note the ways that law-and-order logic tends to bolster police power at the expense of women's agency and alternative institution-building,[46] and reinforces racist stereotypes about work, sexuality, and violence perpetration and victimization. They work to counter how the politics of disgust and work-first common sense reproduce contemptuous "controlling images" of poor women, especially women of color.[47]

Instead, feminist structural analysts focus on perpetrators and the structures, logics, legacies, and dynamics that make battering possible, rational, and even rewarding for men. In this framework, battering "takes two": an abusive man and a system of inequality and disadvantage that reinforces a woman's vulnerability and limits her options for resistance and escape once he has "reeled her in."[48] Individual men's establishing coercive control over their wives and girlfriends is not rooted in anything natural about masculinity, but is backed by political, economic, and social inequalities.[49] Structural inequalities, rather than individual characteristics or even vaguely defined "cultural differences," explain diverse women's experiences of violence and the law-and-order system.[50] What battered women need, according to such a view, is public recognition and support of their human right to define and pursue their own life projects, without the violent or coercive interference of men or the restrictive stereotypes and systematic disadvantages that render them vulnerable to coercive and controlling men.[51]

Similarly, feminist structural analysts do not focus on individual failings, bad choices, or lack of work ethic, fiscal restraint, and sexual discipline as the causes of poverty. Rather, they address the ways that race, class, and gender hierarchies organize work, family, community, opportunity, and politics. They view gross inequalities, exploitation, and poverty as systemic properties of unsustainable socioeconomic regimes and undemocratic governance strategies. According to these analyses, the remedies for battering and poverty need to focus on the same systemic phenomena that cause them. Thus, feminists call for structural changes in class, race, and gender relations; safety, justice, and human rights for those histori-cally exploited and violated; and accountability, redistribution, and reorganization of resources and power toward less exploitative and more economically, ecologi-cally, politically, and socially sustainable modes of production and reproduction. For example, feminist structuralists Jane Collins and Victoria Mayer note that work-first programs push poor mothers into the job market without recognizing that they are embodied and encumbered workers and beleaguered and impover-ished parents. What poor mothers deserve, Collins and Mayer claim, is the right to employment that is "compatible with the care they must provide" and organized around "societally agreed-upon protections" of safe working conditions and living wages.[52]

A feminist structural analysis also views the connection between poverty and battering as the material basis for both. That is, women are "trapped by poverty, trapped by abuse."[53] Consequently, work is a particularly important site for contesting the vulnerability of women to men's abuse. For feminist structural analysts, battering is a means for men's enforcing women's economic dependence. Interfering with women's work and education is a specific tactic abusers use to exploit and control women. Work can be the material basis for women's solvency, solidarity, social participation, and autonomy, and it can be the site of tremendous exploitation and conflict as women struggle to escape poverty and battering.

To alert readers, the feminist structuralist argument that women are trapped by poverty and abuse may sound uncannily similar to the hegemonic explanation with which I opened this chapter and that I termed inadequate for grasping the complexities of the lives of women like Tonya, Alice, and Georgia. Although in the feminist structural account women's employment plays an important role in their being trapped by poverty and abuse, feminist structuralists do not *reduce* women's being trapped by poverty and trapped by abuse to the issue of employment and especially not to individual issues of work effort or work ethic. The difference may seem subtle, but it is crucial. Moreover, when policy institutionalizes work requirements for maintaining welfare eligibility, men's battering in general and their work-related control, abuse, and sabotage in particular are no longer solely an obstacle to women's employment. Battering also becomes an important fulcrum of men's leverage over women's access to welfare benefits, education and job training, and supportive services.

Evan Stark, an activist-researcher involved for over three decades with feminist efforts to stop battering, counters law-and-order logic, criminological expertise, and the various incarnations of victim empowerment folklore, and his work exemplifies the feminist structural approach to the joint traps of poverty and abuse.[54] Using intensive clinical interviews with women on trial for killing their husbands or boyfriends, Stark thoroughly rethinks "domestic violence." He argues persuasively that partner-perpetrated abuse is "neither 'domestic' nor primarily about 'violence.'"[55] Instead, Stark urges researchers and advocates to consider men's abuse of their current and former wives and girlfriends as *coercive control*, "a course of calculated, malevolent conduct" that interweaves physical violence with the tactics of coercion: intimidation, isolation, and control.[56] Coercive control, for Stark, constitutes a criminal violation of women's fundamental human right to self-determination of their life projects and how to fulfill them.

What causes coercive control, for Stark as well as other feminist structuralists, is a set of historical conditions that give women as a group a set of vulnerabilities and give men as a group a set of capacities that render some men ready, willing, and able to exercise coercive control in a subset of couples. Stark's analysis of "how men entrap women in personal life" is sensitive to change over time in gender relations and the economic and social sources and organization of men's power and women's subordination and domestication. In fact, Stark makes a strong case that coercive control is the characteristic form of men's abusing women in the contemporary period, in which women have dramatically increased their labor force participation rates, contributions to household income, and participation in public life.

Given his innovative view of the harm and causes of battering, Stark argues that "[C]oercive control is a liberty crime rather than a crime of assault."[57] The fact that episodic physical assault plays a minimal role in coercive control, Stark claims, largely explains why the "no hitting" rhetoric of feminist antiviolence campaigns—and the protective-order-and-misdemeanor approach institutionalized through the VAWA legislation set out below—is ultimately a blind alley. Stark proposes that researchers and activists instead have to perceive and grapple with the chronic and cumulative violations of personhood—of women's dignity, autonomy, and integrity—that constitute individually devised regimes of men's coercive control. He recommends that researchers, activists, and the law view battering as a human rights violation. In the context of twentieth- and early twenty-first-century changes in gender relations in the labor force and beyond, Stark sees women's work as a site of great potential for contributing to the material basis for women's self-direction. But he also recognizes the extent to which men's coercive control can extend to the workplace, and women can find themselves vulnerable to men's efforts to destroy or exploit women's earnings capacities, work-based social connections, and capacities for self-determination.

The overlapping concerns with battering, poverty, work, and policy that I set out in the Introduction and depicted in Figure 2.1, and my own analyses and feminist politics, lead me to adopt a feminist structural approach. In the next and final section of this conceptual chapter, I use this critical framework to characterize the two pieces of legislation and the key shifts in the policy regime at the intersection of the welfare state and the law-and-order state, where they address battering and poverty by championing work as the one best means for women's achieving safety and solvency.

THE CURRENT U.S. POLICY REGIME

Institutions are time- and place-specific constellations of organizational structures and practices; policies articulate and establish institutional rules, goals, and limits for individuals and organizations. Policy can promote innovation or reinforce existing structures through the incentives, sanctions, and values that shape everyday routines in institutions such as welfare offices, workplaces, police stations, and courtrooms. Hegemonic[58] policy regimes facilitate governance in part by connecting people's common sense understandings of society, politics, economics, and daily life to the apparatus of rule through particular constellations of strategies, signs, subjects, and sanctions.[59] That is, different regimes deploy and call forth different *strategies* for maintaining or challenging the status quo. For example, suffragists might strategically invoke women's purity, piety, domesticity, and maternity as the grounds for their suitability for participation in public life; separatist rebels might renounce armed struggle in favor of nonviolent civil disobedience; dissidents might boycott elections and organize mass demonstrations instead. Hegemonic regimes propagate ideal and controlling images,[60] such as the iconic welfare queen,[61] the hockey or soccer mom, or Joe Sixpack, as shorthand *signs* to inform political discourse and simultaneously mobilize and channel the energies of aggrieved constituencies. Hegemonic regimes address and construct specific state *subjects*, such as the alternately lauded and berated character of the working mother or the perennial bad boy of welfare policy, the deadbeat dad.[62] And policy regimes impose characteristic *sanctions* on those who do not conform, for instance, through mass incarceration[63] and welfare benefit cuts and eligibility restrictions.[64]

In this section, I address two major policy responses to—and implicit and explicit characterizations of—the intersections of battering and poverty, as well as the role of the state and women's employment in addressing the social problems that are central to understanding poverty, battered women, and work in the United States today: the Personal Responsibility Act of 1996 (Pub. L. No. 104-193, reauthorized 2005) and the Violence Against Women Act of 1994 (Pub. L. No. 103-322, reauthorized 2000 and 2005). My account of this legislation—and the policy regime they jointly help to constitute—is informed by my critical understanding of conventional wisdom sketched above, a critical understanding generated by the feminist structural approach.

Welfare Rescission

In 1996, Congress rescinded individual and familial entitlements to federal income assistance. The Personal Responsibility Act (PRA) replaced a New Deal Social Security program (originally called Aid to Dependent Children [ADC] and known since the 1960s as Aid to Families with Dependent Children [AFDC]) with a new program called Temporary Assistance for Needy Families (TANF). Congress intended TANF to provide assistance to needy families so that children may be cared for in their own homes or in the homes of relatives; end the dependence of needy parents on government benefits by promoting job preparation, work, and marriage; prevent and reduce the incidence of out-of-wedlock pregnancies and establish annual numerical goals for preventing and reducing the incidence of these pregnancies; and encourage the formation and maintenance of two-parent families.[65]

The statistics justifying these legislative concerns were widely known, at least in their broad outlines and political implications. Thirty-two percent of registered live births in the United States in 1996 were to unmarried mothers; 13.1 percent were to teenage mothers. In 1950, two thirds of adult women in the United States were married and 2 percent of adult women were divorced. In 1996, when the debate was in full swing, only 55 percent of adult women were married and nearly one in 10 adult women was divorced.[66] In the early 1990s, one in five children younger than 18 lived in a household where the family income was below the poverty line. Children in mother-only families are much more likely to be poor, and therefore to be receiving income support from the government, than children in married-couple families.[67]

The statistics about single motherhood, teen motherhood, out-of-wedlock births, divorce, and child poverty added weight to the simplistic, individualistic, and moralistic remedy for poverty behind the repeal of entitlements espoused by conservative pundits and politicians: Stay in school; postpone pregnancy; get married and stay married; get a job, any job.[68] To fulfill the stated purposes of rescinding welfare and the entitlement to income support that the federal government had provided to poor mothers and their children since 1935, Title I of the Personal Responsibility and Work Opportunity Act limits lifetime access to income support to 60 months (or less at state lawmakers' discretion). Time limits constitute the "temporary" part of Temporary Assistance to Needy Families. The federal TANF legislation also imposes more stringent work requirements on all able-bodied adult recipients of cash assistance, starting after just 24 months on welfare (or less at state lawmakers' discretion). Work requirements, especially for women, constitute the "work opportunity" part, as well as half of the "personal responsibility" part, of the PRA. Title III bolsters child support enforcement through mandatory paternity establishment and, in Subtitle B, through expanded location and case tracking mechanisms. The child support provisions, along with the rhetoric about marriage (and, in the reauthorized version in 2005, substantial taxpayer-funded grants for "marriage promotion" programs), constitute the rest of the "personal responsibility" part of the legislation, and for men, also constitute a major portion of the "work opportunity" part of the welfare overhaul. That is, welfare restructuring mandates paternity establishment and child support obligations as a way of imposing work and sexual discipline on both women and men.[69]

Through the PRA legislation, Congress transformed fundamentally the organization of social provision in the United States. Instead of assessing eligibility for entitlements and cutting checks, staff members of welfare offices are to promote and enforce waged work, marriage, paternity establishment, and child support payments.[70] Politicians and commentators justified these much more intrusive[71]— and conceivably far more expensive—missions in moralistic terms that emphasized the failures and indignities of the 60-year-old system of support for the poor.[72] Central to welfare rescission were claims about the nonpecuniary value of, as well as the economic rewards for, waged work, sexual restraint, and community and paternal involvement[73]; a rhetoric of "empowerment" that focused on discipline and self-help[74]; and an effort to restore American economic competitiveness in an era of globalization.[75] The key idea was to eliminate the perverse incentives that purportedly discouraged employment and marriage for poor mothers and fathers and to impose on poor people the self-restraint, discipline, and work ethic that pundits pose as the keys to middle-class success.

Violence Against Women Legislation

The Violence Against Women Act (VAWA), Title IV of the much larger Violent Crime Control and Law Enforcement Act of 1994 (Pub. L. No. 103-322), set out three key priorities. First, VAWA posited law enforcement as both a deterrent and a punishment or measure of accountability for perpetrators of violence and abuse against women. Second, VAWA instituted federal legislation, training requirements, and funding appropriations as a signal of social consensus about the seriousness of violence against women in general and battering in particular. Third, VAWA articulated a social commitment to recognize, grapple with, and reduce violence against women. In its main subtitles, VAWA created federal mandates and mechanisms to promote "Safe Streets for Women,"[76] "Safe Homes for Women,"[77] "Civil Rights for Women,"[78] "Equal Justice for Women in the Courts,"[79] "National Stalker and Domestic Violence Reduction,"[80] and "Protections for Battered Immigrant Women and Children."[81] The key provisions of Subtitle B—Safe Homes for Women are most directly intended to address battering. Those provisions include a national "domestic violence" hotline,[82] provisions for interstate enforcement of protection orders,[83] encouragement of arrest policies,[84] grants for battered women's shelters,[85] funding for data and research,[86] and provisions for youth education,[87] community programs,[88] confidentiality,[89] and rural "domestic violence" and child abuse enforcement.[90]

The language and structure of the legislation combines expert analysis, advocate positions, and everyday understandings of both battering and policing. For example, the distinction between "safe streets" and "safe homes" reproduces the hegemonic distinction between public and private. Congress inscribed in legislation the hegemonic notion that the victims, perpetrators, forms, causes, harms, and remedies for violence against women are completely different at home from everywhere else. Distinguishing public and private as sites of violence against women is not controversial when it comes to grants for capital improvements to prevent crime in public transportation and national and public parks.[91] However, the legislation reifies assumptions about women's vulnerabilities and the distinction between public and domestic in more harmful ways. VAWA institutes federal penalties for sex crimes,[92] creates law enforcement and prosecution grants to reduce violent crimes against women,[93] and mandates federal "rape shield"[94] and sexual assault victim assistance programs.[95] These innovations are important, but they all fall under the "Safe Streets" subtitle, implying that rape, violent crimes against women, and sex crimes all happen in public spaces. In contrast, the provisions that address partner-perpetrated abuse are under the "Safe Homes" subtitle.[96] This distinction relegates partner-perpetrated abuse to the "domestic," reproduces a marital exemption for rape in particular, and reinscribes a distinction feminists have long criticized as central to gender inequality.[97]

Congress summarized the empirical data supporting the need for "improving services for victims of domestic violence, dating violence, sexual assault, and stalking" in the findings section of the VAWA Reauthorization Act of 2005. Congress found the following:

- Nearly 1/3 of American women report physical or sexual abuse by a husband or boyfriend at some point in their lives.
- According to the National Crime Victimization Survey, 248,000 Americans 12 years of age and older were raped or sexually assaulted in 2002.
- Rape and sexual assault in the United States is estimated to cost $127,000,000,000 per year,[98] including–(a) lost productivity; (b) medical and mental health care; (c) police and fire services; (d) social services; (e) loss of and damage to property; and (f) reduced quality of life.[99]

Much of the research that produced these findings was conducted under Chapter 9 of Subtitle B of the original VAWA legislation. The findings affirmed the seriousness of violence against women as a widespread social problem with heavy social and economic costs, thus justifying a strong government response.

The findings and the inclusion of VAWA in a broader crime bill focused political and media attention and resources on crime, law enforcement, and criminal justice as remedies for the harms of violence against women and key interventions to reduce or prevent it. For the advocates and activists who pushed for resources, training, and organizational changes to better protect and support victims, stop and punish perpetrators, and instruct and guide court and law enforcement personnel, this focus yielded mixed results. Arguably, VAWA encourages the law-and-order, surveillance, and services bureaucracies of the state at the expense of mobilization of feminist resources and support for broader social change.[100] The focus on episodic misdemeanor-level physical violence obscures battering as a chronic pattern of coercive control that deprives women of basic human rights to self-determination of their life projects.[101] VAWA takes much-needed steps to overcome the assumption that men's lives, experiences, and interests are the norm and that women's are invisible, trivial, or peripheral in the law, the courts, and the police state. However, VAWA leaves untouched the economic and cultural foundations of women's subordination through men's violence.[102] The official response to violence against women instantiated in policy, institutions, and practice through VAWA at best undercuts and at worst delegitimizes the analyses and movement-building work of feminist advocates and activists.[103] It organizes thought and talk about battering around a bureaucratic "crime and punishment" response of arrest and prosecution that occludes "the ideological, political, strategic vision as well as the activism of the anti-violence movement."[104] The result: what criminologist Evan Stark characterizes as the "stalled revolution" in the struggle to end violence against women.[105]

In addition to the provisions of VAWA, many jurisdictions in the past three decades established pro-arrest and pro-prosecution provisions for dealing with partner-perpetrated violence, which are important elements of the safety net for battered women. *Pro-arrest policies* allow or require security officers to make warrantless arrests at the scene if there is reasonable evidence of a crime even if the police did not witness it.[106] Critics have raised concerns about dual arrest patterns (in which security officers fail or refuse to distinguish between victim and perpetrator and arrest both members of the couple) and the potentially disempowering effects of mandatory arrest for women who want the abuse to stop, not the relationship or financial and parental support.[107] Also known as evidence-based or no-drop prosecution policies, *pro-prosecution provisions* give prosecutors the ability to pursue criminal assault and other charges against perpetrators without testimony from the victim and even against her wishes.[108]

The good news is that pro-arrest and pro-prosecution policies can send a strong signal to perpetrators about the seriousness and unacceptability of men's violence against their current and former wives and girlfriends. Pro-arrest and pro-prosecution policies moreover provide important incentives for police and prosecutors to respond with alacrity to reports of partner-perpetrated assaults. In addition, being able to blame the police and prosecutor for the arrest and pursuit of charges may help women avoid retaliatory abuse. The bad news is that women's lack of control over the legal processes of the security state could reproduce the loss of control they experience in abusive relationships, could discourage some women from seeking help from the security and health care systems, and could escalate abuse, especially as women signal their intention to leave. Moreover, the "incident-specific and injury-based definition of violence" at the heart of pro-arrest and pro-prosecution policies mischaracterizes the dynamics, harms, and remedies for the most devastating coercive control abusers exercise without resorting to even a single incident of misdemeanor-level physical violence.[109]

Both VAWA and PRA were the legislative dimensions of major institutional shifts—that is, shifts in the practices and organization of the welfare and law-and-order branches of the state, and in the signs, sanctions, subjects, and strategies that constitute the current U.S. policy regime. VAWA sought to change practice and rhetoric throughout the criminal justice system, moved federal money and official attention in new directions, and signaled a cultural shift in the seriousness with which Washington politicians, law enforcement, and courts approach violence against women. PRA reorganized the logic, practice, and meaning of poor support and ushered in a new regime for welfare administrators, front-line case workers, and recipients alike. Both the development of the law-and-order state through the full faith and credit provision of VAWA and the development of the welfare state through enforcement of paternity establishment and child support orders in PRA relied on technological advances in the state's capacity for interstate tracking, surveillance, and intervention in family life. In many respects, legislators in the 1990s realized the efforts of much earlier reformers to build public systems to respond to social problems like battering and poverty.

The Big Picture: Regime Change

The policy regimes that characterized the U.S. approach to poverty, battering, and work both before and since the Violence Against Women Act of 1994 and the Personal Responsibility Act of 1996 feature a *gendered bargain* between families and employers.[110] What changed to make possible the legislation in the 1990s were the specific class and gender terms of the bargain. Under the old bargain, employers expected families to send a worker into the labor force to be available for full-time, year-round employment. Employees invested in firm-specific skills, increased their productivity, and committed to a career of full-time labor without distractions from home or family. In return, employers recognized seniority, granted incremental pay increases tied to internal labor markets, continued to employ workers until retirement, and tied benefits to continuity of employment.

When the worker that a family sent into the labor force was a man married to a full-time housewife, the old gendered bargain between families and employers reinforced the distinction between public and private, work and home, marking the former as essentially masculine and the latter as essentially feminine. Under the old regime, the welfare state insured against those situations—disability, divorce, abandonment, widowhood, and, to a much more limited extent, out-of-wedlock births—where the gendered bargain fell into disarray. The entitlement programs of the New Deal maintained the gendered division between public and private and continued to treat women as primarily mothers and wives attached to (or tragically detached from) a breadwinning man. The private character of home and family under the old gendered bargain meant the old law-and-order policy regime similarly secured men's abuse of their current and former wives and girlfriends behind a veil of privacy.

Large-scale shifts in the material basis and organization of the U.S. economy (from manufacturing to consumer and producer services, known as deindustrialization), pressures from global economic competition, diverse feminist movements, and a sustained attack on the legitimacy of the welfare state have all contributed to the breakdown of the old gendered bargain and prompted the development of a new policy regime, institutionalized in large part through the legislative initiatives of the PRA and VAWA. Under this new regime, the old breadwinner–housewife family form (only imperfectly achieved even by middle-class White heterosexual couples, often inaccessible to working-class families and families of color, and forbidden entirely to same-sex couples) and the old gendered bargain between employers and families have been replaced by the expectation that all adults (not just men) will spend most of their lives in the labor market.

The old expectations about job security, benefits, and other rewards to seniority and loyalty to a specific firm have eroded, along with the basic social safety net provided by the New Deal welfare state. These changes have distinctly different consequences for people employed in different parts of the labor market. At the high end of the labor market, workers now expect opportunities for continuous skill building, participation in workplace decision making, and creative work in return for uncertainty, insecurity, and ever-expanding demands on their time from "greedy workplaces."[111]At the low end of the labor market, workers now face stagnant or sinking wages, irregular work schedules, and no affordable health insurance, paid sick time, paid vacation, or paid family leave. The new service economy increases demand (but not remuneration) for supposedly unskilled labor in health, elder, and childcare settings. Low-end service sector workers support high-end workers through personal and business services, and perform custodial labor on a crumbling public infrastructure.[112] In the face of these changes, the work-first programs of the Personal Responsibility Act undermine some aspects of the gendered division between public and private, for example, by requiring employment even of mothers of very young children. Contradictorily, the PRA also promotes heterosexual marriage and a traditional assignment of men to breadwinning and women to marriage and family.[113] The changing gendered bargain between families and employers, along with demands from feminist social movements and increasingly intrusive policing and imprisonment practices, similarly made room for the victim empowerment folklore and expanded law-and-order state capacities institutionalized in the Violence Against Women Act.

Under the old regime, *government* interests in "protecting soldiers and mothers"[114] and defusing popular demand for buffers against the risks and costs of joblessness, disability, old age, and other sources of "dependency" converged with *business* interests in public subsidies for social reproduction, a reserve army of labor, and a labor force unencumbered by care responsibilities. The old regime drew women into public policies and institutions as "worthy widows" and "welfare cheats,"[115] reproduced the "career mystique" and the "feminine mystique"[116] on which the myth of the breadwinning husband and housewife rested, and protected men's violence against women behind a veil of privacy.[117]

In the new regime institutionalized in the PRA and VAWA legislation and their organizational consequences, *government* interests in policing labor, reproduction, and violence to enhance discipline and social control converge with *business* interests in invoking rhetoric of globalization to justify a "race to the bottom."[118] The new regime draws women into workfare programs as "temporarily needy" and into the police and court systems as "battered women" with a new bargain, in which they have "both hands tied."[119] This striking image of the lack of political and economic citizenship for poor mothers in the contemporary policy regime vividly captures the consequences of three decades of market fundamentalism and welfare state bashing in U.S. politics and policy. Advocates of the new regime (including President Reagan as well as President Clinton) dismantled both the social programs of the New Deal welfare state and the century-long "family wage" bargain so that individuals bear the costs of uncertainty and responsibility for care work. Neither the government (through adequate public investment in education, housing, or health, elder, and childcare) nor employers (through living wages, flexible schedules, or multiple and easy points of entry and exit between education, work, and family responsibilities) bear any significant costs of social reproduction. As sociologists Jane Collins and Victoria Mayer put it, "… failure on the part of both the state and employers to address the new realities of family care prevents women, on the one hand, from parenting as they feel they should and, on the other, from performing as ideal workers"[120]—hence "both hands tied."

The PRA rescinded entitlements to income support for poor mothers and their children and recruited poor women to police men as fathers and workers. The VAWA instituted full faith and credit provisions and recognized the harms to women of violence perpetrated by their current and former husbands and boyfriends. Temporary Assistance to Needy Families mobilizes market discipline and global competition to replace solidarity and social insurance for risk of market failure, and the Violence Against Women Act mobilizes a policing model and professional services to replace autonomous feminist organizing.

There is a basic contradiction at the intersection of battering, poverty, and the state, a contradiction illuminated by the Venn diagram and the feminist structural account of the relevant policies on poverty and battering. The contradiction is at the heart of explaining the inconsistent findings of research on the effects of battering on women's labor supply. In short: Government institutions and policies create exemptions from *work requirements* and *time limits* on welfare benefits for battered women through the Family Violence Option (FVO) *at the same time* that they *mandate work* as the route to both safety and solvency. The states that adopted the FVO opened several possibilities for local welfare administrators and caseworkers to respond to battered women. Welfare offices could offer waivers from work requirements and time limits to battered women who applied for welfare and disclosed abuse to caseworkers.[121] Welfare offices could hire experts on battered women to train caseworkers in issues that battered women face and their options in implementing the new welfare law.[122] Experts on battering could also serve as consultants to welfare officials and caseworkers, provide direct services and referrals to battered women in welfare offices, and act as liaisons between the law-and-order and welfare branches of state and federal government.

The basic contradiction here occurs when the moral condemnation of the welfare recipient, as well as efforts to discipline her to the rigors of the low-wage labor market, actually endanger the relatively worthy battered woman. Sometimes, the despised welfare recipient and the worthy battered woman are one and the same.[123] Battered women can find themselves subjected to welfare eligibility requirements of cooperation with paternity establishment and child support enforcement or enrolled in welfare when they enter a shelter for battered women. As a result, welfare workers may inadvertently endanger battered women by revealing their location and contact information, by requiring contact with an abusive current or former boyfriend or husband, or by adding to men's leverage over women by holding women's welfare benefits or housing hostage to men's coercive control or work-related control, abuse, and sabotage.[124] Welfare recipients can find themselves, as was Tonya in the previous chapter, expected to be in two places at once in order to protect their children from an abusive partner *and* work for wages, or required simultaneously to attend mandatory job-search programs *and* appear in court to obtain a protective order. The Family Violence Option described in the Introduction addresses some of these issues. Even if advocates raised the issue of battering strategically[125] in the mid-1990s in order merely to complicate a welfare "reform debate" that was steamrolling ahead with little attention to the real challenges facing low-income women, what they accomplished through Murray-Wellstone and the provisions of the FVO was both more subtle and more difficult to contain. It built into the welfare state's accommodation for battered women a strong set of doubts about work as the universal solution or "silver bullet" for poverty and battering.

We live in a context of an economy and restructured welfare state where the poor are taking a beating. An increasingly disciplinary state expects women simultaneously to identify and track down "deadbeat dads" and to rely on court-based protective orders against them. My research at the intersection of poverty and battering suggests several problematic consequences that I explore empirically and thematically in the rest of the book. One consequence is that the empowerment myth that poses waged work as the solution to every personal and social problem severely restricts women's inclusion in democratic deliberation and inhibits women's claims to economic, social, and political rights. Similarly, heightening the stigma of "dependency" threatens women's eligibility for inclusion in job creation/stimulus programs coming through the current economic crisis. Finally, the categories of rights and needs are increasingly gender polarized as the rhetoric of *petitioning* (for economic aid, for protection from coercion and control at home and at work) replaces hard-fought *entitlement*.

In the next chapter, I turn to a phenomenon at the intersection of poverty, battering, and the welfare and law-and-order states suggested by Figure 2.1: the crucial question of what happens when abusers follow women to work.

What Happens When Abusers Follow Women to Work?

Just two weeks before we met, 22-year-old Larnice[1] had a run-in at the courthouse with her former boyfriend. Her ex, most of whose income (Larnice explained) came from selling drugs, was angry about having to pay for the blood test to establish paternity of their 3-year-old child, a requirement of Larnice's welfare application.[2] A couple of weeks before that, in the most severe incident of physical violence she had experienced, he tried to strangle her after he saw her getting out of the car with her new boyfriend.

Larnice was on welfare and enrolled in a "work-first" program because she faced many hurdles on her path toward finding and maintaining living-wage work. She was young, Black, and sole custodial parent of a preschool-age child. She had about the average amount of education for her work-first program cohort, a few months of training after high school. Along with almost two thirds of her job training program cohort, Larnice had no driver's license.[3] In addition to slack labor markets and discrimination, many workers face obstacles (as well as motivation and support) in the form of their own family relations (between young workers and their parents and siblings, or between working parents and their children).[4] In part as a consequence of these issues, Larnice had worked for a total of only 23 months in the past six years; she had been on welfare almost as long, for 20 of the 36 months since the birth of her child. She had held a job for only four weeks in the past year.

The conventional wisdom about the causes of poverty and battering and the connections between them set out in the previous chapter assumes that work requirements give women an escape route or greater leverage in their abusive relationships and give men material incentives to support and encourage women's employment. Larnice's case shows some flaws in that conventional wisdom. Although Larnice's partner clearly thought poorly of Larnice because she had been on public assistance and she reported his telling her, "welfare is ignorant,"[5] he also disliked her working. "He always wanted to know where I was," Larnice said when asked about relationships and work. When she was at the two jobs she had held, which paid $9 and $10 per hour, she noted, ". . . that was hard for him. He wanted me to work but he wanted to work [in the same place], too, so he could watch over me." Larnice had to cope with his calling while she was on the job. She had to contend with his tendency to "just come in and bother me" when she was at work. Larnice had grown sufficiently fed up with the abuse and harassment that she had filed for a civil restraining order[6] against him.

My purpose in this chapter is to contribute to understanding poverty, battering, work, and the connections among them by presenting and interpreting evidence about the characteristics and dynamics of specifically work-related control, abuse, and sabotage. Interrupting, controlling, or thwarting women's employment or their transition from welfare to work are all significant methods, means, and mechanisms of men's directly establishing dominance, enforcing control, and exercising coercion in relationships. I define and describe work-related control, abuse, and sabotage as they shape the lives of Larnice and other members of this cohort of welfare-to-work program participants. I present the workplace as a significant site of partner stalking. I explore employment and earnings as a site and material basis for men's subordinating and domesticating women. As I show in this chapter, work-related control, abuse, and sabotage turn out to be important factors in understanding variations in the ways poverty and partner-perpetrated abuse shape some women's lives, in explaining women's transitions from welfare to work, and in exploring what the varied experiences of poor women tell us about the policies and practices of the welfare and law-and-order arms of government where they intersect.

"WORK–FAMILY CONFLICT" GETS LITERAL

Only five of the 40 women in Larnice's cohort described their partners as supporting their employment. LaShauna, 21, Black, and never married, reported that the father of her two preschool-age children viewed her working as her doing something for herself. Four other women similarly reported that their partners supported their working because the man cast a woman's employment as her being responsible or doing something positive for herself. For example, Philippa, 29, Black, and never married, noted that the father of her three children (ages 10, 7, and almost 1 year) supported her working because "he knows I hate sitting at home," and her working "means that we are accomplishing things," such as saving to buy a house together.

The comments that LaShauna and Philippa recalled were among the most positive and supportive reports that this cohort of welfare-to-work transition program participants made about their perceptions of their partners' responses to their working outside the home. Far more (about 35 percent) reported that their partners were indifferent or at best lukewarm toward their getting and keeping a job. Janice, 30, a Black mother of three, reported of the father of her oldest child that "he don't care" about her working. Janice was one of 14 out of the 40 women in this cohort who reported that at least one of her past or current partners was indifferent to her employment. Marketta, 37 and Black, said her teenager's father "was OK with it" and a more recent partner "didn't mind" her working. Others could not say what the fathers of their children thought about their working now because they were no longer in touch with them.

Politicians, pundits, and local welfare officials and service providers had high hopes for positive effects from the dramatically changed incentives and practices of a work-focused welfare system, not least on the possibilities and alternatives facing battered women.[7] These high hopes were generally rooted in two theories of violence in relationships: exposure and exchange models. *Exposure* models predict that women's increased labor force participation will reduce battering by reducing women's exposure to abusive men. *Exchange* models predict that women's increased earnings will shift the balance of power between women and men, thus reducing men's leverage over women and increasing women's capacities for negotiating in abusive relationships.

Exposure theorists predict that work requirements should get women out of the house and therefore away from the site of "domestic" abuse. According to exposure theory, the more time women spend at work, out of the household, the less partner-perpetrated violence they will experience.[8] Congruent with this expectation was the experience of Nancy, a White, divorced, 43-year-old mother of one 7-year-old and one adult child. Nancy noted that, "[When I was working, I] would get dressed up and be out at work, not under his control." Nancy's sense of using work to get away from a controlling partner, an example confirming exposure theory, was unfortunately rare; only Nancy and one other woman in the cohort[9] of work-first program participants reported such effects.

Exchange theorists argue that negotiations in relationships are based on the partners' relative assets and contributions. In this model, victimization motivates women's employment because increasing women's work outside of the home and their absolute and relative contribution to household income should increase their bargaining power (or "voice") within and ability to leave ("exit") an abusive relationship.[10] No woman in this study explicitly observed or reported the effects predicted by exchange theory. However, nine women reported that the fathers of their children supported their working because they seemed to think women's earnings got men off the hook for some of their financial responsibilities, thus reducing one common source of relationship stress and strife. For instance, Frankie, a Black 42-year-old high school dropout, had been on and off welfare since the birth of the first of her four children, more than 20 years before. At the time of the interview, Frankie's youngest child was still preschool age (only 4); Frankie had a very spotty work history and had not worked at all in the past year. When asked what her working meant to the father, Frankie said, "He's cool with it. He thinks it will make it easier for him." Brenda, 19 and the never-married mother of an 18-month-old, also reported that working (and receiving welfare) enabled her to contribute financially to their household. She reported that her baby's father was "not too happy about it, but it is saving him money." Such attitudes suggest the centrality of financial concerns to the fathers of children whose mothers wind up on welfare. However, Brenda's and Frankie's experiences provide only slim support for the "independence effect" of employment as a deterrent to abusers assumed by exchange theory.

In addition to lukewarm support (much of it apparently motivated by men's pecuniary interest in avoiding sharing the costs of children or sharing their income with their children's mothers[11]) or indifference, I find in these women's life histories evidence of three distinctly negative dynamics concerning women's employment. All fall under the broad category of "work–family conflict," a concept that scholars have coined to capture the conflicting demands of combining responsibilities for earning and caring that particularly but not exclusively beset mothers. In their studies of the connections and contradictions between work and family, researchers have identified several sources of potential conflict, including time allocation, role overload, and spillover of tasks or feelings from one site to the other.[12] Most feminist accounts focus on the institutional or organizational barriers—such as lack of childcare, inflexible work schedules, and gendered divisions of labor—that make it especially difficult for women to reconcile earning and caring, and that therefore reproduce the traditional assignment of breadwinning to men and intensive mothering and housewifery to women.[13] The notion that women's work can be a source of conflict in relationships is consistent with a third theoretical account: a *backlash* model. Contrary to the predictions of exposure and exchange theory, a backlash model predicts that abuse will start or escalate as a woman takes steps toward increased independence from her husband or boyfriend by applying for welfare or increasing her labor force participation and earnings.[14]

Recently, workplace organization scholars have introduced the work–family conflict framework to add new dimensions to how researchers and activists understand the antecedents, consequences, and costs of battering.[15] Even as they lament the lack of reliable data on the prevalence and cost of battering,[16] they register the abuse-related costs to work organizations of higher turnover, increased health expenditures, workplace security, and litigation.[17] My interviews with Georgia, Alice, Tonya, Larnice, and others begin to fill the gap in what we know about the causes of poverty and battering and the connections among battering, work, and welfare. In the women's accounts that follow, I focus on different types of work–family conflict: family conflicts *about* work, conflicts and abuse that *interfere* with work, and abuse and abusers who *follow* women to work. I give examples of all three types of literal work–family conflicts and concentrate on the third and least examined: what happens when abusers stalk, harass, or assault their current or former wives or girlfriends in the workplace.

Conflicts *About* Work

The first category of work–family conflict salient for my purposes involves conflicts *about* work. A job is a source of money, social connections, organization, and physical and emotional space outside of home and family.[18] Women's employment is therefore a potential source of conflicts over resources, power, and control in relationships. In addition, couples may disagree about the gendered division of labor (within the home and between home and workplace) and about the rewards of waged work (in terms of entitlements to leisure and deference at home, for example). Researchers have documented these conflicts in many couples trying to juggle work, family responsibilities, and what sociologist Barbara Risman calls the "gender vertigo" of uneven social change.[19] For example, researchers have shown how women's labor force participation changes the level of conflict in immigrant couples from Mexico. Women's employment challenges the "breadwinner" element of hegemonic masculinity, undermines men's control over financial decisions, disrupts housework and childcare responsibilities traditionally assigned to women, and (as exchange theory predicts) shifts the balance of power in interactions.[20]

Couples' struggles over the logistics and meanings of women's employment become partner-perpetrated abuse when they cross the line from simple fights and conflict tactics to efforts to diminish and destroy individual women's integrity, dignity, and autonomy.[21] Research studies of women who have left abusive partners[22] or are living in refuges for battered women[23] reveal the extent to which women's labor force participation—and the economic resources, social networks, and potential for independence it represents—can be an important source of relationship strife (as the backlash model predicts).

A common source of conflict *about* women's work is men's jealousy, which may be either financial or sexual. Seven of the 40 women interviewed mentioned conflicts over their employment that included their partners' being "jealous." Harriet, Black, never married, and 30 at the time of the retrospective interview, said the father of her toddler let her know: "He was the man and he wanted to provide. . . . He was jealous that I had a job and he didn't and he wanted to take care of me and he didn't want me to be independent." Of the father of her middle child, Janice (also Black and 30) said that although he had never stopped her from working, she "always felt he was a little bit jealous." Alice, introduced in the first chapter, noted that the reason the father of her older child objected to her working was that "he was jealous and scared that I'd find someone else." Of her fiancé, 18-year-old Karen said, "[He] is a very jealous person and always has been." Nevertheless, she added, he wanted her to get a job and start working so that they would have more income; he was impatient with her efforts to get additional training (in computers) before trying to work full time. The impressions Harriet, Janice, Alice, and Karen reported of work–family conflict notably included issues of masculinity, including both adherence to the ideology of male breadwinning ("he was the man and he wanted to provide") and heterosexual possessiveness ("he was jealous and scared that I'd find someone else").[24] These are all cases in which work–family conflict takes the form of conflicts *about* women's employment, consistent with the backlash model.

Some women's lives combine these issues. For instance, Sally, a White 44-year-old grandmother legally separated from but currently living with her husband, described the conflicts about work that developed early on in her long-standing, off-and-on relationship in this way: "He didn't like me working—he said he made enough money to take care of me." She said he was unstable and sometimes violent during their early years together, hitting and strangling her on several different occasions, and he was "very jealous. When the phone rang, he was jealous. He worried that I'd find someone at work and leave him." Sally explained his erratic and aggressive behavior in terms of a medical condition: "[H]e had some sort of seizures that made him do stupid stuff and then forget about it. Like one time, he set the curtains on fire, left, and then came back and read the paper." In the worst incident of physical violence during their early years, he attacked her in the kitchen when he came home late and Sally did not have dinner ready. He banged her head against the rim of the sink and cut her with a kitchen knife, resulting in her having to go to the hospital emergency room. After that incident, Sally explained, her husband was in prison serving three years of an unrelated 10-year sentence; they didn't see each other for a long time. For the last three years before the retrospective interview in 2001, however, they had been living together again and he had changed for the better. "It was better [for me] not to work to keep the peace back in the old days," Sally said during a follow-up interview, "but now it's ok. . . . He's changed a lot, and the grandkids are his babies. . . . Now, he gives me his money. He wants to control me, and understands now that he can't do that, but back then he didn't understand it. We've had counseling[, and] that's helped." Besides, Sally concluded, "No one tells me what to do anymore. No one raises a hand to me. I'd kill 'em first."

Conflicts That *Interfere* With Work

Sally's past conflicts with her husband about her working, apparently rooted in his fear that she would meet someone new on the job and in his desire to maintain a traditional gendered division of labor and his breadwinner status, did not keep her from working at off-the-books waitress jobs for much of her adult life. The coercive control that results from conflicts *about* women's work may be intended to restrict women's labor supply, but the cross-sectional finding, reviewed in the Introduction, that a history of battering is not associated with lower levels of women's employment is consistent with the accounts in the previous section. In some cases, however, violence and abuse can *interfere* with women's waged work. Research results, some conventional wisdom, and feminist structuralism all suggest that partner-perpetrated harassment, physical violence, injuries, and their emotional fallout complicate women's labor force attachment.[25] Control tactics that interfere with or sabotage women's obtaining or maintaining employment include men's forcing women to quit their jobs or getting them fired, making them chronically late or absent (for example, by backing out of promises to provide childcare or transportation, or by showing up drunk or high, demanding sex, or picking fights when the women need to leave for work), undermining their educational or job certification efforts or their efforts to obtain a driver's license, and appropriating their paychecks.[26] In addition, coercion and control that draw women into criminal activity can land them in jail or give them records that make it much harder to find legitimate employment.[27]

Surveys and ethnographic studies of women in poor neighborhoods[28] and public housing projects[29] document the effects on employment, earnings, welfare receipt, and poverty of women's experiences living with or depending on abusive men, especially the fathers of their children. Similarly, findings from studies of welfare recipients specifically designed to shed light on the intersections of partner violence, work, and welfare in the context of the 1996 welfare restructuring[30] confirm what early advocates observed: Some men use physical violence, stalking, and other technologies of coercive control to limit women's labor force participation, prevent their compliance with welfare requirements, and hinder their transitions from welfare to work.[31] Even when violence and abuse are not explicitly intended to interfere with employment, compared to women without such histories, women coping with present or past violence and abuse report more injuries and poorer physical and mental health, more often report using illegal drugs to self-medicate, and report longer and more frequent spells of unemployment, poverty, and homelessness.[32] As I noted in the Introduction, this picture is complicated by the fact that poor physical and mental health, problems with alcohol and other drugs, and other problems associated with women's being battered are of course also associated with trouble obtaining and maintaining employment; there are complex feedback loops among poverty, battering, and the symptoms and troubles that may contribute to vulnerability as well as follow from these plights.[33]

The physically violent manifestations of work–family conflict that could interfere with women's employment were widespread in this cohort of welfare-to-work transition program enrollees. Two thirds reported at the retrospective interview that the father(s) of their child(ren) had done at least one of the following (lifetime rates): hit, kicked, or threw something at her (32 percent); made her fear for her safety or the safety of her children (28 percent); demanded to have sex with her or forced her to have sex (26 percent); cut, bruised, strangled, or seriously injured her (19 percent); or threatened her with or used a knife or gun to hurt her (12 percent).[34] Recall from the Introduction that Tonya worried about being able to fulfill her work requirement and maintain her eligibility for income assistance because her ex-husband had injured her neck over the weekend and because she was supposed to appear in family court to apply for a restraining order at the same time that she was required to attend her job readiness/job search program in order to maintain her welfare eligibility.

In response to open-ended questions, the women in this cohort of welfare recipients matter-of-factly described incidents of physical violence. Said Donna, when asked to describe and explain such physical abuse: "He punched me in the stomach when I was pregnant. He was just angry—I don't remember why, but probably because I . . . came home late. . . . He was just sick. He was controlling and possessive. He would follow me and not let me to talk to anybody." Donna, a self-identified White 22-year-old who had never been married, did not attribute this physical assault to her employment, and it occurred at home rather than at work, so although it might have *interfered* with her going to work the next day, her experience in this instance does not represent work-related control, abuse, or sabotage that was either *about* work or *at* work.

The notion that physical violence has more to do with alcohol and drug use by the abuser than with any victim characteristic or "precipitating factor" such as the woman's labor force participation is reinforced by several women's accounts, whose experiences help to distinguish between conflict *about* work and conflict likely to *interfere* with work. For instance, LaShauna (who said the father of her children approved of her working) said of the timing of the physical abuse she endured: "He did it when he was drunk, so it didn't really have to do with work." Similarly, Barbara (39, never married, Black) told us, "When he was using drugs more, then it would get worse—but the abuse was not changed by [my] working or not working."[35] Pat (never married, Black, age 20) said of the father of her young child: "He was obsessed, crazy, a stalker, a mentally deranged person in general. His abuse did not have anything to do with my starting work." Between 33 and 46 percent of *physically battered* women we interviewed said their working seemed not to be related to the onset, frequency, or severity of physical violence and injury. The women in this category did not experience their partners as abusing them in response to, or in order to prevent, their working. This finding is consistent with the notion that although batterers often blame women for provoking violence ("if you would just do/stop X, I wouldn't have to hurt you"), women's actions seldom precipitate physical abuse.[36] Some women, however, find themselves the targets of specifically work-related control, abuse, and sabotage.

Work-Related Control, Abuse, and Sabotage

It is in the description of specifically work-related control, abuse, and sabotage that the notion of coercion and physical violence as enforcing men's economic exploitation and control of women becomes most analytically useful. In addition to the ways that work–family conflict can take the form of physical violence and other abuse that interferes with women's work, interviews with battered women reveal forms of coercive control that appear deliberately to extend men's surveillance, coercion, and control of women into the workplace.[37] There is strong empirical support for the feminist observation that some abusers consider work and economics part of the terrain on which they are determined to exercise control over women.[38] Researchers find widespread work-related control, abuse, and sabotage in samples of women taking refuge in shelters[39] and among welfare recipients.[40]

There is considerable anecdotal and interview evidence of men's using physical violence and other abuse to thwart the work effort or undermine the performance and employability of their partners.[41] The issue is clearly on the minds of welfare program officials. When I first embarked on this project, shortly after the passage of the Personal Responsibility Act of 1996, a conversation with the top county welfare administrator revealed that a welfare recipient enrolled in a local computer-repair training course failed to take her certification exam because her boyfriend threatened to break her fingers if she did so. The top county welfare administrator, many program directors, and the staff I surveyed were all aware that the women enrolled in welfare and work-first programs often faced abuse.[42]

In our retrospective and follow-up interviews, we found that the current or former boyfriends and husbands of these 40 welfare recipients sometimes failed to provide promised childcare (43 percent), withheld the car keys or a promised ride to work (32 percent), picked fights when the women needed to leave for work (55 percent), and took or wrecked women's work clothes or other possessions important to performance and comfort at school and work, such as eyeglasses or dental appliances (30 percent). They kept the women up late or interrupted their sleep (47 percent) or needed time or help because of being drunk, high, or in trouble (42 percent), all when the women needed to go to work, be with their children, or just be alone. They threatened to withhold money or gifts if the women persisted with job training or work (40 percent) or threatened to hurt the women or their children if they continued with job training or work (45 percent), and the vast majority (75 percent) seemed jealous that the women might meet someone new at work. They undermined the women's confidence and self-esteem by telling them that they "could never keep a job, learn, or accomplish things in life" (43 percent).

Recall from the first two chapters that a central assumption of the advocates of the Family Violence Option (the main policy provision for battered welfare recipients) is that men's violence and abuse of their current and former girlfriends and wives makes compliance with welfare requirements difficult and even dangerous. Specifically, battering obstructs work and therefore women's compliance with the work requirements of the Personal Responsibility Act. It is also possible that working triggers or escalates relationship conflicts and therefore starts or aggravates physical violence and other partner-perpetrated abuse.[43] Evidence from our interviews suggests that conflicts about women's employment vary a great deal; in fact, the women we interviewed reported that their working had different effects on different sorts of abuse. It appears that *for women who experienced specifically work-related control, abuse, and sabotage*—that is, the women where work–family conflict took the specific form of conflicts *about* work that were also likely to *interfere* with work—going to work precipitated or aggravated the abuse rather than ameliorating it (by getting women out of the house, for example, as predicted by the exposure model, or increasing women's resources and contribution to household income, as predicted by exchange theory) or having no effect. Women's subjective assessments of the temporal and causal relationships between their going to work and being abused reinforce the notion that what researchers consider "work-related" control, abuse, and sabotage are indeed related to work. Abused women perceive a difference between men's acting instrumentally through these forms of control and sabotage and the more common physical violence that expresses anger, jealousy, or other emotion.[44]

There were a few significant differences by racial-ethnic category in patterns of work-related control, abuse, and sabotage. A few White women reported that their partners strongly disapproved of their combining employment and motherhood. For example, two of the six White women we interviewed matter-of-factly reported that their partners told them they could only work outside of the home if they kept up with the housework. In contrast, Black interviewees often scoffed at questions about their partners' gendered expectation about women's domesticity or combining motherhood, housework, and employment. One remarked (after she stopped laughing) that she would kick a man out if he ever talked that way. This is not to say that no Black woman reported that the father of her child objected to mothers' working. For example, Reena, whose experience I describe in some detail at the beginning of the next chapter, said of the father of her second child that he argued that she should not work because working mothers are bad mothers, and reported: "He's caused me to lose jobs, and when I was changing jobs, he would hide the letters saying I got the job. He would make bruises so I'd be embarrassed to go to work." But the fact remains that Black and White women responded quite differently to the series of questions we asked regarding men's expectations about how women combine responsibilities for earning and caring or how women juggle being workers, mothers, and wives or girlfriends.

The racialized cultural and economic organization of employment, motherhood, and marriage contribute to the observed differences in patterns of work-related control, abuse, and sabotage. Black and White welfare recipients face different gender expectations about both employment and maternity. Welfare workers and husbands or boyfriends of Black women are more likely to assume Black women are available to combine motherhood and waged work, while welfare workers and husbands or boyfriends are more likely to construct White women as not in the labor force or unavailable for employment.[45] More intense surveillance, restrictions, and enforcement characterize local welfare offices with a higher percentage of recipients who are people of color.[46] In addition, welfare recipients (like all job seekers) encounter racially stratified labor markets, with important effects on their ability to find and maintain employment and therefore fulfill work requirements. Black women therefore may be even more vulnerable to coercion and control centered on their labor force participation than White welfare recipients, who "are more likely than Black recipients to successfully leave welfare, to stay off of assistance once they have left, and to have better options and referrals for education/training."[47]

Finally, some of the observed differences in women's experiences with work-related control, abuse, and sabotage are no doubt due to racial patterns of men's incarceration rather than to differences in experiences and expectations of work, motherhood, and marriage. For example, Barbara, introduced above, whose children were 10, 14, and 21, reported that their father "would call *a lot* or just show up" when she was at work, and even after she ended her relationship with him, he forced his way into the house and physically abused her. However, at the time of the interviews, he was in prison for a stabbing unrelated to their relationship and he could no longer threaten her or her children or interfere with her employment. Similarly, Angela, age 34, a mother of five children under age 10, reported that the father of her oldest child supported her working but had been killed (in a drug-related incident), as had the father of her fourth child; the father of her third child, with whom she had traded sex for drugs and housing, was in prison at the time of the interview, on charges not related to battering. A total of 10 of the 40 women in this cohort said the father of one or more of their children was in jail or prison, and all but Donna, introduced briefly above, self-identified as Black. The racialized dynamics of violence and imprisonment, especially related to the urban drug economy of the 1980s and 1990s, clearly created profound differences in the experiences of the Black and White women in this cohort of welfare recipients in 2001, not least in their partners' efforts and ability to control or sabotage their employment.[48]

Conflict *at* Work

The third—and least studied—form of work–family conflict that researchers and advocates have identified includes abuse that happens *at* work. As I noted above, Jody Raphael's interviews with Bernice included stories detailing how Bernice's partner threatened, followed, and harassed Bernice and her supervisor, sometimes at their worksite.[49] TK Logan and her collaborators also found that the workplace was a site of partner surveillance and harassment in their study of stalking victims in rural Kentucky.[50] Other researchers have used workplace (rather than shelter-based) samples to document the presence and work-related costs of battered women in work organizations, but have not studied incidents of partner-perpetrated violence and abuse that occur on the job.[51]

Larnice, whose story opens this chapter, combines all three possible meanings or types of work–family conflict. Her ex made her employment a source of conflict in their relationship by being so jealous that he tried to extend his surveillance of her from home to work. The remainder of the empirical material in this chapter focuses on the least studied of these forms of work–family conflict: what happens when abuse and abusers follow women into the workplace.

VIOLENCE AND ABUSE IN THE WORKPLACE

Research on occupational health and safety reveals violence in the workplace. Some workers produce violence as part of the job (for instance, professional hockey players or prison guards[52]). Workplaces are sites of bullying and racial, sexual, and gender harassment by employers and co-workers.[53] "Going postal" is a slang term for the explosive anger some disgruntled employees direct at current or former employers or co-workers; the term refers to a series of fatal shootings at U.S. Postal Service offices in the 1990s.[54] According to the U.S. National Crime Victimization Survey, in the period from 1993 through 1999, an average of 1.7 million violent victimizations per year were committed against people age 12 and over while they were at work or on duty.[55] As is the case generally for violent crime in the United States, far more of those victims were men than women. Although women are increasingly close to half of the U.S. labor force, the average annual rate of workplace violence victimization (rape and sexual assault, robbery, aggravated assault, and simple assault) per 1,000 in the workforce is 9.6 for women and 15.0 for men, the average annual workplace homicide rate per 100,000 employees from 1993 to 2002 was 0.26 for women and 0.96 for men, and women are only 19 percent of the annual average 900 workplace homicides.[56] However, women are much more likely than men to be harassed or killed at work *by their current or former spouses or lovers*. What the Department of Justice calls "intimates" are perpetrators in 18,700 nonfatal workplace violence incidents per year.[57] Unfortunately, because the Bureau of Justice Statistics (BJS) does not report perpetrator relation to nonfatal violence victim by sex category, it is impossible to know how many are men assaulted by their wives or girlfriends. However, the BJS data indisputably show that more than one in six workplace homicide victims who are women (16 percent) are killed by their current or former husband or boyfriend, compared to only 3 percent of workplace homicide victims who are men killed by relatives or other personal acquaintances. Moreover, in the seven years from 1993 through 1999, 40 times the number of work-related homicides were committed by the husband of the victim than the number committed by the wife of the victim.[58]

It is in this broad national context of partner-perpetrated workplace violence that I note that during the retrospective interviews, one in four of the 40 women enrolled in this work-first program reported incidents in which their current or former partners harassed them at work.[59] Mostly, men extended their surveillance and efforts to control their partners from home to the worksite. Incidents of harassing, threatening, and stalking by batterers were widespread not just at workplaces but also on the employment training program sites where the research team conducted interviews. Information about disruptive and potentially dangerous incidents circulated among program staff. Staff at an interview site informed me upon my arrival one morning that the day before, the boyfriend of one of the program participants had frightened staff and clients alike by pacing on the sidewalk outside, brandishing a knife, and shouting threats. Anecdotal evidence of such incidents had reached the top of the county welfare administration, which contributed to the openness of administrators and staff to my conducting this research.[60]

We asked the women about both behaviors by their partners and responses by their co-workers and employers. Some employers and co-workers were supportive, as in the following examples. Alice, introduced in the first chapter, said of her ex-husband: "He would show up every day at lunchtime, call 20 times in an hour, and harass me constantly. One time, I was at work and he showed up. He . . . made an idiot out of himself while I cried. . . . He left voluntarily because they were gonna call the cops. My co-workers were shocked and felt bad for me, and tried to calm me down. They didn't like him, and were angry when he called or showed up." Larnice, from the beginning of this chapter, described the conflict and abuse that followed her to work in these terms: "He would keep calling. Or he would just come in and bother me. At my last job, we had a fight in the parking lot at work. [My co-workers] knew something was wrong and my supervisor let me go home for the day."

Responses ranged from co-workers' sympathetic emotional and protective physical reactions to employers' calling in law enforcement. Reena recalled, "He would show up and want me to go home. He'd make a scene sometimes. [The people at work would] try to make him leave or get me away from him. He [fought his way] through five people to get to me once." Protective responses from co-workers and employers send the message that the woman is experiencing something stressful or dangerous from which she deserves protection. The women reported informal employer remedies such as the instructions to Larnice to take the rest of the day off. Such informal remedies may not actually protect the woman, but from the employer's perspective, telling her to take the rest of the day off temporarily resolves a potential or actual crisis by expelling a troublesome trespasser and an upset employee from the worksite. These women—whose employment was often tenuous—were grateful not to be reprimanded or fired for the disruptions their abusive partners caused.

Only one woman reported that her employer responded with specific safety measures on her behalf. Barbara, introduced above, whose drug-abusing former boyfriend was in prison at the time of the interview, said of his earlier attempts to monitor and harass her when she was at work: "He would either call a lot or sometimes show up. My employer was very supportive—changed my office phone and pager and everything was on file with security there." Barbara's experience illustrates some of the contradictions these women often face. On the one hand, controlling partners insist on having uninterrupted access to women and demand phone and pager numbers so they can monitor women on the job. Women may be out of sight but not out of mind or out of reach for controlling, coercive men. Increasingly sophisticated and mobile telecommunications technologies aggravate the situation. On the other hand, giving out such numbers is generally against workplace policy. Barbara had clearly complied with her partner's original demand that she provide these numbers, and he used workplace technology to extend his control from home to work. Her employer used the tactic of changing her numbers as a safety measure.

The employer's tactic may have stymied her partner's efforts to extend his surveillance of her whereabouts and activities to the time she spent at work. At the same time, the fact that he was able to obtain the numbers from her in the first place and used them to harass her on the job exemplifies the ways in which abusive men position themselves as omniscient and omnipotent even when their wives or girlfriends are out of the house.[61] Evidence of work-related control, abuse, and sabotage thus explicitly rebuts the exposure theory I set out above; leaving home to go to work does not necessarily reduce men's efforts to exercise coercive control or women's exposure and vulnerability to men's abuse.

Other employers were less understanding or supportive than Barbara's and threatened to fire or actually dismissed workers whose current or former boyfriends harassed or abused them while they were on the job. For instance, Edna (22, never married, Black) noted of her partner's harassment: "He called and watched me at work and called in a bomb threat. I almost got fired. They traced his call and he went to jail." Georgia, introduced in the first chapter, recounted that when her partner harassed her at work and stole merchandise from her employer, his actions "got me fired. . . . My boss threatened he would press charges on him and take him to jail." Pat (Black, never married, age 20) reported of her boyfriend: "He would be there at my lunch break just to see what I was doing. He was a pest—calling all the time to see what I was doing. They fired me."

A woman's being fired because of a man's abusive or controlling behavior, or her being held accountable for his trespassing or theft, is a serious consequence. In an era of work requirements and mandatory employment activities to maintain eligibility for income assistance, being fired can lead to caseworkers' terminating benefits, including not only cash and food stamps but also housing and medical aid.[62] These are among the major concerns that originally motivated activists to lobby for the Family Violence Option, the provision in the 1996 welfare rescission legislation that allowed states to grant battered women temporary exemptions from work requirements and child support enforcement provisions, to exclude battered women from some stringent time limits, and to allow battered women to count safety planning, petitioning for protective orders, and attending counseling for themselves or their children as "work-related activities" to fulfill the new contracts between welfare recipients and the restructured welfare bureaucracies.[63]

"He'd make a scene" (Reena's phrase), "He was a pest" (Pat's term), and "He made an idiot out of himself" (Alice's expression) are euphemisms some women in this study used to refer to times that their boyfriend or husband yelled at or physically assaulted them in public settings such as the parking lot or lobby of their place of employment. These expressions draw attention to the man's behavior and signal the woman's perception that the man should be ashamed of behaving inappropriately, without actually mentioning herself or his threats to her safety, dignity, and employment. Her implicit disdain for the abuser and erasure of herself and her suffering is consistent with the rhetorical strategies of battered women, which include minimization, dissociation, and low-key reportage.[64]

Nevertheless, even these low-key reports demonstrate how work-related control, abuse, and sabotage fit into patterns of coercive control. They exemplify the extension of surveillance, isolation, and other control tactics from home to the workplace.

Work-related control, abuse, and sabotage form part of the surveillance repertoire of controlling and coercive men's practices of obliterating women's autonomy, privacy, and personhood by injecting fear into women's "perfunctory choices," by delivering threats, and by monitoring women's whereabouts, behavior, social contacts, and access to money and other resources.[65] Moreover, these incidents make clear some of the gender dynamics of coercive control and the central place of work in those gender dynamics. That is, men's efforts at work-related control, abuse, and sabotage are based in part on normative expectations of men as breadwinners able to support women, and of women as appropriately domestic and dependent—the old gender bargain reviewed in the previous chapter.[66] Women can have profoundly contradictory responses to men's enforcing women's domesticity. Initial delight with the traditional assignment of breadwinning to men can turn to concern over control. This problem is exemplified in a documentary about battered women who killed the men who had abused them. In the film, one woman recounts her initial gleeful response to her boyfriend's suggestion that she quit her job: "I was like, 'Girl, my boyfriend told me I don't have to work, he's going to take care of me so I don't have to go to work nowhere.'" She goes on, "I didn't know he was in the process of putting me in his own little prison."[67]

Women's accounts of what happens when abusers follow them to work suggest that what are still considered in conventional wisdom to be separate spheres of home and work are not so separate. Work–family conflict sometimes takes the specific form of men's efforts to obstruct or control women's labor force participation. When abusers and abuse follow women to work, it compounds their vulnerability, especially if they are low-income mothers and abuse interferes with their complying with work requirements and therefore jeopardizes their future employability and welfare benefits as well as their safety, integrity, dignity, and autonomy.

WHAT ELSE HAPPENS

In the rest of this chapter, I place work-related control, abuse, and sabotage in the context of other obstacles to work for the Black and White welfare recipients whom we interviewed. I attend particularly to what the evidence from the lives of welfare recipients participating in a mandatory work-first program that I present in this chapter suggests about the causes, source of harm, remedy, and role of work in both poverty and battering. I also explore the implications of this evidence for the applicability of exposure and exchange theory to the situations of battered women in general and of those enduring work-specific control, abuse, and sabotage in particular.

One of the connections between poverty and battering is literally through work. Abusers follow women to work, either in person or via telephone, with measurable consequences for women's employment (hours worked, stability of employment, or earnings). In terms of economic costs, mean wages for women in this study who reported physical violence were 76 cents per hour less than mean wages for respondents who did not report physical abuse. Similarly, the women who had ever filed a restraining order against an intimate partner (including one woman who filed during the follow-up period) averaged a 53-cent-per-hour *decrease* in their hourly wages over the follow-up period. The women who had not filed a restraining order averaged an *increase* in their hourly wages of approximately the same amount.[68] At first blush, 76 cents per hour may not seem like a big wage gap between welfare recipients who do and welfare recipients who do not report having been physically abused. However, it was nearly 15 percent of the minimum wage at the time when we conducted these interviews. In many of the low-wage occupations in the U.S. economy, the wage gap between women and men is less than 15 percent, and feminists still think of it as a significant material as well as symbolic problem.[69]

In addition to the work–family conflicts and abuse that literally spills over into the workplace and affects women's performance and safety on the job, battered women sometimes carry anxiety, fear, and anger related to abuse from home to work. Persistent physical, mental, and emotional abuse can cause symptoms of traumatic stress. Trauma has multiple, cumulative, interactive consequences for cognition, affective regulation, and belief systems. Traumatized battered women report symptoms of intrusive memories, flattened affect, and hyperarousal plus feelings of worthlessness and profound doubt in the orderliness and trustworthiness of reality.[70] In response to a list of posttraumatic stress symptoms she might have experienced as a result of being the target of her partner's abuse, one woman I interviewed remarked, "That's why I'm on Prozac."[71] The consequences of traumatic stress—in the form of symptoms—follow women from the putatively private realms of the family and mental health into the realm of work. Such symptoms can derail women's progress in public settings such as school and work, thus thwarting women's achievements and aspirations. However, the picture is more complicated than seeing battering simply as an obstacle to work. On the one hand, women who reported having angry outbursts as a symptom of posttraumatic stress dropped out of welfare-to-work and job training programs at a significantly higher rate than other women enrolled in work-first activities, a negative outcome when attending work-first activities is a condition of welfare eligibility. On the other hand, women whose posttraumatic stress symptoms included intrusive memories of their abuse reported positively that work gets them out of the house and thinking about something else, and these did not appear to increase their drop-out rates.[72] This diversity underlines the importance of acknowledging that different kinds of *abuse* and different *symptoms* of traumatic stress have different effects, and thus require different approaches and remedies. This is another complicated connection between battering and poverty through the mechanism of work.

In the incidents reported here, the man's gendered controlling behaviors—including his concerns about being a "good" provider and especially his sexual jealousy—sometimes obstructed women's labor force participation. These findings are consistent with important aspects of exchange theory: Work is related to independence and therefore to the balance of power and potential for control and coercion in relationships.[73] The evidence I presented in this chapter—of conflicts *about* women's work, conflicts that *interfere* with women's work, and conflicts *at* work—shows that, along with behaviors and feelings, men's specific *ideas about controlling masculinity* and *dependent, domestic femininity* also follow women into the workplace. Some men use abuse to (re)assert control over women, others to compensate for the erosion of masculine privileges of breadwinner status or exclusive social and sexual access to the mothers of their children.[74] Women's employment—and therefore their transition from welfare to work and compliance with the work requirements imposed by the Personal Responsibility Act—can be a central terrain of struggle in their relationships with the fathers of their children, some of whom appear to enforce women's accountability for their interactive enactments of femininity[75] by sabotaging their work effort through abuse. Gender power is central to the connections among battering, poverty, and work, with important implications for welfare policy; the Family Violence Option moves the fulcrum of controlling and coercive men's leverage with women by extending time limits, including services for battered women as work-related activities, and offering battered women at least temporary exemptions from work requirements. Even temporarily relaxing the demand that mothers enter the labor market—for some couples, a demand that constitutes a serious source of work–family conflict—can make a difference in men's holding women accountable for fulfilling their expectations of women's dependence, domesticity, and submission. The connections among poverty, battering, work, and policy resound with gender politics to which exchange theorists tend to turn a deaf ear.[76]

Many factors increase the likelihood that women will be poor and depend on public assistance such as Temporary Aid to Needy Families, food stamps, medical assistance, and housing subsidies. Women we interviewed cited lack of job experience, no transportation, and having been on probation or otherwise in trouble with the law as obstacles to meeting their goals and factors that made and kept them poor. Many mentioned the need for education and training—and the time that education requires—as obstacles to finding work. Some connected the simultaneous need for money and time as an obstacle to maintaining employment; for instance, they noted that going to school requires both time and money. Health problems were a significant obstacle to work for some women. Alice cited her diabetes. At the second follow-up interview, Virginia (Black, separated, age 43) said that since the previous interview, she had been diagnosed first with high blood pressure and then with uterine cancer. Others said problems with addiction to alcohol and prescription or street drugs were almost insurmountable obstacles. Mary, whose experience I recount and interpret more extensively below, put it this way: "Getting treatment has to come first, so I can deal with my drug and alcohol problems. There is a little open door I can see."[77] For those able to find employment, lack of childcare was a significant problem. Three quarters were living alone with their children and therefore could not depend even theoretically on a coresident adult for consistent help with housekeeping and childcare responsibilities. For the two thirds of this work-first program cohort that had either an infant or a preschool-age child at home, finding safe, reliable, affordable childcare was no easy task.

As a consequence of these difficulties finding and maintaining work, a significant proportion of these work-first program participants had limited work histories. I noted in the Introduction that one in four had worked fewer than four months of the past year, and another quarter had not worked at all during the same time period. Employment for most had been highly unstable. At the time of the retrospective interviews, they averaged four jobs, and more than one third had held six or seven jobs since they turned 16. Employment is obviously connected to poverty as well as to social connection and democratic participation in a society that increasingly mandates waged work and conditions health and citizenship benefits on employment (as well as marital status).

Individual work histories are not in fact purely personal, however. The rate at which the regional economy generates job openings in largely low-wage occupations with little upward mobility outstrips the rate at which it generates jobs in higher-paid, full-time, stable occupations with direct connections to internal labor markets or job ladders.[78] Consequently, young adult workers like Larnice and many of the other women we interviewed generally face short internal job ladders with little hope of increasing wages through developing skills, experience, and commitment to a specific employer. As a result, most welfare recipients cycle off and on welfare and in and out of work and remain poor either way, subject to the "churn" at the bottom of the labor market.[79] Changing jobs or employers can be an important strategy for increasing wages. However, although frequent job changes and intermittent employment are common among entry-level workers at the low end of the labor market, over time they tend to characterize the trajectories of those who wind up stuck in low-wage employment rather than those who manage to find higher-wage jobs.[80]

Those who had held jobs worked in retail sales, clerical work, data entry, food preparation and service, nonprofessional health care services, cleaning, or personal services—generally, "women's work" in the relatively and absolutely poorly paid service sector.[81] One in five last worked in retail or personal services sales. Another fifth worked in food preparation and food service jobs, although several women recounted having quit the training programs for highly regimented, poorly paid positions in fast food franchises that they sneeringly called "McJobs." One in five also worked in the "pink collar" ghetto, with jobs in administrative support, clerical and financial records processing, or data entry. One quarter worked for temporary employment agencies, generally as either clerical or financial records processors. Hourly earnings at the most recent job (before the retrospective interview) ranged from the minimum wage ($5.15 per hour at the time of the interview; 10 percent were earning at this level) to one who earned $13.00 per hour. Indeed, virtually all of the women we interviewed earned the low wages typically associated with predominantly female occupations with low education and minimal skill requirements; at the retrospective interview, the mean hourly wage was $7.55 for the most recent job. Although significantly above the minimum wage, this level of earnings is below the "living wage" standard debated in Allegheny County during the period of the interviews. Earnings under $8 per hour are unlikely to lift women above the poverty line or enable them to leave either welfare or abusive intimates, especially if they are unable to work full time. Of the 25 percent of women in this cohort of work-first program enrollees whose most recent job was part time, half said they would have preferred to work full time. Finding full-time work that pays—especially for full-time childcare, especially for young children—is unlikely to be a realistic goal or requirement for these women, at least without significant support.[82] In all of these ways, these interview data shed light on the causes, consequences, and meaning of poverty and battering and the problematic centrality of work in both.

Mary, a White mother of three, age 41, and divorced at the retrospective interview, exemplifies the complicated lives that place battering in the context of other obstacles to work for women in work-first programs five years after Congress rescinded the federal entitlement to income assistance for poor women and their children. Mary was trained as a copy machine repair technician and had worked doing copier set-up and repair, with a salaried job paying $1,200 per month. She had the potential to escape low-waged "women's work" because she had trained in a skilled technical trade generally considered "men's work." But Mary also had a serious drug and alcohol problem, and she was one of several women at the retrospective interview who had lost her driver's license for driving drunk. When we talked about relationships, Mary reported that her ex-husband "laid down the law about not working." Their child was born when Mary was in ninth grade, and they were married for four years.[83] In Mary's observation, his physical violence (which included his raping her and putting a gun to her head) came at random rather than as a consequence of her employment, "and he didn't give me bruises to keep me from working." He nevertheless objected to her employment outside the home and kept her from working just by insisting she not do it. "My husband wouldn't let me work, although I don't know why," Mary said. "I was very young. Perhaps he wanted to keep me at home so I wouldn't end up like the prostitutes in the neighborhood." Her husband's (and perhaps Mary's) associating women's employment with prostitution is part of a pattern of his holding Mary accountable for a certain way of "doing" gender.[84] Feminist criminologist Evan Stark persuasively argues that the ability of men to coerce and control their partners without even intermittent physical violence is paradigmatic of current patterns of abuse, as is holding women accountable to stereotypes of feminine domesticity.[85] Although Mary apparently saw no causal connection between her ex-husband's physical violence and her (not) working, her speculation on his motives for preventing her from working is consistent with Stark's model of coercive control.

Limited education, limited childcare, early childbearing, addiction, trouble with the law—all contributed to the problems Mary had maintaining employment. They also are all entangled in complex feedback loops with her vulnerability to coercive control. But the abuse she suffered at the hands of her ex-husband, and his objections to her working, are now 20 years in her past. Her current partner, in contrast, is "happy" with Mary's working because it means "I can help with expenses, he don't have to help out as much. When I didn't work for four-five months, I had to rely on him, and he didn't like that much." At a follow-up interview, Mary (who had a strong sense of the absurdity of life) said of her current partner: "He's supportive and always has been, a workaholic himself—we hardly see each other because he works so hard, which probably makes the relationship work." In fact, Mary said, "He expects me to work, take care of the house, take care of the kids, everything—[he wants] Wonder Woman." Gendered expectations and traditional notions of feminine domesticity still inform Mary's relationships to men and to waged labor, even though they are combined with a typical awareness of the contours of the new gendered bargain and the concomitant reality that most families need two earners to make ends meet.

Mary and other women's accounts of what happens when abuse follows them from home to work reveal both the variation and the banal consistency in work-related control, abuse, and sabotage and their consequences for women's labor force participation. The range of controlling and abusive behaviors men use to sabotage women's work effort and compliance with requirements of welfare reform is limited; there are only so many variations on "He bothered me at work." But employers' responses—whether, as in Pat's case, it is to fire the woman, or, as in Larnice's case, it is to send her home for the day with the abusive man, or, as in Barbara's case, it is to file a report with security and change her work phone and pager numbers—make a difference in women's ability to maintain employment. And in an era where welfare eligibility depends on women's maintaining employment, employers' responses can make the difference in women's ability to use work and welfare as resources within or as they try to escape from abusive relationships.[86]

As I remarked earlier in this chapter, most feminist accounts of work–family conflict focus on the lack of childcare, inflexible work schedules, and gendered divisions of labor that make it especially difficult for women to reconcile earning and caring. In several ways, describing what happens when batterers follow women to work continues long-term feminist critiques of work–family conflict and lends itself to political efforts to end violence against women, including battering.

First, these women's accounts of conflict *about* work, conflicts that *interfere* with work, and conflicts that happen *at* work help to explain the contrasting predictions from different theoretical frameworks, such as exposure, exchange, and backlash models of the relationship between battering and work. In terms of posttraumatic stress symptoms, the evidence suggests that getting out of the house helps some women to cope with their symptoms, a finding that might be construed as consistent with the exposure model. However, the finding that men and abuse follow women from home to work specifically undermines the central proposition of the exposure model, that is, that battering is specifically "domestic" and that encouraging women to go to work will get them out of the house and away from the batterer.

Similarly, the complex ways work enables women to bring increased resources to abusive relationships provides some empirical support for the exchange model; some men clearly appreciate the ways women's employment reduces their perceived responsibility for contributing to household support. According to exchange theory, abuse that impairs or obstructs the participation of women in the labor force reduces women's earnings and social networks. Obstructing women's employment keeps women from accumulating the resources associated with work—resources that might help them to leave or give them leverage to insist on a reduction in abuse. This is a useful way of thinking about the connections among poverty, battering, and work, and about abuse as an obstacle to employment, so far as it goes. However, exchange theorists take the additional step of fusing this account with victim empowerment folklore. Exchange theory thus implicitly or explicitly predicts that victimization motivates women to increase their earnings as a source of power within the relationship or as a means to leave the relationship. The evidence of specifically work-related control, abuse, and sabotage I present in this chapter calls into question the assumption that *women* have to make batterers stop, and renders problematic the notion that waged work is the best route to safety and solvency.

In addition, the evidence of work-related control, abuse, and sabotage I present in this chapter complicates both work and family as sites of ongoing interactions that produce and reproduce notions and practices of masculinity and femininity. Whether or not women seek, find, obtain, and maintain paid work is one element in a set of everyday arrangements between men and women. As exchange theory proposes, the arrangements couples make, and the conflicts that arise in the course of everyday life, concern bargains that have both determinants and consequences at the household level. But there is something much bigger at stake. Work-related control, abuse, and sabotage blur the distinction between public and private. "Domestic" abuse is clearly not something that only happens at home. Men's expectations about domesticity, social and sexual fidelity, and emotional availability follow women to work. The bargains women and men strike at home are constrained by and in turn shape broader social bargains about the possibilities and constraints for women's combining earning and caring. When wedded to victim empowerment folklore, any version of exchange theory that poses waged work as the solution to every personal and social problem fails to recognize the conflicts at home and the tensions between home and work that are central dilemmas for contemporary families.[87]

Finally, focusing on work-related control, abuse, and sabotage contributes to understanding the economic and personal costs of the ways men and women enforce and acquiesce to difference and dominance based on naturalized notions of what it means to be a "real man" or a "proper woman." Women whose current or former husbands and boyfriends try to control them by invoking traditional duties of motherhood and housewifery (in this study, mostly White women) are especially vulnerable to dropping out of programs designed to move poor mothers from welfare to work.[88] Women less subject to these traditional notions of domestic femininity and therefore more pressured to go to work (in this study, mostly Black women) are paradoxically therefore especially vulnerable to losing their welfare eligibility when men harass or abuse them at work. The work requirements and time limits imposed by the welfare rescission of 1996 have some of the most costly consequences for women whose efforts to conform with those requirements put them at added risk for abuse, a group that includes both Black and White women. The revised gender expectations of welfare policy—that all able-bodied adults shall work for wages in order to be considered for the benefits of citizenship[89]—contradict abusive partners' notions of domestic maternity and dependent femininity. The expanded work requirements also give coercive and controlling men an additional point of leverage against women who seek independence through welfare, work, or their combination. Women's accounts of work-related control, abuse, and sabotage—and what happens when abuse and abusers follow them from home to work—illuminate the likely futility of using welfare policy for marriage promotion and the ironies of using poor women to control poor men, as called for by victim empowerment folklore and the politics of disgust.[90]

Calculating the Costs
of Taking a Beating

Many women in the cohort enrolled in the "work-first" program we studied had an extensive history of attempting to draw on state resources—in the form of welfare benefits, on the one hand, and in the form of civil orders of protection, on the other—to escape poverty or abuse or both.[1] For example, Reena (a Black, 37-year-old mother of two introduced briefly in the previous chapter) had spent three separate "spells" on welfare, for a total of over 11 years since the birth of her first child, 17 years before. Progressive economists and advocates argue that people with limited education, skills, and earnings, or with extensive care obligations, or with mental or physical health problems, often resort to welfare. Neo-liberal economists argue that welfare perversely discourages work and fosters poverty; people will rely on the state safety net if they can use it to avoid hard work and sexual responsibility. No matter which theory applies, however, Reena was clearly one of the long-term welfare recipients targeted by the 1996 welfare legislation. As I observed in the second chapter, both time limits and work requirements were designed to change the incentives and therefore the behavior of women who had spent long spells on welfare.

In addition to three long spells on welfare, Reena reported that the father of her younger child (age 8) made her fear for her safety if she went to work, and she had petitioned for a restraining order against him. Again, whether you think poverty traps women in abusive relationships or abusers sabotage women's education and earnings and thus keep them dependent and poor, or some complex combination of the two, the fact that one quarter of the women in Reena's work-first program cohort had petitioned for protective orders suggests that these civil remedies for physical abuse are important resources for welfare recipients and other women coping with coercive and controlling partners. The question is: What do patterns and differences in women's earnings and in their appeals to the state for income support and protective orders tell us about the relationships among poverty, battering, work, and welfare? The details of Reena's experiences, and the accounts of the complex conflicts *about* work, conflicts that *interfere* with work, and conflicts *at* work from the previous chapter, enrich the technical questions of calculating the costs of taking a beating that are the focus of this chapter.

Reena was a high school graduate, and she had participated in training programs at two of the regional contractors to which the welfare office referred recipients before stringent work requirements and time limits went into effect in March 1997. Through those programs, Reena had completed a six-month certificate in hairdressing, and she had "worked in hairdressing shops off and on, but [she] mostly did hair out of [her] house in between" formal jobs. But six months of certificate-level training after high school did not equip Reena to earn her way out of poverty. Reena had—for a number of family and health reasons—dropped out of two different culinary training programs and completed only four months of a six-month clerk-typist certificate program. Reena viewed her lack of typing skills in particular as a serious liability in the local job market. For six years prior to the retrospective interview, Reena had worked part time, up to 36 weeks per year, as a clerk, mail handler/sorter, and letter carrier for the U.S. Postal Service, "good jobs" in which she earned as much as $11.60/hour.[2] But Reena knew that in order to be competitive for full-time employment at the post office, she had to supplement her sorting and number pad skills with the ability to use a QWERTY keyboard. By the time of the final follow-up interview in early September 2002, not having gained the requisite skills, Reena's wages had fallen to only $6.25/hour and she still only worked part time.[3]

One goal of this chapter is to put Reena's (essentially stalled) pattern of education, employment, and earnings into the broader perspective of welfare recipients who did and who did not petition for a civil order of protection during the five years before and after Allegheny County implemented the new welfare rules, time limits, and work requirements. For now, it is necessary to note that Reena's employment history and educational attainment were fairly typical of the women in this cohort. Reena was a high school graduate, had completed a postsecondary certification program, and had established an employment record with the post office. Reena was therefore in a somewhat better position in the labor market than the one in five members of her cohort who had only a high school diploma or equivalent as their highest educational attainment. She was significantly more likely to be able to work her way to solvency than the 12 percent of her cohort who had only completed 10th or 11th grade and had no GED. One in five women enrolled in the work-first program with Reena had not worked at all in the previous year, and another one in four had worked between one and 16 weeks in the previous year. Recall that the average wage at the most recent job for those who had earnings was $7.55/hour, well above the legal minimum wage of $5.15/hour but below the "living wage" threshold for Allegheny County.[4] At times, Reena had made far more than that, although at the final follow-up interview, she was making only $1.10/hour above the minimum wage and earned $1.30/hour below the average wage of the cohort, with an even larger gap between her wage and the "living wage."

Reena, whose housing situation was stable, who had postponed her first birth until she was 20, who had been married to the father of her first child, and whose youngest child was already in school, did not face many of the obstacles to work that are common in her cohort and in the lives of welfare recipients across the country.[5] In this cohort of women, one quarter had been evicted or had to move in with someone else. A few had significant literacy problems. Recall from the Introduction that

40 percent had a preschool-age child living with them, and one in five had an infant at home. The mean age at first birth was 19, and 60 percent reported becoming mothers for the first time when they were teenagers (by age 20).[6] What Reena shared with a quarter of the women in her cohort was having petitioned for a civil restraining order against the father of one of her children. In this chapter, I set out further evidence about the connections between battering and poverty in the context of policy changes. I answer a series of empirical questions using administrative data about poverty and battering in Allegheny County, including: Which comes first, petitioning for a protective order or going on welfare? How do welfare recipients who petition for a protective order differ from other welfare recipients? Did changes associated with welfare rescission have the same effect on the earnings of welfare recipients who do and do not petition for protective orders?

From the perspective of the work–family conflict model explored in the previous chapter, Reena faced a complex and contradictory set of expectations about earning and caring.[7] In addition to raising her two children, ages 8 and 17, Reena was responsible for helping to take care of her aging mother and stepfather. The restructured welfare system expected her to seek and maintain employment. At the same time, the father of her youngest child felt that working mothers are bad mothers—a classic example of conflict *about* work, rooted in conventional views of feminine domesticity and maternity. He also tried to *interfere* with her working: "He would make bruises [*sic*] so I'd be embarrassed to go to work. I wasn't fired because of something he did, but he prevented [me from] being hired. He would hide the letters saying I got the job. . . . He'd lie [and say he was sick] to get me to leave work." Finally, he would abuse her *at* work: "[He would s]how up and want me to go home. He'd make a scene sometimes. . . . He went through five people to get to me once." Jealousy was at the root of his objections to her employment. Reena said, "He didn't want me to work because he thought that I'd leave him. . . . He didn't want me to have a job, and he's that way about his new wife. He's very insecure." The administrative data I analyze in this chapter do not allow me to distinguish among the types of work–family conflict explored in the previous chapter. They also do not allow me to track the stability of women's employment, a very important outcome in research on poverty, battering, and welfare.[8] But they do allow me to calculate the cost of taking a beating by looking at differences in the earnings trajectories—that is, the starting points and growth over time in earned income—of welfare recipients who did and who did not petition for a protective order in Allegheny County between 1995 and 2000.

As I sort through the different ways of calculating the costs of battering, keep in mind the image of Reena's ex-husband hassling her in the parking lot of the regional supermarket chain where she had finally found a job. Picture her younger child's father bruising her face and arms so she would be too ashamed to go to work. The administrative data I use to explore the connections among work and battering for women on welfare are not nearly as rich as the interviews with Reena and her cohort. However, the administrative data allow me to ask and answer an important set of questions about the costs of taking a beating—and the answers will be more meaningful in the context of Reena's experience.

COST ACCOUNTS

There are several different ways of calculating what I am calling the costs of taking a beating. One reason the estimates of these costs vary so widely is because different researchers are counting different things in their efforts to answer different questions. In this section of this chapter, I review the empirical and theoretical work researchers have done to define and calculate the cost of battering.

Recall from the second chapter that Congress recorded among its findings in the Violence Against Women Act that, "Rape and sexual assault in the United States is estimated to cost $127,000,000,000 per year."[9] Where does an estimate like $127 billion per year come from? To calculate the annual cost of any set requires four operations: defining the unit, estimating the number of units per year, estimating the cost per unit, and multiplying the estimated number of units per year by the estimated cost per unit. This is an exercise in *aggregate* social cost accounting. In the case of rape and sexual assault, defining the unit means specifying what counts as rape and sexual assault. Estimates of the number of units per year are relatively readily available for some definitions of rape and sexual assault; official crime statistics provide reasonable estimates of reported rapes and sexual assaults. Estimating the cost per unit also requires specifying what counts as a cost; the economic costs of medical and mental health treatment, law enforcement and court costs, and lost wages and productivity might all be included. The definitions and estimates are the difficult and potentially controversial part; multiplication is simple. Similarly, calculating what Wendy Max and her collaborators call "the economic toll of intimate partner violence against women"[10] involves defining "intimate partner violence" and estimating its prevalence, then adding up the estimated economic costs per victim and multiplying the cost per victim by the number of victims in the country over a particular time period.

Estimating the cost of taking a beating in this sense is an important part of the social problems rhetoric for mobilizing support to the cause of ending violence against women. The idea is to generate cost estimates that support activists' assessments of the widespread and consequential character of violence against women as a social problem.[11] Using data from national surveys of violence against women and medical expenditures, Max et al. estimated that annual intimate partner violence against women in the United States cost somewhere between $3.9 billion and $7.7 billion in 1995 dollars. That range included the direct and indirect "monetary burden to society of physical and mental health consequences, time lost, and premature death resulting from" partner-perpetrated rapes, physical assaults, stalking, and murders. Updated to 2003 dollars, their point estimate is about $8.3 billion per year.

Of course, researchers who include a broader range of relationships between victim and perpetrator (child/parent and violence against men), and who include "lost quality of life" in their calculations, produce significantly higher estimates of the aggregate costs of "domestic violence." For example, in 1996, researchers from the National Institutes for Justice (NIJ; the research branch of the U.S. Department of Justice) estimated the costs associated with "domestic violence" (including child/parent and violence against men) at $67 billion.[12] This figure is an order of magnitude higher than the estimate produced by Max's research team, but still only about half of the estimate Congress included in the Violence Against Women Act (VAWA) legislation. The NIJ researchers considered a wider range of victims than Max et al. did, which accounts for some of the difference. More important, though, $58 billion of the NIJ estimate is for lost quality of life, a factor Max et al. did not include in their estimate. Again, the estimates you get depend on what you count.

The U.S. Centers for Disease Control and Prevention (CDC) reported that health costs of partner-perpetrated rape, physical assault, stalking, and homicide of women totaled $5.8 billion in 2003.[13] Economists estimate that employers lose $96 million/year when battering undermines the productivity of the women they employ.[14] The cost estimate of $127 billion that Congress included in the VAWA Reauthorization Act of 2005 covered rape and sexual assault only, but was not limited to partner-perpetrated sexual violation. What added significantly more to the VAWA 2005 figure was the fact that estimated costs included not only medical and mental health care, social services, and reduced quality of life, but also lost productivity, public expenditures for police and fire services, and loss of and damage to property. Additional costs, therefore, might include policing, prosecuting, and incarcerating perpetrators, and legal, social, and protective services for battered women and their children. The bottom line: It is very difficult to compare research-ers' estimates of the aggregate costs of partner-perpetrated abuse and other violence against women, for example, to see if they are changing over time, because they cover different victim groups, count different crimes, consider different costs, or otherwise constitute apples and oranges rather than comparable figures.

Whatever you count in the *aggregate*, advocates, researchers, and service provid-ers alike acknowledge that battering diminishes *individual* women's health, lives, capacities, and possibilities. Physical injury, emotional damage, and traumatic stress all take their toll on women's capacities for earning, employment, and the "self-sufficiency" reformers hoped to promote by rescinding welfare entitlements and requiring poor mothers to seek and maintain work.[15] For U.S. women aged 15 to 44, physical violence perpetrated by a current or former partner is the most common source of injury and mortality, surpassing injuries and deaths from automobile accidents, cancer, and muggings combined.[16] Vocational rehabilitation specialists and advocates argue that battering not only causes debilitating physical damage (especially through head injuries) but also diminishes the experiences and choices that girls and women have as students, workers, mothers, and lovers.[17] Mental health specialists note that intrusive memories, sleep disturbances, inability to concentrate, hair-trigger startle reflex, dissociation[18] and flattened affect,[19] and other posttraumatic stress symptoms are frequent consequences of battering.[20] It therefore makes sense that another strategy for making the argument that battering is a costly social problem is to apply similar accounting and estimating techniques to the *individual* level, and to thus estimate the average cost per victim of various types of interpersonal violence while doing an end-run around the preva-lence problem.

For example, Ann Coker and her research collaborators conducted an epidemio-logical study of the physical health consequences of psychological forms of partner-perpetrated abuse. The implication is that there is a "health toll" facing battered and abused women.[21] Researchers eager to bolster the case that stopping batterers will save taxpayers' money point to the additional finding that health care costs are 19 percent higher for women who have a history of "domestic violence" than for women without such a history.[22] Rivara and colleagues estimate that victims require an average per person expenditure of $439 more on medical care than nonvictims.[23] Wisner and her team estimate the additional health care costs for battered women at $1,775 per woman per year.[24] Arias and Corso went a step further and applied unit cost estimates to measures of the utilization of health care services. They found that the average cost per man victimized by his heterosexual partner was $80 in mental health services and $83 for medical services; for a woman victimized by her heterosexual partner, the average cost per woman was $207 in mental health services and $483 for medical services.[25] Rothman and Corso looked at the workdays and on-the-job productivity of a small sample of men working for a state agency, and they found that greater propensity for abusiveness is associated with costly missed days and decreased productivity, yet another dimension of the cost of battering.[26]

One way economists approach the problem of calculating the costs of taking a beating is by using *game theory* to explore the incentives that might explain why abusive marriages continue, change their level of violence, or break up. Economists give central importance to a person's *utility*, that is, the net benefits (income and consumption) someone gets out of a situation. In this context, the benefits of marriage are *marital utility*, the benefits available outside a marriage make up a person's *external utility*, and the minimal level of benefits a person is willing to accept is his or her *reservation utility*. Game theorists use a bargaining model, in which resources not tied to her husband shape the decisions a woman makes about whether or not to "put up with" his violence.[27] Thus, income and consumption and anything that improves her quality of life—from work, but also from outside family and friends, welfare and other social support systems, and perhaps even a neighborhood or community culture that supports women's autonomous household formation and their dignity and integrity as workers, mothers, and sexual beings—increase a woman's external utility. And when a woman's external utility rises, economists figure, "the man's ability to 'buy' violence from her decreases and the violence falls." Labor economists Amy Farmer and Jill Tiefenthaler make a clear presentation of this analysis.[28]

This way of thinking about the situation facing a battered woman can help to explain both why she might stay and why and when she might leave as well as the effect of her independent access to resources on her decision to stay or go and even her bargaining power within the relationship. For example, Farmer and Tiefenthaler posit that, "[I]f services and the divorce settlement [and, presumably, her own income] adequately compensate her for the loss of his transfers [that is, the resources, consumption, and good feelings (including validation of her as a good mother) she receives from him], she will not remain in the marriage."[29] Similarly, they propose, "If a woman believes her children are better off in an intact family, [her children] will increase her marital utility relative to her reservation utility[,] which will lead to an increase in violence. However, if a woman believes that the violence has a negative effect on the children[,] her marital utility falls below her reservation utility and the violence will decrease"[30] or she may try to exit the relationship.

In some ways, economists who present game-theoretic analyses are trying to work through yet another approach to the question, "Why do women stay in abusive relationships?"[31] Game theory in some respects represents an advance over psychopathological accounts that invoke feminine masochism, cognitive dissonance, learned helplessness, or other individual-level psychological explanations for battering and for women's staying in relationships with abusive men.[32] Economists' ways of thinking about welfare and work—as resources for consumption and other components of a woman's utility outside of marriage that increase the probability that she leaves and therefore that lower the level of violence if she stays[33]—yield predictions they call "intuitive."[34] That is, these predictions are consistent with what economists think garden-variety rational actors would do. The predictions economists produce are also consistent with elements in "feminist resource theory," which "also predicts that as women's incomes increase and their alternatives to violent marriages improve there will be less wife abuse."[35]

But there are several difficulties with the game-theoretic approach to understanding the cost of being in an abusive relationship. Foremost, as economists are the first to point out, violence affects income at least as much as income affects violence. This problem of endogeneity or reciprocal causality makes it very difficult to sort out the costs and causes of battering. Second, a controlling or coercive man may use abuse (some of it physical violence, but much of it not) to belittle his wife or girlfriend, trying to convince her that no one else would ever want her. Men also sabotage their girlfriends' or wives' education, job, or promotion prospects. In economists' terms, a man seeks to diminish a woman's external utility in order to keep her from leaving the relationship. The game-theoretic model could take this dynamic into account, but economists have not contributed much to the social science research about work-related control, abuse, and sabotage that might go into such a way of calculating the costs of taking a beating.

Finally, when Congress and President Clinton rescinded federal welfare entitlements in 1996, they raised women's "threshold" or "threat point" (that is, the point at which game theory predicts a woman's utility from leaving the relationship finally exceeds her utility from staying) by potentially increasing the impact of violence on women's long-term earnings. After all, if an abusive man can undermine a woman's work effort, get her fired, or sabotage her performance at school or on the job, he can simultaneously reduce her earnings and undermine her eligibility for public assistance, thus reducing two external factors in her income and consumption. Congress increased women's vulnerability, or raised women's threshold or tolerance for abuse (they amount to the same thing), in two ways. First, by rescinding federal entitlements, Congress reduced the availability of welfare benefits as an alternative to low-wage work, thus aggravating the economic consequences of poor women's experiences of work-related control, abuse, and sabotage. When the partners of women like Edna, Georgia, and Pat extend "domestic" abuse to the workplace, they decrease women's ability to obtain and maintain employment and therefore earn income and increase consumption (that is, reduce women's external utility and thus their leverage in the relationship and raise the amount of violence or abuse they are willing to tolerate).

Second, by requiring states to show that an increasing percentage of welfare recipients were spending an increasing number of weekly hours engaged in work or "work-related activities," Congress raised the stakes of poor women's employment to include compliance with work requirements. Noncompliance with work requirements, along with bumping up against time limits also instituted through the 1996 legislation, can lead to sanctions that reduce a woman's welfare benefits and therefore her external resources, thus (in this model) increasing her tolerance for abuse. Although their model can accommodate changes in external resources (including both welfare benefits and earned income), Farmer and Tiefenthaler never actually discuss the ramifications of changes in welfare benefits, policy, requirements, or sanctions, even though they published their article about the employment effects of "domestic violence" well after Congress rescinded welfare entitlements and thus dramatically shifted women's external utility.

In their game-theoretic analysis, Farmer and Tiefenthaler model the woman's utility[36] as a function of a combination of her earnings and the income and consumption available to her from other sources (welfare, family, shelters) if she leaves. They note:

> The greater the impact of violence on the woman's long run earnings, the higher his [the abuser's] utility. In addition, the woman's external utility is now lower than it would have been if her long run earnings were not affected by the violence. . . . Thus, if a victim of domestic violence would continue to suffer earnings losses even if she left her abuser, his knowledge of this effect will permit him to commit more violence. . . . If violence only lowers a woman's income temporarily[,] while she is in the relationship, then we predict that amount of violence is lower relative to the model in which violence has no impact on income. Since the woman's threat point is unaffected, the man must compensate her for the lost income by lowering the violence. However, if violence permanently lowers a woman's earning potential, we expect more violence. The abuser can weaken her credibility of leaving the relationship by limiting her future earnings potential. Thus, we predict that violence will be the greatest when the damage to the woman's income is the most permanent.[37]

The prediction that a man will commit the most violence against his wife or girlfriend when he can successfully undermine her external resources is intuitive. This is true both in terms of the man's incentive (which is to escalate the violence in part *in order to* damage her outside earnings) and the importance of work requirements as an external issue. He winds up with an incentive to sabotage her work effort and her compliance with work mandates so that the resources and consumption that do not depend on the abuser decrease under a work-first regime.

To their credit, Farmer and Tiefenthaler in this analysis are less asking, "Why does she stay?" than they are asking, "Why does *he* stay—and abuse?" From a feminist perspective, the latter is a far more interesting question to ask and answer; moreover, game theory provides an alternative to natural, religious, or criminological conventional wisdom explanations of what causes men's violence against women.[38] What Farmer and Tiefenthaler seem not to notice is the ways work requirements and time limits perversely constitute policy support for women's increased vulnerability and men's increased leverage and incentives to abuse. This is a paradoxical outcome of a welfare policy ostensibly designed to increase women's "self-sufficiency" by eliminating perverse economic incentives presumed to discourage employment, sexual restraint, and parental responsibility.

In the face of these problems with conducting an economic analysis of partner-perpetrated violence, abuse, and coercive control, economists have also worked to calculate the cost of taking a beating specifically by estimating "the *employment effects* of domestic violence."[39] The economic costs of battering to individual women and their families include reduced wages, work hours, job experience, employment stability, and earnings[40]; increased food insecurity and trouble paying rent or utility bills[41]; chronic individual and intergenerational cycling between work and welfare and in and out of abusive relationships[42]; and what researchers term "dangerous dependencies" on abusive men for job supports such as childcare and transportation.[43] The personal costs—education and training foregone, physical and mental health compromised, dreams deferred, life possibilities stunted—are part of the uncalculated and uncompensated price of women's subordination. Both safety crises and the traumatic physical, sexual, and emotional aftereffects of battering may obstruct women's transition from welfare to work, and poor women report not only high rates of battering but also high levels of distress rooted in trauma.[44] Battering and posttraumatic stress symptoms may thus impede school and job performance, career planning, and ability to conform to work requirements and time limits imposed by welfare reform through short-term safety crises, inter-mediate-term sabotage of compliance, and long-term physical and emotional effects.[45]

It is also clear from a growing set of research findings that there are strong associations between battering and poverty in general and specific hardships (such as homelessness) or other problems (such as drug addiction). In one study, metha-done users who are women were both extremely poor and likely to have been abused by their partners; some women use heroin, "crack" cocaine, alcohol, and other drugs to numb the pain of having been battered.[46] Formerly homeless women report mental health, substance abuse, "domestic violence", and family changes as the concurrent issues associated with homelessness.[47] Interviews with low-income women in temporary or public housing show strong associations among home-lessness, poverty, and "domestic violence".[48] The Worcester, Massachusetts, study of housed low-income and homeless women found widespread, recent partner violence.[49]

It is less clear from this research what type of barrier abuse represents to working, escaping poverty, or avoiding material hardship. Strong anecdotal evidence from nonrandom interview studies suggests that some abusers sabotage women's waged work, limit their earnings capacity and career development, and prevent poor women's compliance with the work requirements instituted with the 1996 welfare reforms.[50] No *national* U.S. studies go beyond estimating prevalence to document or explain the difference "domestic violence" makes in women's experiences of poverty, work, and welfare. The data simply do not exist at the national level.

As I note in the Introduction, findings from *local* U.S. studies that include current or recent abuse as a possible correlate or predictor of employment are often contradictory or counterintuitive.[51]

An example of a counterintuitive finding comes from a study of domestic violence and welfare receipt in Maryland. Maryland welfare recipients who disclosed "domestic violence . . . were more likely to be Caucasian, be separated, and receive assistance in jurisdictions with mid-sized caseloads" than those who did not disclose domestic violence to a case manager.[52] The women who disclosed abuse also spent *less time* on welfare than their nondisclosing peers. It would be simplistic to argue that moving poor mothers from welfare to work will automatically reduce battering, but it is realistic to think that women who disclose battering might receive services that will help them to make a speedy transition. Clearly, there are differences between women who do and do not disclose, just as there are important differences between battered women who do and do not seek protection from the police and court system; those differences are likely correlated with variations in the effects of abuse on employment patterns and earnings.[53] Furthermore, no one would suggest that policymakers should encourage battering as an incentive to move women off welfare. Nevertheless, the Maryland study raises questions about the relative importance of work, solvency (through welfare or employment), and safety planning for poor and abused women.

Examples of contradictory findings come from other research. In the Michigan Women's Employment Study (WES), "domestic violence" was not one of the barriers significantly associated with working 20 or more hours per week.[54] Moreover, in the WES, a recent, first-time incident of violence was not associated with specific hardship experiences or the overall level of hardship, including food insecurity, homelessness, and utility shut-offs. These specific findings notwithstanding, the researchers concluded that "domestic violence of a severe, recent and persistent nature is a factor in lower economic well-being for women who have received welfare benefits," and "domestic violence that is both recent and persistent is associated with numerous indicators of hardship."[55] Contradictory and counterintuitive findings about the ways battering increases hardship and poverty specifically by obstructing work are typical of research on these issues.

The contradictory, mixed, and counterintuitive findings from this research are the results of confounding at least three different aspects of the employment effects of battering. I and many other researchers interested in the relationship between battering and employment have investigated effects on *labor supply*, that is, on the probability that a woman will be employed or looking for work at any given time.[56] This is consistent with the observation that battering is an obstacle to work. In the context of that observation, the repeated finding that a history of battering does not significantly reduce women's labor market activity appears not just "mixed" but downright anomalous.

Farmer and Tiefenthaler observe that, "[R]esults are mixed. While the empirical evidence supports the [economic, game-theoretic] model's assumption that violence has a negative impact on the labor market productivity of working women, it also indicates that being a battered woman does not significantly decrease the likelihood that a woman participates in the labor market."[57] This finding is partly an artifact of using cross-sectional data, which only provide a snapshot at one point in time. As they note, "[E]ven after controlling for other confounding effects, battered women are no less likely to work for pay than other women" (that is, labor supply is basically the same in the immediate term), *but also* the negative effects of battering on women's employment show up in even brief longitudinal studies: "[B]attered women have significantly lower odds of working 30+ hours per week for at least six months."[58]

But the employment effects of "domestic violence" also include the toll abuse takes on working women's *productivity* (including absenteeism, distraction, needing help to complete assigned tasks, etc.). Women who participated in two different studies of partner stalking reported that, "[S]talking by a partner interfered in their work through on-the-job harassment, work disruption, and job performance problems."[59] Farmer and Tiefenthaler "estimate that 2.8 million work days are lost each year as a result of domestic violence . . . [and] estimate the total pay lost by battered women to be $96 million."[60] Similarly, Arias and Corso estimate the average cost per man victimized by a female intimate partner was $244 in productivity losses, and per woman victimized by a male intimate partner was $257 in productivity losses.[61] Combined with the results of efforts to calculate the costs of battering as a social problem reviewed above, findings on the negative effects on productivity and labor force participation of physical violence and the sorts of work-related control, abuse, and sabotage featured in the previous chapter contribute to understanding the price individual women, employers, and society as a whole pay when the "work–family conflict" discussed in the previous chapter becomes literal.

Researchers derive still another way of calculating the costs of taking a beating from trying to understand partner-perpetrated *economic exploitation and control.* Interviews with battered women and their abusive partners reveal the financial, economic, and employment dimensions of men's coercive control and abuse of their wives and girlfriends. Sociologist Angela Hattery points out the complex gender and race dynamics of economic dependency, exploitation, and what she calls intimate partner violence. Some men seek to maintain control over and sexual access to women by interfering with their employment, and—consistent with aspects of the game-theoretic model—some women trade sexual access and put up with physical and emotional abuse in return for a measure of economic support. But Hattery also finds that men who have trouble maintaining steady "family wage" employment or getting and keeping a "straight" job because they have a history of incarceration[62] or other discrimination sometimes encourage their wives or girlfriends to bring in income from waged work and welfare—and then compensate for their "failures" as breadwinners through physical violence and other abuse.[63] Discriminatory patterns of employment and incarceration make this pattern particularly common for men Hattery identifies as African American, as in the example of two of Hattery's interviewees, Wanda and Chris. The jealous Chris "tries to physically assert what he sees as 'his right to his woman,'" only to have Wanda "'remind' [him] that he is not the breadwinner in the household and therefore has no claim to enforce the 'rules.'. . . In an attempt to reassert his masculinity the argument escalates and often becomes physical."[64]

Similarly, criminologist Evan Stark notes the ways men can benefit from controlling the work effort and wages as well as spending patterns of their wives and girlfriends, and gives an extended example of a woman whose partner coerced her into stealing from her employer.[65] Criminologist David Adams documents variation in patterns of economic abuse by men who murdered their wives or girlfriends; some of his interviewees were abusive men deeply invested in exploiting women's earnings capacity, while others seemed coldly indifferent to the income-generating activities of their wives or girlfriends.[66] The stakes in men's work-related control, abuse, and sabotage are of course higher when the earnings potential of the woman is higher. This might explain why the more highly educated members of a group of welfare recipients I interviewed reported more conflict about work, work interference, and stalking and harassment on the job than did their less educated peers.[67]

Most recently, Adrienne Adams and her research collaborators have developed a Scale of Economic Abuse, a 28-item checklist designed to measure the character, prevalence, and frequency of partner-perpetrated economic exploitation and control. They included in the checklist those items that were reported by at least 25 percent of a sample of 103 women receiving residential or nonresidential services from a "domestic" abuse victim service agency. They included those items from the Work/School Abuse Scale, a checklist of tactics abusers deploy to restrain women or interfere with their work and school activities,[68] that met their criteria for clarity, psychometric properties (high item-total correlation), and conceptual contribution. They conducted an extensive measurement analysis, but did not in fact report the scale scores of this sample; we still know very little, empirically, about specifically economic abuse.[69]

Finally, there are effects of battering on *household income* or *earnings*, either through reduced wages, missed promotions, firings, or reduced work hours, or through sanctions or time limits that reduce cash, food stamps, and medical benefits from welfare. Recall Tonya's concern that the neck injury she received from her abusive ex-husband might interfere with her employment and therefore with her compliance with the eligibility requirements of the work-first system. Failure to comply with attendance requirements would have jeopardized her welfare benefits and potentially her earnings. In addition, failure to petition for a protective order (which she had to do during the same morning hours that she had to attend the work-first program) would have jeopardized her safety. On that particular Monday morning when I interviewed Tonya, it made sense to observe that battering lowered her earnings potential, rather than to argue that her economic dependence led to her being battered. But this question of causation—of which came first, economic dependence or battering—remains a vexed one in research and theory.[70] Causal arguments become especially complicated because life is not a single event; life is iterative and staggered, with intricate feedback loops among what might seem like separate incidents.

The problem of attributing causality to two related or correlated phenomena, when they may be operating simultaneously, creating a feedback loop (known colloquially as a vicious cycle or virtuous spiral), mutually constitutive, or otherwise related in a complex causal chain, is technically called endogeneity.[71] That is, both elements in the potential causal story are endogenous or inside the circle of causality, and both could be either cause or effect or both. One way to picture this problem is to set out explicitly the two causal relationships economic theory suggests are "likely" and the pathways or mechanisms through which one factor causes the other. In the first causal relationship, abuse is the cause and low earnings the effect (perhaps through the ways abuse interrupts education, training, or job continuity and thus lowers productivity and therefore earnings). In the second causal relationship, low earnings cause abuse, or at least vulnerability to abuse, through exactly the opposite mechanism: Low education, occupational status, educational attainment, and earnings mean women have little leverage within and limited resources to leave abusive relationships. Both stories are plausible, and the only way to adjudicate between them is to observe the actual ordering of battering and earnings changes in particular cases. Figure 4.1 sketches some of these relationships.

Researchers and policymakers know that welfare receipt reduces earnings, principally by reducing work hours.[72] As I review below, it also appears that, at least in Salt Lake City in the years right before Congress rescinded welfare entitlements, about the same percent of women who file "domestic incident" reports do so *before* as do so *after* they apply for public assistance.[73] What is less clear is the effect on earnings of petitioning for a Protection From Abuse (PFA) order. Having reviewed the various approaches to calculating the costs of taking a beating and sorted through the findings of previous research, in the rest of this chapter, I first report what the work-first program enrollees we interviewed told us about physical abuse, petitions for protective orders, and work-related control, abuse, and sabotage during their transitions from welfare to work. In the last section of the chapter, I report findings from an analysis of administrative records that contribute empirically to the task of assessing not only the extent but also the causal dynamics of the relationship between battering and women's work and earnings.

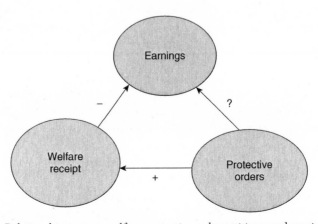

Figure 4.1. Relationships among welfare, protective order petitions, and earnings.

ABUSE DURING THE TRANSITION FROM
WELFARE TO WORK

Overall, data from the follow-up interviews we conducted with Alice, Georgia, Tonya, Reena, and the other women in their work-first program cohort showed sharp *decreases over time* both in physical violence and in work-related control, abuse, and sabotage. As noted in the previous chapter, lifetime histories of physical abuse were widespread. At the time of the first follow-up interview, four women (10 percent of the cohort, 13 percent of the 31 women for whom we have follow-up interview material) reported their partner hit, kicked, strangled, or threw something at them in the interval since the retrospective interview. That dropped to a single woman at each of the second and final follow-up interviews. Two of the women at the first follow-up reported having petitioned for a civil order of protection from abuse in the interval since the retrospective interview. Edna (introduced in the previous chapter) still worried that her daughter's father would come after her. She had petitioned for a protective order, she said, ". . . but he doesn't pay any attention to that." Tyronda, a Black 33-year-old separated from her husband, explained that her relationship with her husband "officially" ended when she petitioned for a protective order because he was being physically and mentally abusive, but she was still involved with him "off and on." No one reported having recently petitioned for a protective order at the second or final follow-up interviews.

As was the case for physical violence, the reported prevalence of work-related abuse shrank appreciably over the 12 to 18 months following these women's entry into the work-first program. Of the 31 women for whom we have at least one follow-up interview, 34 percent reported some abuse during the follow-up period. On most of the items in the checklist we administered, prevalence was lower in the follow-up periods than with reference to the current or most recent relationship at the retrospective interview (the recall period with which the follow-up interviews are most comparable).

The exceptions to the decrease in reports of work-related control, abuse, and sabotage include one of the gender conformity items ("tell you that you could only work outside the home if you kept up with the housework") and one threat item ("threaten to hurt you or your children or threaten to leave you if you continued with job training or your job"). It appears that the forms of work-related control, abuse, and sabotage most likely to arise or persist through the transition from welfare to work are those that represent the man's holding his current or former girlfriend or wife accountable to traditional standards of feminine domesticity. This finding is consistent with feminists' observations about the ways men entrap women in personal life by micromanaging their performance of domestic and maternal tasks.[74] In an era of work requirements, a man's enforcing a woman's domesticity increases the likelihood of her being sanctioned and thus losing the (paltry but nevertheless important) income assistance and other benefits of welfare.

It is good news that, overall, welfare-to-work transition program participants reported fewer incidents of physical violence and work-related control, abuse, and sabotage over the first 12 to 18 months of their transitions from welfare to work than in their lives up until the retrospective interview. It is possible that some of this decline came because enrolling in a work-first program lowers women's risk of abuse, either through encouraging her to spend less time at home (as the exposure model predicts) or by increasing her income and other resources (as the exchange model predicts). However, this finding must be interpreted with some caution. Yes, their being out of the household to attend employment training, search for a job, and otherwise comply with the work requirements imposed by the Personal Responsibility Act (PRA) may reduce women's exposure to abusive men. As Edna hypothesized at a follow-up interview, "He has not been physically abusive recently, but . . . that is probably because I have not been around much." But on many indicators, a significant number of welfare recipients report that going to work aggravates abuse.[75] Moreover, the plausibly ambiguous causal relationship between work and abuse means it is also possible that the decline in abuse facilitated the women's participation in the follow-up interviews and smoothed their transition from welfare to work.

There are several likely explanations for the observed declines in women's reports of physical violence and work-related control, abuse, and sabotage over the follow-up period of this research. Most obviously, to the extent that attrition from the follow-up interview schedule is correlated with physical violence or with work-related control, abuse, and sabotage, the declines in women's reports of physical violence and work-related control, abuse, and sabotage may be artifacts of bias. In other words, it is possible that the women most likely to experience and report such abuse during their transitions from welfare to work were the women who dropped out of the study. The finding that the women who dropped out of the study did not differ on the relevant measures from those who completed the prospective longitudinal interviews suggests attrition is not necessarily a large factor, however.[76] Methodologically speaking, the recall periods are different for the retrospective and follow-up interviews; the former is a lifetime rate, while the latter covers a much briefer period. Moreover, an unknown amount of the decline is probably due to unmeasured reporting bias; women are more likely to report abuse in former than current relationships.

More substantively, as a practical matter, toward the end of the prospective interviews, very few women reported maintaining old relationships or starting new ones. Many mentioned that finding and maintaining work and mothering responsibly meant they were simply too busy for a relationship. Thus, one explanation supported by the pattern of declining abuse over the course of women's transition from welfare to work concerns the greatly reduced risk of abuse (related to work or not) that comes from a woman's not being in a heterosexual relationship at all. In addition, as I reported in the previous chapter, 38 percent of the women we interviewed reported that the father of their child was incarcerated (generally but not always on charges unrelated to battering) at the time of the retrospective interview and through the follow-up period. Men in prison, at least, were not directly interfering with these women's training, job search, and employment activities during this particular transition from welfare to work. For instance, Keshauna, a 22-year-old mother of two, reported that the father of her children was in prison. So did Hera, a 30-year-old mother of four, who said that when people recommended she seek counseling to deal with relationship conflicts, she responded, "I don't have time for that," meaning perhaps both counseling and a relationship, and observed that, "He is in jail right now and can't bother me." Incarceration is a more specific version of reduced exposure as an explanation for the drop in reports of experiencing work-related control, abuse, and sabotage 12 to 18 months after initial enrollment in a work-first program. As incarceration rates are highly racialized, the prevalence of incarceration as an explanation for the decline in abuse as women made the transition from welfare to work is no larger than should be expected given the highly skewed racial-ethnic composition of this group of respondents.[77]

EARNINGS AND PROTECTIVE ORDERS IN THE CONTEXT OF WELFARE RESCISSION

In this final section of this chapter about calculating the costs of battering, I use a unique longitudinal data set to answer five empirical questions about the connections among poverty, battering, and work in the context of policy change. The data are from three sources, covering Allegheny County during the period from 1995 (before Congress rescinded welfare) to 2000: all of the petitions for protective orders,[78] all of the welfare records, and earnings for all protective order petitioners and all welfare recipients. I combined the data in a hierarchical person-period data set—that is, a data set with variables that provide information for each welfare recipient (whether she petitioned for a protective order or not) in every quarter from 1995 to 2000. Importantly, the data set organizes information about both the *unchanging characteristics* of the women that might affect their earnings (such as their age in 1995 and their race-ethnicity) and also the *changing characteristics* of the women in each quarter of the year (such as their earnings, whether or not they were receiving welfare, the number of people in the household, and whether or not they petitioned for a protective order).[79]

What Percent of Women Who Petition for a Protective Order Have a Welfare Spell?

It has become almost an article of faith among advocates for poor and battered women that "violence affects poor women in two critical ways: it makes them poor, and it keeps them poor."[80] The evidence that supports this position is mostly anecdotal. But in a pioneering study of "domestic violence" incident reports from the Salt Lake City Police Department and public assistance benefits records from the Utah Department of Human Services Office of Income Support, social work activist-researcher Ruth Brandwein reports,

> Of 3,147 unduplicated reported domestic violence incidents in Salt Lake City from January 1993 to February 1996, between 24% and 31% of women reporting these incidents had sought AFDC [Aid to Families with Dependent Children].[81]

As the rate of AFDC in the general population in Salt Lake City was far below 24 percent, Brandwein's study offered evidence that battered women were more likely than nonbattered women—or, in this case, women who do not report a "domestic incident"—to seek public assistance. There are no national data sets with individual-level measures of both welfare and battering (or even proxies for battering, such as the "domestic incident" reports Brandwein used). However, I matched Allegheny County court records of protective order petitions with welfare records and earnings reports[82] to figure out: What percentage of women who petition for a protective order have a welfare spell? In Allegheny County, 10,875 women petitioned for a protective order between 1995 and 2000. Of those, 2,640 (24 percent) had at least one spell on welfare during the time period. The rate of welfare receipt for petitioners is much higher than the rate of welfare receipt in the total population in Allegheny County in the second half of the 1990s, just as the rate of welfare receipt for women who report a "domestic violence" incident is higher than the overall rate of welfare receipt in Salt Lake City in the mid-1990s. A significant fraction of women willing to seek state protection by filing an incident report or going to court to obtain a protective order are also willing (and need) to seek financial support from state welfare programs. The percentage of women who petition for protective orders who also receive welfare is an important piece of the puzzle about the connections among poverty, battering, and work.

What Percentage of Welfare Recipients Petition for Protective Orders During the Period?

Brandwein appears not to have data appropriate to asking the logical next question in figuring out the relationship between poverty and battering: What percentage of welfare recipients petition for protective orders during the period? In Allegheny County during the five years between 1995 and 2000, 2,640 welfare recipients also petitioned for a protective order. The petitioners were 8.4 percent of the total of 31,341 adult women welfare recipients. Recall from the Introduction to this book that in May 2001, the month that we started the interviews featured in the previous chapter, the Pennsylvania Department of Public Welfare website had classified only 30 Allegheny County families who were receiving Temporary Aid to Needy Families (TANF) as "domestic violence"–related cases. This represented just four tenths of 1 percent of the 7,000-family TANF caseload in Allegheny County that month. A significant percentage of women receiving welfare are also protective order petitioners, and the vast majority of them appear to be slipping through the safety net that temporarily exempts battered women from work requirements, time limits, and child support enforcement.[83]

Which Comes First, the Protective Order or Welfare?

Brandwein is not only interested in the percentage of women involved in "domestic violence" incidents who use welfare, and I am not only interested in the percentage of protective order petitioners who use welfare and the percentage of welfare recipients who petition for protective orders. Advocates, policy analysts, and researchers are all interested in understanding the relative *timing* of the two events: reporting a domestic incident case or petitioning for a protective order, on the one hand, and receiving welfare benefits, on the other hand. Brandwein collected the first data on the timing of "domestic incident" cases and the start and end points of welfare spells. She reports:

> ... between 8.5% and 11.2% of domestic incident cases began to receive AFDC within 6 months *after* the violent incident and ... up to 22% started on AFDC within 1 year *after* the incident.[84] ... Between 11% and 14% began to receive assistance 6 months *before* the domestic violence incident, and between 19% and 26% within 1 year *before*.[85] ... Examining the combined figures of commencement of AFDC within a year before or after the incident report, we found that between 38% and 41% of all those women reporting domestic violence who had used welfare had their AFDC cases opened within 1 year of the reports.[86]

Timing matters because of the light it sheds on causality. Brandwein carefully reminds readers that the high percentage of women who were on welfare before reporting a "domestic incident" does not mean that being on welfare causes battering, but her analysis stops short of making the case convincingly. To explain why requires a quick review about causality. A glance back at Figure 4.1 will help readers to recall the discussion of endogeneity and causation that motivates this section. Philosopher David Hume set out the classic criteria for arguments about cause.[87] The first is *determinism*: A plausibly causes B if A is necessary or sufficient to make B happen. More complicated versions of this criterion involve A in various combinations with other factors,[88] but the basic issue is that it is only logically plausible to claim A causes B if they have a deterministic relationship. Hume's second criterion is *proximity*: A plausibly causes B if the action of A happens near enough to B to have had an effect. Chaos theory aside, it stretches our ordinary conception of causation to claim that the flutter of a butterfly's wings in Australia meaningfully *causes* a hurricane that hits the Florida coast. The third of Hume's criteria is *temporal asymmetry*: A may plausibly be among the causes of B if A happens before B, but A cannot plausibly cause B if B happens first.[89] Comments above about reciprocity and feedback loops notwithstanding, Hume's temporal asymmetry criterion raises the third empirical question, one that can only be answered with longitudinal data (that is, repeated observations of the same individuals over time[90]): Among Allegheny County women who petition for protective orders who ever have a welfare spell, which comes first, the protective order or welfare?

For Allegheny County welfare recipients who petition for protective orders, of all person-months that fall two months *prior* to protective order petitions, 43 percent are spent on welfare. This rises to 45 percent for months directly before protective order petitions, and increases further, to 47 percent, for months in which women actually petition for a protective order. That is, *the closer that women who eventually both petition for a protective order and receive welfare get to the month in which they appear in court, the more likely they are to be on welfare* (by nearly four percentage points). This pattern suggests that *welfare is increasingly important as a resource to women as they approach the point of petitioning for a restraining order.* Of all person-months that directly *follow* protective order petitions, 51 percent are spent on welfare, which increases to almost 53 percent of months falling two months after petitions. Overall, the majority of months leading up to protective order petitions and months in which women appear in court to petition for a protective order *are not* spent on welfare. In the months following protective order petitions, however, the majority *are* on welfare; the initial increase in the month immediately following the filing is 3.6 percentage points, and grows within two months to 5.1 percentage points more than in the month immediately prior to the petition.

The temporal pattern of the ways welfare recipients who ever petition for restraining orders use welfare is one of the most important findings from the analysis of longitudinal administrative data, for two reasons. First, and not surprising given Brandwein's results, the pattern *supports advocates' claim that welfare is a vital resource for battered women.* Second, and a critical empirical and methodological improvement on previous research, the pattern *rebuts the notion that welfare receipt somehow causes battering* by discouraging work, undermining women's agency, or giving men incentives to abuse.

How Do Welfare Recipients Who Petition for a Protective Order Differ From Welfare Recipients Who Do Not Petition?

Brandwiein makes the important point that, "... women receiving public assistance are frequently the same women who are victims of domestic violence. Economic dependence is one reason women cite for remaining in abusive relationships. Public assistance has been a way out, at least temporarily, for such women."[91] However, Brandwein does not consider the notion that battered women who go on welfare might be different from other welfare recipients. If they are different in ways that we think are related to earnings, then we cannot really address the connection between poverty and battering—or the basic question about the cost of taking a beating that is the core of this chapter—because there might be other important sources of differences in earnings. This leads to my fourth empirical question: How do welfare recipients who petition for a protective order differ from welfare recipients who do not petition?

The two groups of Allegheny County welfare recipients—those who do and those who do not petition for a protective order—are similar in terms of age and household size (two important factors in earnings). However, the racial-ethnic compositions of the groups differ. The majority of women who petition for a protective order are White (54 percent), while the majority of women who do not petition for a protective order are Black (54 percent). In addition, the women who petition for a protective order between 1995 and 2000 have *higher initial quarterly earnings* ($624.50) than women who do not file during this time period ($488.96), a statistically significant difference ($p < .001$) that persists in multivariate models.[92] Women who petition for a protective order spend significantly *more total time on welfare* over the period than the nonpetitioning group, a difference of more than seven months. Welfare receipt reduces earnings, principally by reducing work hours. Therefore, this difference in time on welfare contributes to significant differences in *earnings growth* between petitioners and nonpetitioners: Earnings across the petitioner group grow at a slower rate (an average total of $1,230.59) than for welfare recipients who never petition over the period (an average total of $1,394.46). The difference between the two groups—$163.90—is statistically significant ($p < .01$) as well as substantively important for poor women.

For women who petition for a protective order, higher initial earnings are more strongly associated with a reduction of the time spent on welfare ($r = -.28$) than for their counterparts who do not petition for a protective order ($r = -.18$). This finding is consistent with the notion that women who petition for a protective order may have different motivations and resources than women who do not, such that their use of welfare is more time limited. For women who never petition for a protective order, absolute changes in wages over the five-year period are more strongly associated with reduced welfare receipt ($r = -.06$) when compared to protective order petitioners ($r = -.02$). The difference could be because petitioners turn to welfare for income support while they try to negotiate with or leave their abuser. It could also be because his abuse reduces her work hours and drops her earnings below the eligibility threshold for welfare, or through some other mechanism; it is impossible to tell from these data. At any rate, it is not surprising that women who petition for a protective have slower earnings growth than women who do not petition. In fact, in the population of welfare recipients in this study, the earnings growth for petitioners is so much slower than it is for nonpetitioners that it completely erodes the higher average initial earnings of protective order petitioners ($135 – $163 = –$28). Consequently, by the end of the study period, the petitioners' average earnings are virtually identical to the nonpetitioners' (see Figure 4.2 below). The point is that although petitioners may be different from other welfare

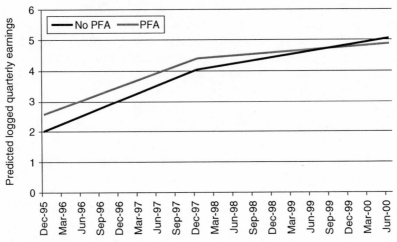

Figure 4.2. Predicted earnings equation, unconditional model, Allegheny County welfare recipients who also petitioned for protective orders (1995–2000).
SOURCE: Hughes and Brush (2011, p. 332).

recipients, the initial earnings advantage of petitioners quickly erodes. Moreover, the difference between the earnings trajectories of petitioners and nonpetitioners works through the mechanism of increased welfare receipt; there is no empirical support for an independent effect, at least among welfare recipients.

How Did Welfare Rescission Affect Women's Earnings?

Consequential as they are, these correlations do not account for differences between petitioners and nonpetitioners in the relationships between welfare and earnings before and after welfare rescission. This leads to an additional question related to the connections among poverty, battering, work, and public policy: Did changes associated with welfare rescission have the same effect on the earnings of petitioners and nonpetitioners?[93] I answer this policy-oriented question through an analysis of changes in welfare recipients' earnings trajectories before and after welfare rescission.[94] Figure 4.2 provides a basic picture of earnings trajectories as they change over time for the two groups. I compared the two groups in the section immediately above; in this section, I am most interested in the bends in the two lines. The bends are what analysts call the "knots" that mark the policy shift. The prerescission time interval is July 1995 to December 1997. The postrescission time interval is December 1997 to June 2000. These intervals capture earnings growth before and after Allegheny County welfare administrators implemented the provisions of the PRA, with some lag time to allow for restructuring to take effect.[95]

For welfare recipients who petition for a protective order, earnings growth postrescission (that is, after March 1997, when Allegheny County implemented the program restructuring mandated by the Personal Responsibility Act of 1996) averages one-third the size of their earnings growth in the time period between 1995 and the program change (0.46 to 0.17). This is the lighter line in Figure 4.2; the slope of the line after the knot is much shallower than it is before the knot. For welfare recipients who do not petition for a protective order (the darker line in Figure 4.2), the change in average earnings growth between the two time intervals is less pronounced, but is still cut in half (0.50 to 0.26). Much of the before-and-after difference in earnings growth between petitioners and nonpetitioners is due to the way welfare rescission changed the association between earnings and welfare receipt for these two groups. In the period *before* Congress rescinded welfare entitlements and instituted work requirements and time limits, the negative correlation between earnings and months on welfare for protective order petitioners ($r = -.36$) is much larger than the negative correlation between earnings and months on welfare for nonpetitioners ($r = -.11$). In the period *after* welfare rescission, the negative correlation between earnings and time on welfare for protective order petitioners *shrinks* to -0.27. For nonpetitioners, in the period *after* welfare rescission, the negative correlation between earnings and time on welfare *grows* to -0.27. This is clearly visible: The two lines representing the two groups' earnings trajectories actually cross after the knot in Figure 4.2.

Welfare rescission attenuates the negative relationship between welfare receipt and earnings for welfare recipients who petition for a protective order. But for women who do not petition for a protective order, the negative relationship between welfare and earnings increases in strength postrescission. Interestingly, the relationship between welfare and earnings in the two groups looks very different prerescission, but the groups converge postrescission. Before welfare rescission, the initial negative effects of welfare receipt on earnings are stronger for women who petitioned for a protective order than for their nonpetitioning peers. However, nonpetitioners experience greater swings across time prerescission. The result of this pattern is that by the end of the first period—before the PRA of 1996—*the effect of welfare receipt on earnings is the same for women in the two groups.* During the second period, after local welfare administrators instituted the time limits, work requirements, and modest work supports associated with rescinding entitlements to welfare, the groups initially maintain their similarity. As advocates of work requirements would predict, both groups see an attenuation of the negative effect of welfare receipt on earnings. But there the similarity ends; the attenuation of the negative effect of welfare receipt on earnings continues for the protective order petitioners but not for the women who do not petition for a protective order. Overall, the negative effects of welfare receipt on earnings diminish over time for the protective order petitioners, but the nonpetitioning group does not see these benefits. Again, this is clearly visible where the earnings trajectories of the two groups cross after the knot in Figure 4.2.

That is, welfare rescission had different effects on the earnings growth of welfare recipients who did and who did not petition for a protective order. The politicians who mandated work requirements expected that people subject to work requirements would have higher earnings than people for whom searching for, finding, and maintaining work is not a criterion for welfare eligibility. Similarly, they expected that time limits would push the lowest earners (nonworkers who are long-time welfare recipients) off of the welfare rolls, at least potentially increasing their earnings. Work supports such as childcare subsidies and extended medical benefits should ease women's movement off of welfare and eliminate perverse disincentives to work. All three changes were designed to change behavior by shifting incentives to work and should attenuate the well-known negative effect of welfare on earnings.[96] This analysis shows that work requirements, time limits, and work supports associated with welfare rescission reduced the negative effect of welfare on earnings over time for women who petition for a protective order, as legislators expected. However, welfare rescission appears not to have had such salutary effects for welfare recipients who do not petition for a protective order.

****

In the previous chapter, I documented what happens when poor women experience conflicts *about* work, conflicts that *interfere* with work, and conflicts *at* work. In the early sections of this chapter, I summarized the aggregate economic and social costs of battering and the individual costs of health care, lost wages and hours, absenteeism, and reduced productivity associated with battering. In the last two sections of this chapter, I documented some of the issues related to battering over the course of women's transitions from welfare to work, and I used longitudinal administrative records to answer five key questions about the connections between poverty and battering.

This longitudinal comparison of the earnings trajectories of Allegheny County welfare recipients who do and who do not petition for a protective order tells researchers, advocates, and policymakers some important things about the costs of taking a beating and about welfare and work as solutions to the problems of poverty and battering. The longitudinal data on the timing of welfare receipt and protective order petitions show no empirical support for the conservative hypothesis that welfare causes battering. The substantive findings about the effects of petitioning for a protective order on the earnings trajectories of welfare recipients suggest that welfare and restraining orders are important safety nets for women seeking to escape the traps of poverty and abuse. The trajectory analysis also shows that the effects of the work requirements, modest work supports, and time limits that Congress instituted with the Personal Responsibility Act of 1996 were distinctly different for welfare recipients who did and did not petition for a protective order, such that the initial earnings gap (significantly in favor of petitioners, for reasons that likely have to do with the ways petitioners who turn to welfare are different from other welfare recipients) erodes entirely by 2000. All told, efforts to calculate the costs of taking a beating reveal a lot about the perils and promise of the two ways that women like Reena can turn to the government for help when they are poor or battered or both: applying for welfare and petitioning for a protective order. In the next chapter, I show some of the interesting lessons available to those who listen when welfare recipients who are taking a beating talk back about their experiences.

Welfare Recipients Talk Back

with the assistance of Lorraine Higgins

Poor mothers are the adults most deeply affected by welfare policy. Abused and coercively controlled women and their families are similarly among the people whose lives—at least potentially—are most profoundly shaped by criminal justice policy and practice and by the limits and possibilities of activism, polemics, and service provision around violence against women. Yet poor mothers and abused women are often excluded from public decision making and critical conversations on the issues. There are few venues for dialogue between policymakers and welfare recipients or battered women. Unfortunately, even when such opportunities emerge, genuine dialogue is difficult. Experts and the people they study, treat, or serve speak different languages. They often share neither perspectives nor purposes, let alone a common vocabulary or communication style.

Moreover, when they use technical language—often, even when they speak accessibly—experts and policymakers talk *about* rather than *with* disenfranchised or victimized groups.[1] At the same time, although marginalized community members often have important insights to share, those insights are often not only personal but partial. Victims' observations and explanations of their own and others' experiences are frequently disconnected from larger issues and questions. Members of disenfranchised groups may be so caught up in the hegemonic way of thinking and talking about things that they cannot notice the way their experience contradicts conventional wisdom. Subordinated people seldom have the time and wherewithal to develop and express their criticisms. Experiences and accounts that go against the kind of hegemonic explanations I set out in Chapter 2 may be so far outside the box of normative conventions that they do not seem credible.[2] Hegemonic ideas about social problems and social change are often based on stereotypes, focused on deficits or pathology, and rooted in moralistic judgments. When that is the case, marginalized or subordinated speakers and writers find it next to impossible to repair their stigmatized identities, overcome the explicit or implicit indictment of their character by expert and mainstream discourse, and win the thoughtful attention of service providers, mainstream media, and policymakers.[3] In short, if poor or battered women are to enter meaningfully into public deliberation, they have to develop the ability to convert their private troubles into social problems.[4] They have to articulate their feelings and analyses in terms both audible and legible to the mainstream and otherwise transform their complaints and experiences into stories and arguments that will get at least a serious, if not sympathetic, hearing from mainstream audiences.

It is tremendously hard work to turn private stories of loss, abuse, and hope into purposeful articulations of a problem, its causes, and possible solutions. It takes preparation and support to create informed arguments that have a chance of being heard. This is the work of citizenship and self-advocacy that poor people and abused women (all too frequently the same person) often have neither the time, nor the wherewithal, nor even the outlines of a process to undertake. This chapter is the fruitful yield of doing this work with a dedicated group of current and former welfare recipients (some of whom had experienced various degrees of coercive control in their relationships) determined to tell their stories of toil and trouble, tenacity and redemption.

STORIES, CAUSES, RIVALS

. . . When I was living with my current boyfriend, he didn't understand my depression and anxiety. Plus, he was a cop, which meant he had a problem with my drug use. To make matters worse, he cheated on me, and I found out. That day I called a Yellow Cab, and I paid the driver with the other woman's VCR, which I found in our place. I paid the cabbie to take my boyfriend's clothes to the other woman's house. At the time, it felt good. It was on my mind, so I did it, but now? I think that it was crazy! Soon after, I came home from work one day, and he showed up. He parked his police car in front of my place. He still had a key, and he was on the lease, so there was nothing I could do to keep him out. We had an argument, and he slapped my face. I called the police, but because he was a police officer, he just got on his radio and told them to disregard the call. I could hear my mother crying as she witnessed this, but all I could see was red. I grabbed his gun and had it at his head. Although she was right next to me, I couldn't see my mother — I could only hear her crying, but that finally made me put the gun down. I put a brick through the window of his police car. Then he left.

This incident was critical. I was trying to hold on to the house. Even though he was often with that other woman, he had still been paying my bills. I was working a little at [a commercial mail sorting company], but my life was chaotic. As it turned out, we split up after this incident. I stayed in the house, but he was no longer supporting me. At that point, I was in my late 30s, and that was when I first turned to welfare for help. . . .[5]

In this excerpt from a story she wrote in a mentored community literacy project, Red[6] (an apparently Black woman in her early 40s) identifies a critical incident in her life. She introduces readers to some of the important characters and relationships in her life, such as her boyfriend and her mother. Even this brief passage includes important elements of *narrative*, that is, of verbal or written storytelling.

Red brings in characters, creates a specific setting, and presents events in temporal order. She also recounts a plot by providing details about the build-up to her boyfriend's slapping her and to her pulling his gun on him and vandalizing his police car and by setting out the series of events that led her to turn to welfare. Red delivers a moral or message in the form of her reflection on the gap between acting on her feelings and understanding the problems she created for herself by acting out.[7] In addition, Red places that critical incident in a broader context, in which poverty, work, and welfare intersect. Red explains the complex situation of economic dependence, insecure housing, addiction and depression, relationship troubles, and police indifference that shape and give meaning *both to the specific course of events* during this particular critical incident in her fraught relationship with her boyfriend *and to the general trajectory* she follows toward welfare. In the process, Red conveys her sense of the connections among poverty, welfare, and work.

Red's story and her causal analysis of this critical incident and her path onto welfare was possible in large part because she participated in a community literacy project that activist rhetoric scholar Lorraine Higgins organized and ran to complement the interviews that I highlighted in the two previous chapters. Higgins had worked previously with activist-rhetoricians Wayne Peck and Linda Flower to develop a process intended to bring into the conversation some of the many people usually excluded from public policy debates and discussions about "social problems," such as "at-risk" youth, poor tenants, medical patients, and welfare recipients.[8] Participants in community literacy projects like the one Higgins and I conducted identify problems that affect them and their communities. With the help of writing mentors and the outline of a process for constructing narratives of critical incidents, they produce narratives to represent how they have experienced these problems (in this case, conflicts affecting welfare recipients' safety, solvency, or eligibility for welfare benefits). Participants then reflect and comment on the larger meaning of these narratives. They analyze the complex network of causes and constraints that underlie these problems. They grapple with the ideas, stereotypes, and causal analyses they confront in the offices of doctors, social workers, and judges; around the kitchen tables of their friends and families; and in the rhetoric they encounter in the media and political campaigns.[9]

In this chapter, to the interview and administrative data that inform the previous two empirical chapters, I add the materials created by eight women who participated in the community literacy project Higgins designed and led, and who therefore had an opportunity to "talk back" to experts and service providers. I place their stories and analyses in the context of the conventional wisdom about poverty, abuse, and public policy; I show their strategies for addressing the myths and stereotypes about poverty, welfare, work, and abuse. I showcase welfare recipients' causal analyses of their situations and I give examples of their engaging in *rivaling*, a literate practice that subordinated speakers and writers can use to make their voices and messages intelligible without automatically reiterating the terms of the dominant discourse.[10]

These materials, my analysis, and the process of rivaling begin to answer the call for activist-researchers to counter the "politics of disgust"[11] with which poor mothers have to contend. I use the community literacy project materials to answer social anthropologist Michelle Fine's call for "alternative images for how feminist scholars might conduct research so as to nurture counterdiscourses that focus popular and policy attention back onto institutions that perpetrate, sustain, and exacerbate violence against women."[12] Rather than treating poor or battered women, single mothers, or welfare recipients as a social problem,[13] I treat policy rhetoric and implementation as *problematic*, in two senses. First, the policy responses to poverty and abuse are sometimes problematic in the sense of being troubling or disturbing, especially in the ways they increase women's vulnerability and jeopardize their safety, dignity, and integrity. Second, the policy responses to abuse and poverty are problematic in the sense that they constitute a cognitive and practical framework; they represent and constitute the limits and possibilities of thinking, talking, and taking action about these issues.[14]

We encouraged participants in the community literacy project to find ways of describing and characterizing their experiences that would allow them to navigate between the rock of the "victim narrative" and the hard place of the "hero narrative." That is, on the one hand, we wanted them not to have to present themselves as hapless and helpless victims of circumstances beyond their control (and only thus potentially worthy recipients of public sympathy, justice, taxpayers' dollars, subsidized goods and services, and employment opportunities). On the other hand, we wanted them to be able to avoid presenting themselves as heroes somehow endowed with exceptional character and fortitude (and only thus avoid the disdain ordinarily heaped on welfare recipients and the pity sometimes grudgingly extended to battered women).[15] We also wanted to help them steer clear of the "victim empowerment folklore," the account that blames abused and coercively controlled women for their plight and encourages them to change their own lives by "taking back their power."[16] The two discursive strategies we encouraged them to use were, first, to *provide their own causal analyses* of their situations and trajectories, and second, to carry on an imaginary *dialogue with rival perspectives and explanations*, through which they could "talk back." This chapter presents and discusses selections from the narratives and from the "contributing factors" and "rivaling" writing that the community literacy project participants produced.[17]

TALKING BACK TO STEREOTYPES AND MYTHS

Women's writing about their experiences and analyses of poverty, abuse, work, and welfare counter the hegemonic explanations I set out in Chapter 2 in several ways. The women's experiences sometimes provide empirical, factual rebuttals of assumptions and stereotypes. Their analyses sometimes point to the faulty logic of hegemonic explanations. Their narratives provide alternative perspectives and important background or context. Storytelling creates space for writers to elaborate examples of honorable choices and actions, thus establishing character in both senses: Poor mothers and abused and coercively controlled women are the *central actors or characters* in their own lives, and they are able to assess and face the consequences of their life situations, thus demonstrating *good character* in the sense of virtues such as perseverance, compassion, and loyalty.[18]

Rivaling demonstrates a grasp of a wide variety of positions on contested social issues. When they articulate and then grapple with rival hypotheses, subordinated rhetors give their own experiences and perspectives equal weight to those of their expert and lay critics. Some of these writers give advice in a sisterly mode. Some demand practical support from the experts, service providers, and systems around them. Some alternately accept and counter mainstream assessments of their situations and behavior. Many focus on individual behavioral change and the rewards of discipline in the form of the work, family, and sexual ethics that constitute the organizing idiom of the welfare and rehabilitation programs in which they have been enrolled.[19] They demonstrate their skills in the especially difficult balancing act of accepting and complying with versus questioning and defying expert opinion and common sense. They also sometimes invoke more structural analyses of the forces and institutions that contribute to their individual dilemmas and trajectories, such as the health care system, cultural notions of gender and marriage, the labor market, the criminal justice system, and the welfare bureaucracy.[20]

IT'S BEEN SAID: Women on welfare are all unwed teen mothers.[21]

It is true that some young women get pregnant and decide to have a child quite early, and that decision shapes their relationships and their trajectories in the labor market. Robin, an apparently Black mother in her early 30s whose two younger, school-age children usually came with her and did their homework during the sessions of the community literacy project, wrote what is probably the classic tale of an ambitious student whose life plan changed dramatically when she got pregnant on the cusp of her high school graduation. In the narrative she composed through the community literacy project, Robin described her situation this way:

> . . . All through grade, middle, and high school, learning seemed to come easy for me; I didn't have to work very hard to get those good marks. I was such a bookworm that I didn't go to socials, concerts, or sleepovers as most of my friends did. I kept my mind on my goals.
>
> In 1986, my final year of high school, I met a guy I really liked. He was older and more mature than I was. I fell head over heels in what I thought was love. Our relationship became serious, and a short time after, I found that I was pregnant. I was very disappointed in myself. At that point I realized that I was not in love with my boyfriend; I was infatuated with him because he was older than I was. I thought long and hard about my situation. I decided to keep the baby and continue with school. I knew it was going to be a long hard battle going to school and raising a child, but I also knew that I could do it.
>
> By the summer of 1986, I found myself 17 years old, a recent high school graduate, and the parent of a beautiful son. On the day of my graduation, I was told that I had a full academic scholarship to a very prestigious college. I turned it down, because I didn't want to leave my son or become a drop-in parent. I wanted to experience every aspect of his life. I didn't want to miss a thing. I realized that if I didn't take the scholarship, it would be much harder

to become a successful lawyer. So that is when I rethought my career aspirations. . . .

Making the Decision: Should I Have a Baby?

I felt confused and scared about making a decision that could affect the rest of my life. I didn't want a baby, because I had very concrete plans about my future. I also knew that I wasn't mentally prepared for motherhood. I was frightened, because I used to watch a lot of after-school specials in which teens became pregnant, and their parents would kick them out of the home. They were forced to live either on the streets or in some sort of home for wayward teens. Usually the teen would begin a life of drugs and crime, struggle with raising the child, or give the child up for adoption. I didn't want to live a life of crime, struggle, or uncertainty. I was fearful of having an abortion, because I might go to Hell and because of my strong Catholic upbringing. I would weigh the consequences of going to Hell or Heaven in my head.

Robin's circumstances fit the brute facts of condemnatory stereotypes about welfare recipients as prematurely sexually active and unwed teen mothers. She became pregnant when she was a teenager, before she finished high school. The pregnancy was unplanned and constituted a serious obstacle to her life plan. She was not married to the father, and the pregnancy contributed to her realizing that the relationship was not built on as strong of a foundation as she originally thought. As she wrote in her "contributing factors" section identifying the causal factors that contributed to the situation she recounted in her narrative, Robin's first, unplanned pregnancy

  . . . was due to the fact that she had more book smarts than street smarts.
  . . . resulted from unprotected sex, even though she knew the facts of life.
  . . . happened because she had sex without being in a committed relationship.
  . . . happened because she was naïve; she was "young, dumb, and fulla cum."

However, at the same time that some aspects of Robin's story fit the stereotypes that animate welfare myths, her story and analyses demonstrate the tensions between career aspirations and social development, between academic and professional desires and ambitions and parental responsibilities, which many mothers face in contemporary America.[22] Moreover, Robin's story defies the stereotype of "babies having babies."[23] Her broader narrative and her causal analysis portray Robin as holding her younger self accountable for her decisions. Although she says she "felt confused and scared" and "wasn't mentally prepared for motherhood," Robin notes that even as a teen, she grappled with ethical and practical decisions that society requires of adults.

Even more counter to the myth that all welfare recipients are unwed teens is the fact that not all welfare recipients are young women. Not all women who end up on welfare had their children out of wedlock. Not all mothers on welfare had their first pregnancy or child as a teenager. This is true both in the aggregate and in the small, nonrandom group of current and former welfare recipients who participated in the community literacy project. For example, writers Jane, J.J., and Nikki (like Robin, a mother when she was a teenager) were all married when they had their children. Although Robin was a welfare recipient as an unwed teen, all of the other participants in the community literacy project waited to have children until they were older, married, or both. The materials written by Jule (an apparently Black woman in her early 40s with a diagnosed learning disability) show that not all poor mothers are teenagers or had their first pregnancy or needed public assistance when they were very young.

> ... I graduated from high school in 1982 when I was 21 years old. I signed up with [program name] to receive job training, and I worked with a chef in the kitchen of a nursing home in [local suburban community]. They paid me while I trained.
>
> I met a man who worked at the nursing home, and we started seeing each other pretty seriously for about two years. When I was 23, two years out of high school and living with my sister, I got pregnant. I didn't plan the pregnancy; I wasn't using birth control, because I had never had sex before. I wanted the baby, because I felt close to the father and don't believe in abortion.
>
> Even before I was pregnant, my boyfriend started staying out late, and I caught him in a lot of lies. He stole some money from me, and at that point I kicked him out. After the baby was born, he didn't come around to help at all. I never went to look for him, because he was involved with other women and wasn't trustworthy. I was without a partner but didn't feel trapped or as though I had made a mistake. I just had to move on with my life.

> ... Two years after my son was born, I had my second child, a daughter, with another man I had met through a girlfriend. We saw each other off and on for about four and a half years, and I thought he was a good person, even though he was married. I hadn't planned the pregnancy. I was using birth control pills for awhile, but it messed up my menstrual cycle, so I stopped taking them. I didn't bother using any other method, because I figured I only saw him once a month and probably wouldn't get pregnant again, especially because I only see one man at a time.

Factually, Jule's story rebuts the stereotype that all welfare recipients are unwed teenagers: Jule postponed sex until she was a high school graduate, in her early 20s, with two years' work experience at a job for which she had post–high school training. Nevertheless, Jule realizes that hers is a hard case to use to counter myths about welfare recipients. She does not argue that she was prepared for motherhood, or that she had efficacious control over her fertility. Her narrative self-portrait reveals Jule as uninformed about her body and pregnancy. In her contributing factors section, Jule attributed her having children without being married to two main factors:

Loneliness. Kids are comforting, and even if he is not perfect, a boyfriend provides company and some support (even if it's only buying Pampers).

Inadequate Birth Control Counseling. The pill made Jule feel sick. She says: *I probably did get some information on other types of birth control, but I thought I didn't need it since we were only together once a month.* Her religious values prohibited abortion.

Jule is straightforward about her motives for having men and babies in her life and about her tenuous grasp on the facts of reproduction. What Jule tries to convey in her story and other materials she wrote and dictated to her writing mentor is that what matters is not the number of fathers, but the amount of love and the quality of parenting. As she said, "I'm their only mother, and I'm their father too. I didn't want that to happen, but it doesn't mean I'm a bad person that I had more than one child [with more than one man]."

In imagining and grappling with rival perspectives, Jule went on to respond to the concerns of resentful taxpayers and welfare skeptics.

Resentful taxpayers might say. . . Stop having babies and babies if you can't support them. Especially out of wedlock.

Women don't always get pregnant purposefully, and the man is part of it too. Jule says: *I never expected I would have to beg the man I lay down with to take care of his kids. I wasn't married, but I had long-term relationships with each of these men. My choice was to stop at three kids.*

A person skeptical of the welfare system might say. . . If welfare hadn't supported her for so long, maybe she would have felt pressured to get a better job or get other help for her child. Is welfare a disincentive? Lack of personal responsibility is a big issue here—on the part of both the mother and the father.

Jule says: *But I eventually did find a better job—one with benefits and all. And welfare helped me get it. It supported me when I was training and getting experience. I was a very responsible person. I worked a lot and always made sure there was a roof over my kids' heads. I wasn't financially dependent on any man.*

Jule was aware of the degree to which her story left her vulnerable to criticism from disapproving rivals (including, sometimes, other participants in the community literacy project, who challenged one another with skillful recreations of moralistic positions familiar from the media and their encounters with family, neighbors, and caseworkers). She carefully established her responsibility, independence, and work ethic. Jule refused the easy option of the victim narrative; she played down her disability, the fact that it took her nearly four extra years to graduate from high school, her sexual ignorance, and her social inexperience and isolation. At the same time, Jule declined to portray herself as a heroic exception to the stereotype, as somehow fundamentally different from other welfare recipients and therefore not legitimately subject to critique.

Like Jule, most of these women were monogamous and only initiated relationships with other men after the fathers of their children had abandoned their responsibilities. In a context where women are economically dependent, relationships are sometimes stressed and unstable. People get lonesome, and poverty ought not to disqualify women from seeking emotional and sexual connection. Jule said when responding to an imaginary rival: "To tell the truth, I didn't really care [about the moral issues]. I was thinking once I had a child, my boyfriend was really going to be with me, but I found out later it wasn't like that." Jule was by no means an irresponsible teenage welfare mother, and she rebuts this welfare myth and conveys a sense of her situation without resorting to either victim or hero rhetoric.

IT'S BEEN SAID: Welfare benefits only help women to avoid the consequences of their sexually irresponsible behavior.

Women are not always sexually irresponsible just because they end up on welfare. J.J., the only apparently White woman writer in the community literacy project, whose story I explore at length below, was married when she had her children. So was Nikki (a Black woman in her late 30s who married her high school sweetheart and had her first child as a married teen). Nikki's story (the only narrative in this community literacy project that the writer composed entirely in the third person) explains that she attempted to plan and time her childbearing by using birth control pills and a diaphragm.

> It was 1990, and Nikki was married with one child and another on the way. *How could I be so stupid to let this happen at this time?* Nikki thought. She couldn't believe that she was pregnant again. She sighed to herself, *One would think that the complications that came along with the first pregnancy would have taught me a lesson.*
>
> She had her first child at nineteen, and he was a miracle baby, because he weighed all of three pounds. Now Nikki knew that there would be trouble throughout this pregnancy too. She also knew that she and her husband couldn't afford the medical bills or another mouth to feed. But Nikki's husband was happy about the child, and he didn't believe in abortions. Nikki knew that things would change because of this baby, but she believed that she had a very strong relationship with her husband, so it would be o.k. He'd always made the right decisions for them.
>
> **Making the Decision: How Should I Plan for a Family?**
> Nikki decided to use birth control pills. She tried many different pills, but the doctors couldn't find a dosage low enough for her. The higher dosages made her sick. Eventually, they took her off because there wasn't a pill for her, and she became pregnant with her first child. She then tried a diaphragm, but her weight went up and down, and she had to be refitted many times. She became pregnant with her second child, probably because of a poor fit. She was not using birth control when she conceived her third child.

Nikki was married to a man who controlled many decisions about their lives, including decisions about the timing and number of their children. In her narrative, Nikki subjects her past self to a lot of criticism. Her internal monologue echoes popular cultural and political messages about welfare recipients' questionable intelligence and ability to learn from experience. She seems incredulous that her past experience did not somehow protect her from an additional pregnancy. However, Nikki also makes it clear that her pattern of childbearing and her eventual dependence on welfare did not result from sexual irresponsibility.

Jule had her children in the context of what she considered committed relationships, and she continued to work and care for her children while she was on welfare. Jule opens her narrative saying, *For one thing, if I had to do it over, I wouldn't go with married men. And married or not, I wouldn't always trust a man to do what I wanted or expected of him.* But for Jule, as for other women in the community literacy project and other poor women, welfare was a lifeline, not a moral hazard. Jule wrote about going on welfare:

Right after the baby was born, I applied for public assistance. That was the only way I could make it, because I needed the health insurance benefits and didn't get them on the job.

It was stressful, but I was able to cope. While I was on public assistance, welfare paid for my training at [local trade school]. I went there for a year, learning about food service. I didn't use my training right away, because I had to take care of my son, who was still young and who had seizures.

Far from being a marker or consequence of sexual irresponsibility, welfare for Jule was the only way she could fulfill her multiple responsibilities to her young child: continuing with job training so she could eventually support them both, receiving health benefits her low-waged job did not provide, and caring for her son, an important job that was complicated by his seizures. About sexual responsibility and relationships, Jule wrote:

Although I know the advantages of being married when you have kids, I'm still not. The first relationship didn't work, because the man was cheating on me with a lot of other ladies. He lied a lot, so I could not trust him. I broke it off when I was about four months pregnant. I took him to court maybe five or six times, but I got nothing [in terms of child support payments] because he didn't have a job, and he was always skipping town. They did put him in jail for non-payment. But now he's running again.

My life was shattered by his betrayal, but I put the pieces together and became stronger. The father of my second child was a nice person, did a lot for my son and me, but I could not [. . .] marry him, because he was already married. We were together all the time, but he didn't live in my home. At least he bought Pampers and extra milk if we needed it and gave me a little money when he could. While I was pregnant and after my daughter was born, he still came around, but then I just got tired of being the "other woman." It was too depressing, especially when he spent the holidays with her. I also found out that he was selling drugs — and that was it. So I was alone again for about four months until I met my third child's father. I still see [him].

I love him, but I'm not married to him, because he's already married too.

I know I can't have him. Though he loves me too, he has too much invested in his wife, a house, property in Florida, and a child of their own. Yet we still love each other, so we've chosen not to break it off for now. Although this doesn't fit the mold of the perfect family, I prefer it to being alone.

Jule's is a tale of second-best choices from among limited options. The loneliness and hard work of single motherhood are palpable in her narrative. But so is her determination to meet her children's needs without entirely sacrificing her own. She clearly prefers the man she knows—imperfect as their relationship is in many ways—to the risks and possibilities of trying to meet someone new. Although she acknowledges the problems of "going with married men," Jule did not have promiscuous sex, or sex with a lot of partners concurrently, which were for her the markers of sexual immorality. Jule practiced a form of serial monogamy that did not conform to her understanding of the highest "family values," but was motivated by a sense of attachment that satisfied her standards for being sexual in the context of committed relationships.

At first, Robin was the community literacy project participant most hesitant to engage in the rivaling process.[24] She was employed as an advocate at what she described as "a well-known anti-hunger and anti-poverty organization," and although Robin was confident in her critique of poverty and welfare and very familiar with both policy and the then-ongoing debates over reauthorization of the welfare legislation, she was reluctant to give airtime to what she saw as pernicious and destructive rhetoric. But once she realized that Higgins and I were serious when we told her she could respond to those arguments and positions in her own terms, Robin enthusiastically identified contributing factors and energetically "talked back." On the subject of the stereotype of sexual irresponsibility, Robin had a lot to say to the rivals she imagined in her writing sessions and our group discussions.

A **welfare reform politician** might say: No one forced her to have children out of wedlock. Why should the taxpayer have to support her children?

[Robin says:] *But what, realistically, were Robin's other options? If you can come up with realistic ones, please do! Living wage jobs that might provide enough income, health coverage, and daycare were not available (and are not) to a woman with low-level skills. Welfare gave Robin the support and training she needed to raise good kids and become a productive taxpayer herself, who is now happy to contribute her tax dollars to others in need.*

Welfare recipients today have to work first, rather than go to school, even if education might help them get a better job. Our hands are tied, now that the reforms have passed.

[Robin says:] *This is one area in which the reforms should be revised! Robin* [who was able to use prerescission welfare benefits to further her education] *is a great example of why.*

A **sexual moralist** might say: She should have used protection. She could have said "no." She should have waited until she was married before having sex.

[Robin says:] *Yes, protection is always smart. Let's make it more widely available in the schools. Let's make sex ed widely available. As for abstinence? You can suggest it as one option, but get real if you think it is the only one. Teens will be teens.*

Note the way Robin straightforwardly presents the views of her rivals, taking on rhetoric rooted in moralistic judgments about justice, money, and sex. Through the process of rivaling, Robin claims the moral high ground and establishes her character (in both the sense of an active agent in social life and debate and the sense of a worthy rival) through a combination of rhetorical strategies. She partially appropriates the rhetoric of the righteous taxpayer and casts herself as now being in a position to be a productive member of society, and therefore as entitled to both the benefits she received *then* and a hearing for her political opinions *now*. She agrees with select points her rivals make, but then extends the point in critical directions, arguing that birth control and education about sexuality and fertility should be more widely available to youth. She invokes realism about teen pregnancy and chides her rival for being out of touch about the effectiveness of abstinence-only sex education. In her narrative and in her rivaling materials, Robin vigorously rejects victim rhetoric. At the same time, Robin determinedly shows that her hard work, intelligence, commitment to involved parenting, solidarity with working people, and efforts on behalf of social justice in the workplace and beyond do not make her a heroic exception. She is simply an important example of the possibilities foreclosed by a punitive welfare system in which "'work-first' common sense"[25] organizes the discourse, the politics, and the programs directed at poor mothers.

IT'S BEEN SAID: Welfare recipients are bad mothers.

Whether women stay at home with their children or rely on care from others, these stories show that women make decisions in what they feel are the best interests of their children. J.J. stayed in her unhappy marriage rather than raise her children as a single mother: "I'd told him I wanted a divorce. We just weren't compatible, but he said we could work it out. I stayed in the marriage mainly because of the children. They were younger, [my son was only 12 and my daughter was 8,] and I didn't want them to grow up in a single-parent home." Throughout her journal, Jasmine (an apparently Black woman in her late 20s) wrote of the difficulties of raising a special needs child, and she concluded with her aspiration: "To be a strong mother who makes the decisions." These women had high standards for mothering and used ingenious combinations of welfare, work, and personal fortitude to try to reach them. The outcomes were often disappointing to themselves, but the source of disappointment was not welfare per se but rather the problems of mothering in poverty.

Jane's narrative tells of her coping with serious issues of physical pain from a work-related neck injury years before, addiction to prescribed painkillers and street drugs, and mental illness that long went undiagnosed. She recounts a series of difficult decisions to entrust her children to the care of others. Jane (an ex-offender in her late 40s who opened her narrative by writing, "I'm a beautiful Black, African-American woman with knowledge of the public assistance system") describes the tough period when she had to figure out how to get the best care for her children.

> ... I was on Worker's Comp during 1992, 1993, and 1994. In the beginning of 1995 they took me off. The time expired. One doctor had given me [a narcotic painkiller] while I still had medical coverage. I didn't know it was a narcotic. When I lost the disability, I lost the medical insurance and the pills, and then I really ran for the street drugs to replace them. . . . At that time, my rent had gone up to $400 a month, and I couldn't afford it. So there I was, homeless, living in shelters and with different family members. I was doing a lot of street drugs to help with the ongoing neck pain. Finally, I tried to get public assistance. They gave me medical and Food Stamps only, because my income from child support and Social Security was too high. But I was still doing drugs. I was hooked by then.
>
> In 1996 I left my kids with my sister, but they didn't like it there, because she mistreated them. She made them eat after her own kids, even though I was the one buying dinner. They had to sleep on the floor even though I gave her beds for them. She made my kids clean up her kids' room even though they had all played there together. They liked my older sister, but she talked about me, and the kids didn't like that. I was still staying in shelters. . . .
>
> [At one point,] I stayed with my cousin, but she was getting high too. I finally applied to get into a [low-income housing] project and did, but I was stressed with no money and the pain. I sent the kids to a friend. At about this time I started hearing voices and believing people were taking my kids from me. I was paranoid. . . .

For Jane, being a good mother and providing "the best care" means not dragging her children through the trials of her homelessness and addiction (and what turned out to be diagnosed as schizophrenia) and trying to put them in a safe environment. But her sister's home was not a viable place for Jane's children to be while she was staying in shelters; she writes that they felt like second-class citizens living with their aunt and cousins. At no point does Jane write about considering formally relinquishing custody of her children, and she clearly does not want to put them into foster care or have them become wards of the state. As she said when she took the stance of someone with a rival perspective on her situation:

> **Shelter staff** might think. . . Being in the shelter is better than being on the street.
> Jane responds: *It was better for my children, because they didn't have to stay with people who mistreated them. They needed to have someplace to sleep, to get up in the morning, and get to school. But it was not better for me, because of the rules and the useless parenting skills classes. I don't take orders well.*

Jane is deeply aware of the ways the combination of her character, drug addiction, homelessness, and mental illness makes motherhood even more of a struggle and heartache than it can be anyway. She realizes she basically could not be available for her children. Jane's herniated cervical disc from a fall at work meant that she was in unrelenting pain. Her addiction and mental illness meant that her skills for coping and connecting were minimal, and she often showed poor judgment. For example, in her narrative, Jane explains that she spent a $20,000 settlement of her work injury suit on "expensive motels and hotels. . . . I gave [the children] $1000 apiece and bought them clothes. I spent about $1500 of it on drugs. After all the money was gone, I was really in trouble." For Jane, the dilemmas of motherhood defy the simplistic stereotypes and default condemnation (especially of mothers of color[26]) endemic to the hegemonic explanation of poverty and vilification of welfare recipients.[27]

The participants in the community literacy project also made the point that in the unstable and dangerous neighborhoods where low-income parents often live, it can be important for mothers to stay home and care for their children, as Jule, Robin, and Takina tried to do. For example, Jule notes the importance—and undeniable pleasures—of being able to give her children some semblance of a steady family life.

> I enjoyed being a stay-home mother. The house was clean, dinner was ready when they got home from school, and I was there to help them. I was able to help out at their school — taking field trips with the class and helping with projects. In my extra time, I was able to be active in church; I sang in the choir and had my Bible study group to the house for dinner.

It took Jasmine time and energy to fight for the appropriate services and programs to care for her son, who has a diagnosed disability (as does Jule's oldest son).[28] For Jasmine, being a good mother was much higher on her agenda than conforming to work requirements. Nikki noted the dangers of public housing projects for children and youth. From a somewhat different perspective, Robin wrote about the prospect of being a good mother and worried about caring for her first child as a teenaged high school graduate.

Making the Decision: Should I Go to School?
I didn't want to be a drop-in parent. If I took the scholarship I wouldn't have been able to take my son to school with me. I knew there were not good accommodations for young parents on most college campuses. I would have had to leave him home with a family member. I would only get the chance to see him on Holidays and during breaks. I would miss his first steps, first words, all of those utterly important firsts that can never be recaptured.

Robin makes it poignantly clear that mothers' desires to experience the milestones of their children's development are not limited to White, married, middle-class women.[29]

In a more cautionary tale, Takina's story shows how easy—and dangerous—it is to let maternal desire to have the best for children turn into working in the underground economy and then dealing drugs.

It was 1987, and I was feeling good. . . . I did not have much money, but I was happy. I had two beautiful children. We were content and living comfortably. I was receiving welfare assistance, which helped me with my rent, lights, gas, water, and sewage. Still, I was definitely struggling. My children's father was not supportive. He would stop by every now and then with a few dollars and clothes for the children. I guess he meant well, but it still was not enough. This means I had to support us on the welfare check I received every two weeks. I managed to pay all my bills, but I had very little to live on after that. I wanted the best for my children, and it was hard to obtain things we wanted — mostly shoes, clothes, and coats for the kids, and cable t.v.

I decided to set up a salon chair in my kitchen. I began building up a clientele of people for hairstyling. My clients would come over every week or two for an appointment. I would have a few women over per week. I did a variety of styles, and each was done with great detail and pride. This was definitely working for me. I was able to save money and buy things we wanted, like cable and video games and other luxuries. This worked out for a while, but in the winter months, my bills went up dramatically, and I started having trouble keeping up.

Three years later, my whole world had completely fallen apart. . . . I moved into low income housing in order to save money. . . . I started off associating with what I thought were good, hard-working people. These new so-called friends lived in my apartment complex. Little did I know, they were involved in drug activity. I soon found out what they were up to, and started selling drugs for extra money myself. Once I obtained a job as a secretary at this housing complex, I got more familiar with everyone. I soon knew exactly who I could come in contact with to obtain drugs. Once I got my connections together, that's when I thought I hit the big time. I started buying drugs from them. I really thought this was the life. I made a lot of money very fast on a daily basis. I became a "hustler." All day and all night I would sell drugs and make lots of money. I got to the point where I was moving ounces at a time. I could make a thousand dollars in two days. This went on for a period of two years.

I thought to myself, "Who needs welfare assistance when I am making triple the monthly check in an hour's time?" Money now was no object. I bought all kinds of clothes, gold chains, a fur coat, and even a car. Everything was good; at least that is what I thought, until the unthinkable happened. I started using.

Takina's initial list of the material markers of being a good mother is modest: "shoes, clothes, and coats for the kids, and cable t.v." She clearly could not provide them on welfare alone and turned first to the underground service economy and then to small-time drug distribution, a business move facilitated by her relocating into public housing and obtaining a job that placed her in the center of the social network of the housing project. As her income from dealing drugs increased, so did Takina's list of desirable goods: "clothes, gold chains, a fur coat, and even a car." All came within her reach . . . "until the unthinkable happened."

Takina's entrepreneurial and business skills, and her constant efforts to support herself and her children, mark her as "definitely not a lazy or passive person" (as she puts it). Moreover, Takina writes that, "my children inspire me to succeed," a common comment about motherhood from the community literacy project participants as well as from the welfare-to-work program participants we interviewed for Chapters 2 and 3. Of course, her children "inspired" Takina to succeed as a drug dealer, which (along with developing a drug habit of her own) landed her in jail. For Robin, her decision to have her first child and not accept the academic scholarship she needed to go to college meant deferred education and diminished career ambitions (as a child, Robin wanted to be a lawyer "like on *LA Law*"). But the vast distance between inspiration and situation—between what the women in the writing project listed as their "ideal" and their "real"—comes not from any lack in their commitment to and capacity for mothering. The gap comes from the multiple obstacles that beset poor women as they try to meet even modest standards of material comfort and maternal care.

IT'S BEEN SAID: Welfare recipients are all undeserving junkies or crazies.

While it is certainly not true that all women on welfare have problems with addiction and mental health, several of the women participating in the community literacy project did. If anything, welfare is even more important for women who face mental illness, addiction, or both.[30] The welfare changes in 1996 made anyone with a drug conviction ineligible for welfare benefits for the rest of her life. These writers thought that was just like kicking someone when she's down, because it is so much harder to find a job when you have a criminal record. Welfare can provide the treatment resources women need in order to overcome their drug addictions or learn to manage their mental health problems. Jane explains that we have a long way to go before we successfully manage mental health care and addiction for poor women. She notes how dangerous it is for addicts who are still "using" to receive cash benefits when their judgment may be impaired and what is "driving" them is their cravings.

These stories also show that women become addicts for many reasons. Both Jane and Red turned to street drugs as a form of self-medication, Jane to cope with physical pain from a work-related injury and Red to deal with emotional pain and stress. Takina's continuing story shows how the drug and party culture seems very exciting and attractive when your horizons are otherwise limited.

It was not long before I got involved with people who used. It seemed exciting to me at the time, going down to the parties, getting dressed up in the fur coats. I began to become very popular. It was not long before I started partying on the weekends with these people. I wanted a car, a Datsun. I fixed it up, got the tinted windows and sounds in it, nice tires. I thought I was "livin' good." . . .

Then one day a female friend told me, "Try this out. This is the bomb, girl." It was a glass pipe with cocaine in it. I said no. I didn't want it then. But I later tried it. I will never forget that first rush. I definitely liked it. I would frequently visit her house on weekends. She would often call me and say, "Takina, you want to go out?" And I would say yes. After we'd go out, we would always end up getting high. . . . I soon started selling less and smoking more. There came a point where I sold nothing at all.

The struggle and social isolation of poverty and single motherhood can make people vulnerable to the desire first to sell and then to use drugs as part of "livin' good." Interestingly, the rival positions these writers engage differ, depending on their path to addiction. Takina, whose recent release from serving time on drug charges was much on her mind, gives voice to numerous rivals and "talks back" to almost none of them.

A **lawyer** might say: A better knowledge of the law/penalties for drug dealing may have deterred Takina from drug activity.

A **drug and alcohol counselor** might say: The attention you get when you have drugs and drug money is not good attention, because people use you.

A **parent** might say: The kids come first, even if that means working under the table or selling drugs. But then again, what kind of example do you set if the kids find out?

A **taxpayer** might say: Working under the table is fraud when you're receiving welfare at the same time.

A **welfare case manager** might say: Being able to manage your money makes it much easier to pay your utility bills. If you need help, you can seek help through debt management programs.

A **best friend** might say: Being on welfare and not having enough money drove her to drug dealing.

A **boss** might say: Why should I take the risk to hire someone with a criminal record? Welfare reform has given me my pick of workers who really need a job and haven't been in trouble. Why should I hire you?

A **judge** might say: Drugs and alcohol use had a lot to do with Takina's repeated convictions. She needs to pay for her crime.

A **probation officer** might say: We all have choices in life. Drug dealing shouldn't be an option.

Takina says: *Addiction takes over your life and makes you lose a lot of things. I would advise anyone who has thought about dealing drugs or using them to think twice.*

The **Drug Czar** might say: Zero tolerance means that the residents of any public housing units where drug activity takes place should be evicted immediately. This is the only way to wage war on drugs.

A **housing advocate** might say: Zero tolerance means that the family members of drug dealers (who may or may not be aware of drug activity) are penalized and rendered homeless for things they didn't do.

The rivaling segment of the community literacy project gave Takina the opportunity to articulate some of the many regrets she acknowledged in conversation, without having to condemn herself and her decisions explicitly. Taking rival stances was a mechanism that allowed Takina simultaneously to recognize and to distance herself from the virtually universal condemnation she faced. Takina's response to the extensive catalog of shame and blame she encountered consists mostly of advice to "think twice." In contrast, Jane, who attributes her drug addiction to misdiagnoses by medical professionals and inadequate systems of workers' compensation and addiction treatment, takes a quite different stance toward her imagined rivals.

> **Doctors** might think. . . I don't believe her. She is an addict and probably lying. She is trying to confuse me on purpose.
>   . . .
> **Psychiatrists** might think. . . Jane changed doctors constantly because of her insurance, homelessness, and addiction. They didn't know her and didn't have time to read her history carefully. They didn't have time to check for themselves about what other doctors had written and whether it was correct. They didn't even have time to call her other doctors and discuss her complicated case.
> Jane responds: *I wonder if the psychiatrists only care that they are getting paid for their 15 minutes.*

Jane questions the care and attention she received from people throughout the physical and mental health services systems. She knows the professional skepticism with which her injury and pain claims might be met, and tries—mostly unsuccessfully—to get specialized treatment. In contrast to Takina's apparent acceptance of much of the rhetoric of addiction and recovery, Jane's response is righteous and cynical.

Red, unlike Jane, did not have a work-related injury to which she could attribute the pain that she tried to self-medicate with street drugs. Red used her contributing factors section to address the overlap of addiction and depression.

> **Red got hooked on drugs**
>   . . . because of her friend's bad influence. She shouldn't have listened to her.
>   . . . because she didn't have enough resources. She got in trouble, because she had to take care of too many people in her family all at once. It made her even more vulnerable.
>   . . . because of stress. People she loved were sick and dying. The stress of the infidelity by her man might also have contributed to her vulnerability, because she was too trusting.
>   . . . because she was looking for comfort and distraction at a point when crack cocaine was flooding the neighborhood where she lived.
>   . . .
> **Red's depression might have been aggravated**
>   . . . by her worries about sick family members.
>   . . . by her worries about money, because she had to quit one of her jobs.
>   . . . because a psychiatrist was not available for a referral.

. . . because doctors use psychoactive drugs instead of other treatment. Mental health resources are limited even if you have welfare benefits.

. . . because her first husband was selling her stuff to buy drugs.

. . . because being on Prozac and crack cocaine at the same time may have made her symptoms worse.

. . . because her cop boyfriend didn't understand her illness.

. . . because continuing to use street drugs mostly likely increased symptoms of depression and anxiety instead of relieving them.

Red directly took on some of the harshest criticism of welfare recipients in her engagements with her imagined rivals.

A **concerned friend or parent** might say: You didn't have to put the drugs in your mouth. Nobody can make you do anything you don't want to do.

Red talks back: *I was vulnerable and thought it would help. I trusted my friend* [who encouraged her to turn to self-medication through street drugs].

. . .

A **therapist** might say: You had no support from your family. You were medicating yourself with street drugs to try to alleviate your symptoms.

. . .

A **psychiatrist** might say: The Prozac doesn't help; you need a psychiatrist. You have been misdiagnosed.

Red talks back: *So help me get the treatment I need!*

A **medical advocate** might say: When you go to the psych ward, they scare you and treat you with force even if you go voluntarily. You can't let that get to you or keep you from insisting on treatment.

. . .

An **advocate** might say: She gave [her cop boyfriend] her [automated teller machine] card because she didn't want to have access to cash so she wouldn't buy drugs, but that makes her dependent on him and vulnerable.

Red talks back: *Until I feel comfortable with myself, I can't trust myself not to deal with my pain by picking up a hit of crack. I can't say what tomorrow might bring, and I don't want the temptation.*

Red's efforts to work, get off street drugs, and simply find some stability in her life were complicated by several factors. She suffered from untreated depression and anxiety: "I . . . started getting sick with depression and couldn't work. I couldn't concentrate. My heart beat fast, I was nervous, I had no appetite, I was fussy, I couldn't stand other people in my space, and little things would bother me. I tried to work, but I had to quit because I just couldn't do it. . . . I couldn't stay anywhere for eight hours because of panic attacks." Working was also hard because of some of Red's occupational choices:

. . . When I was younger, I went to school to be a nurse's aid, but I had to quit my first nursing job. I worked for awhile at nursing before realizing that I did not like that kind of work. I didn't know that I would have to work with cadavers. After patients died, I had to clean them and put tags on their toes. I couldn't perform these required duties once I was turned loose in the field. I was scared of dead people, but I didn't realize this until I actually got the job. I had gone into nursing because my mother was a nurse. What she told me about nursing turned out to be different from what I had to do, so I did private duty nursing for awhile to avoid dealing with dead bodies.

In addition, Red had to deal with complicated family crises that proved distressing and distracting. Red was caring for the beloved stepfather who had raised her and now had cancer, as well as for an aunt who had a stroke. She came home from her job at a nursing home to find the sheriff putting her furniture out of her apartment because her husband had squandered the rent money. Red writes,

I took all of this very hard. When my stepfather was in the hospital, dying, a friend introduced me to crack. I was very vulnerable, and I didn't know which way to go. My friend told me, "This will make you feel better. Try it." I was naïve and believed her. I didn't think that she would lead me wrong in life. She was older than I was, and I thought that because we grew up practically family, she wouldn't do anything to harm me. It turned out she was using me so she could use, too. The f***ing shit was part of the reason I got addicted and crazy and in all kinds of trouble.

Red's resorting to strong language is a way for her to express her frustration with addiction and mental illness in the context of stresses of marital strife and family crisis, an unhappy work situation, and poverty. Her account of her situation far exceeds the narrow confines of stereotypes of welfare recipients as junkies and crazies.

IT'S BEEN SAID: Get off welfare–there are lots of jobs out there!

In the 1990s and 2000s, the U.S. economy was renowned for generating jobs at the low end of the labor market. As I noted in Chapter 2, contingent, involuntarily part-time, low-wage employment in the service sector was the precarious complement to the bubble of high-wage, high-tech, "information age" jobs in finance and other business services, insurance, and real estate that burst into the global economic crisis of 2008–2011.[31] And even in the midst of the crisis, there are minimum-wage jobs to be had, if one can compete for them.[32] But there is a difference between the minimum wage and a living wage. Moreover, the structure of the bifurcated labor market and mechanisms of discrimination mean that many workers at the bottom of the labor market tend to churn through entry-level jobs without ever having the opportunity to step onto the next rung of job ladders in internal labor markets or to accrue the kinds of experience, recognized responsibility, or seniority that might lead to decent employment.[33] The participants in the community literacy project underscored this point, showing how they could not support themselves and a family on $5.15/hour (the minimum wage during the period about which most of them write). Such jobs did not offer them the important health care benefits and help with housing that they needed. Securing safe and affordable childcare for their children proved to be an insurmountable obstacle when relying on a low-wage paycheck. One after another, these women noted the lack of "good" jobs as a major obstacle to their living their lives and raising their children in safety.

For example, among the factors Nikki listed that led to her spell on welfare were:

Low Paying Jobs. My husband's pay alone wasn't enough to survive comfortably as a family. And once I was the sole supporter, I also couldn't raise my kids on minimum wage jobs alone. Neither of us alone could earn enough to support our three kids.

Lack of Benefits for the Working Poor. With a minimum wage job, I couldn't find housing I could afford, nor did I have health benefits. This made welfare a necessity.

Nikki's points about low wages and benefits certainly generalize to much of the U.S. population during the 1990s and 2000s. Stagnant or even falling earnings, especially for men with low levels of educational attainment, contributed to general pressures on women to work to contribute to their households whether they were married to or living with the fathers of their children or not. The kinds of structural changes in the economy I outlined in Chapter 2 have made it increasingly difficult for one earner to serve as the sole breadwinner.[34]

Takina also makes multiple points about the wide gap between the jobs for which she was qualified and the lifestyle she could afford when she was a small-time drug distributor in her housing project.

Easy Money

Takina was a young lady struggling to pay bills. Not having enough money was a problem. She wanted to buy nice things for herself and her children. She decided to start selling drugs for extra cash. It was easy money. With welfare alone, you're not making enough for nice things. You can get tired of waiting for the check instead of making your own money.

Power and Prestige

The so-called "glamorous life" can be just as addictive as drugs; it isn't what it seems to be. You can be deluded into thinking you're on top with all the attention and power — something many poor women crave. But it's false and temporary power. Having money and materialistic things can mislead you from what's real and what counts. Dealing drugs is not a good idea for anyone. You can become addicted yourself. You can get incarcerated. And where are your "friends" then?

Meeting Difficult Job Standards

Takina went on welfare because she lacked the job training she needed to get a decent job. To complicate matters more, now she not only lacks skills but [also] has a criminal record, which makes it even more difficult to get employment. Many employers do extensive background checks. That is why it is very important to keep your record clean.

The attractions of working under the table were considerable for Takina. The lure of cash to supplement her welfare benefits made work in the underground economy—doing hair and selling drugs—appealing and perhaps necessary forms of economic activity.[35] The glamour of the lifestyle available only through illicit gains (given the limits of Takina's earnings power in the regular economy) contributed to the pull of the drug trade. And of course, obtaining a "straight" job was much more difficult after Takina's drug conviction and incarceration. Moreover, Takina's status was all the more precarious because her drug conviction also jeopardized her eligibility for welfare. The apparently straightforward "work-first common sense"[36] that greeted Takina when she was released after serving her drug sentence was in fact rife with contradictory demands and constraints, leaving her with very few options.

In contrast to the lure of the underground economy that Takina describes and the perils of low-wage work that Nikki notes, Red catalogues a number of causal factors in her precarious economic position.

Red had trouble working

. . . because she was depressed and anxious. Her symptoms made it hard to sit still for eight hours.

. . . because she had severe conflicts between her need to do family care and her work for wages.

. . . because she had unrealistic expectations about the work of being a nurse's aid. She only went into nursing because of her mother. She did not get adequate career counseling.

. . . because she was on drugs, which made her not care about work and probably made her symptoms worse in the long run.

The variety of factors Red lists—from mental health problems to gendered care expectations to addiction—reflects both the complex reality of her situation and her ability to grasp it in the supportive context of the community literacy project. Red also shows the capacity and willingness to imagine extensively and address directly the representation of her plight by welfare caseworkers.

A **caseworker** might say: You had no clear plans for your life — you've just been reacting to things instead of being proactive.

Red talks back: *I had plans in life, but I didn't know what it was really going to be like until I got there. I also didn't get good advice for career planning.*

A **caseworker** might say: Don't think someone offering you drugs was being caring or helpful. People who are older or like family often are the ones who can cause you the most harm.

Red talks back: *That's right. It was not OK for her to offer me drugs, and it's not OK for her to tell me, "get over it" now.*

A **caseworker** might say: You don't "owe" it to your stepfather to care for him just because he raised you.

Your husband's selling your stuff did not make it impossible for you to return to work; your drug addiction did.

Red talks back: *There were many reasons it was hard for me to work, including total lack of support from my husband.*

A **caseworker** might say: You don't have to wait until you can work a whole day. Try to work part time, one or two days a week. Time limits are incentives for people to get off welfare. If there were no limits, people like Red would never work.

Red talks back: *Different people have different barriers to work and need different supports to overcome them. Welfare should treat people on a case-by-case basis, not as though we are all the same.*

Red responds extensively to the comments of an imaginary caseworker. Red implicitly critiques the contradiction internal to the caseworker's argument that any work is better than none and the caseworker's judgment that punitive incentives are the only forces to which "people like Red" will respond. Without trying to portray herself as special or heroic, Red unequivocally asks for help and insists on individualized assistance in facing the substantial barriers that obstruct her ability to "get a job, any job."[37]

IT'S BEEN SAID: Poor women are used to rough living.
They give as good as they get in relationships.

The women participating in the community literacy project articulated safety concerns about themselves and their children. They explained how troubled relationships could disrupt their life plans and derail their work effort. As Jule put it, speaking of the dilemmas facing a single mother without many resources:

I know I'm getting older, and our relationship does not seem to be moving toward marriage, so it may have to end. But I'm afraid. It's hard nowadays to trust someone new. There are so many people who are violent to women and children. What scares me is all the crazy stuff going on in the world, and I don't want to expose my little girl to it.... I feel more secure bringing my kids up my way, without fear of what a strange man might do.

Although she ritually invokes the hegemonic notion that relationships ought to be "moving toward marriage," Jule's situation—like the situations of the rest of the women writers in the community literacy project—is unlikely to be improved by the focus on marriage that characterized much of the policy debate when she was writing. Indeed, in her contributing factors section, Jule attributes her situation in part to dependency and failed expectations. Jule trusted in men who ended up leaving or were untrustworthy; she had no back-up plan other than welfare and her low-wage job.

Nikki also turned out to need a back-up plan when her husband failed to support her through a difficult pregnancy, two-timed her with another woman, stole her money and her dignity, and left her to deal with his own ailing and abusive grandmother. When Nikki found herself having a difficult pregnancy that required her to "go on bed rest,"

... Her husband assured her that they could make it, but that turned out to be what she called a lie from the bottom of the pit of hell.

Here is what happened. A few weeks went by, and the landlord started acting up. He was one of those landlords who thought he was the boss of everyone. He would come into the apartment and look through their personal belongings and help himself to anything in the house. He was a heavy drinker and felt as though he could treat his tenants any old way, because they needed a place to live. After about two months, her husband told her that they needed to move out, because the money was very tight. She didn't know the truth. The true story was that he wasn't giving the money she had given him for her part of the rent to the landlord, which would explain why the landlord was coming into the apartment. As it turned out, Nikki's husband had been spending the money on drinking and hanging out with friends. He was going out after work and acting as if he had money like that all the time.

Nikki cried for a while, because she didn't want to go back to her parents' home. Her husband decided to move her to his grandmother's house, across from their apartment. Nikki agreed to move in with her grandmother-in-law, but eventually things grew very rocky. After they moved in, her husband told her that he would be working a lot more, maybe two jobs, to pay his grandmother's rent. Nikki didn't like it, but she had no choice. She no longer worked [because of the difficult pregnancy]. For several months, Nikki's husband told her that he had to work all the time. He sometimes wouldn't come home for several days. She never realized that he, in fact, was living with another woman in the same neighborhood. She found out later that his grandmother, sister, friends, and even her mother knew that he was running around. She was devastated. The main person she put all her trust in had broken her heart.

Nikki had the baby, and it was premature, but healthy. She moved back in with her parents, because they insisted that she needed to be around them, her own family. After about a year, though, Nikki went back over to her husband's grandmother's home. Her husband had begged her to come back to him, because he couldn't live without her, and Nikki agreed if he would be there for her and the kids.

About five months after she moved back in, Nikki called for a doctor's appointment, because she felt really sick, and something was really wrong. She was talking to the nurse on the phone, and the nurse asked her when her last period was. She told her that she was still having it, but the nurse told her that she needed to come in right away, because she could be pregnant. Nikki was so upset that she started crying. She felt like her husband was trying to trap her. *He knows I'll leave him if he cheats again, but I'll have to stay if I am pregnant. What else can I do? He's entrapping me with this pregnancy,* she thought. The doctor told her yes, she was in fact about five months along, but that she also had cervical cancer. Nikki called her mother to tell her she wanted to get rid of the pregnancy, and they argued for a while. Her mother thought it was wrong. Nikki knew that there was no way out of the situation. She felt as though she had to get rid of the problem, but at the same time it was against her religion. Her husband told her parents that he wanted the baby, and it would be unfair for her to go out and get rid of his child. Nikki eventually decided to keep the baby, and she stayed again at the grandmother's house.

Then one day her husband's mistress called looking for him. Nikki asked why she was calling. The woman stated that she didn't have to talk to her, because Nikki's husband told her she was a "crazy psycho-bitch" that wouldn't leave him alone and get on with her life. Nikki was heartbroken. He had also told this woman that their second child was dead from complications in child-birth. Nikki told her that she was now pregnant with their third child, and she wasn't going anywhere, so this woman had better leave them alone. Then she confronted her husband and ended her relationship with him, but had to stay with the grandmother until something better came along. She went on welfare and sued her husband for support. He was agreeable and helped when he could. Welfare took money from his checks for child support — $300 per check — plus he would help pay for clothing and food for the kids when he could, but he went in and out of their lives.

Nikki was so embarrassed and ashamed. She felt that no one was to be trusted at all. She started thinking about standing on her own two feet and get-ting her own place. She tried several times before, but there was no success, because she would always be put on a waiting list. She grew emotionally drained. She knew that she had to keep fighting for the kids, because she was all that they had in life and vice versa. Then her husband's grandmother started her shit. She retired from her job and started to get real money hungry. Nikki was already giving her money and Food Stamps, but she still wasn't happy. She had health problems and was an alcoholic. She was also jealous, because every-one was paying attention to Nikki, who she called Ms. Goodie Two Shoes. She told a few of the family members that Nikki was sleeping with her man, the man that Nikki called grandpa. Nikki was really mad at this point anyway, because she felt like she was the grandmother's personal maid. She was tired of picking up after her and cleaning up after she defecated and urinated on the bathroom floor (deliberately, Nikki thought). She had enough of her family, his family, and the whole damn situation. Nikki decided, *I'm going to pack my shit and get the kids together and move to a shelter away from all these crazy sons of bitches.*

Nikki's life with her husband carried many of the classic markers of what sociolo-gists call "hard living": Her husband was frequently absent, he stole her share of the rent money, he drank, and he manipulated her emotions. She felt that he used money, housing, emotional blackmail, and pregnancy to keep her dependent and in the relationship—a formidable mix.[38] Writing about unstable relationships as a contributing factor in her situation, Nikki says, "I moved to low-income housing and went on welfare to get on my feet, because I wanted my own place. Getting subsidized housing meant I could afford my own rent even if my husband was not reliable." She addresses a wide variety of potential rival perspectives on her story.

A **Counselor** might say... Nikki had low self-esteem, because she was treated so poorly, and she needed someone whom she could trust and confide in daily. She needed to know, *I'm normal and there is nothing wrong with me; it's not my fault.*

A **Parent** might say... Nikki, if you first would have gone to college and thought about an education instead of a family, maybe things could have been different. But you have discovered as a parent that the kids' needs come first. Too bad your husband didn't realize that sooner!

Nikki Responds: *I would advise anyone who wants to get married right out of high school to enjoy life to its fullest first. Get your degree, find a job, and travel, before you decide to include a significant other or start a family. Never rely on anyone other than yourself, and always know that there is a lesson to be learned in every difficult situation.*

A **Taxpayer** might say... Well, if she has a husband, then why can't they make it without the welfare system? Can't they live off of his job like other men and their families?

Nikki Responds: *In today's society it takes two incomes, and my husband's wasn't enough. When we were separated, his financial support was erratic.*

A **Welfare Worker** might say... Women like Nikki can do it if they don't give up on themselves. You have to crawl before you walk.

A **Girlfriend** might say... Nikki, why don't you just leave your husband and get someone else? You deserve better. It's not like you can't find another guy. Get a man on the side. Ya gotta do whatcha got to do!

Nikki Responds: *Whether I'm with him or anyone else, all relationships are risky. I feel it's better to stay with who you know than take a risk with a new man. Women in the past swept things under the rug to hold their marriages together. I admire that they stayed together, but you can't ignore problems. I held it together by speaking out. This helped my husband to change. He's scared now and respects me more, because he knows that I can do it with or without him. I am stronger willed and make more money than he does. With my salary and his, we can buy a house.*

A **Family Division Judge** might say... If you and your husband truly separate, he'll have to pay a lot of child support for three kids. You'll just be another statistic in the eyes of the court. Many couples who get married before the age of 20 get divorced.

The practice of rivaling allowed Nikki to render an elaborate set of perspectives on her situation, some supportive and some critical. Her cautionary advice is proportionate to the moralistic, "I told you so" tone she attributes to some of her imagined rivals. Nikki uses the rivaling process to convey information about marriage and parenthood that acknowledges both the powers of desire and the serious consequences of traditional gender expectations about feminine deference and dependence. The evidence of her heartache at her husband's betrayal and of her rejection of glib or tit-for-tat responses rebuts any welfare myth that dismisses poor women's concerns with their integrity and dignity in relationships.

In addition, Nikki's narrative, causal analysis, and rivaling demonstrate the short-comings of the hegemonic explanations of, and standard remedies for, poverty and abuse. On the one hand, "work-first common sense" fails to recognize the obstacles to family-supporting employment that both Nikki and her husband face. Her prob-lems obtaining and maintaining living-wage work are rooted in problem pregnan-cies, care responsibilities for both children and needy adults (such as her grandmother-in-law), and a husband who lied to her, robbed her, and cheated on her, not her having lack of incentives to work or lack of personal responsibility. On the other hand, Nikki's situation put her under the radar of the standard mecha-nisms of the criminal justice, welfare, and shelter systems. Protective orders and the shelter system are poorly suited to address Nikki's experiences of dependency, betrayal, and loss of control over her housing, finances, and fertility.

Red's narrative shows her surprise when her marriage started to go deeply awry, and emphasizes the extent to which life and relationships can take unpredictable turns.

> One day my girlfriend called me at the nursing home where I worked and told me to come home right away. The constable was going to set my furniture out. The constable and my girlfriend sat there until I got home. The constable demanded the rent, which I paid with my paycheck and my mother's help. My husband showed up and gave my mother a ride home in his new Cadillac. That's when I learned that he had used the rent money to buy the Caddy.
>
> . . . I started having more problems with my husband. He was on crack and started selling all my stuff. He was reliable until he got on drugs, which he didn't do until after we got married. You never know what's going to happen with these guys.

As was the case for Nikki and J.J., part of Red's problem was the way her husband undermined her living situation, tested the limits of her fragile coping mechanisms, and contributed to her high stress levels. The writers in the community literacy proj-ect used different ways to express these issues. Jasmine referred to the father of her son as "the sperm donor," while Robin wrote disparagingly: "By 1993, I found myself the parent of three children, four if you count my fiancé." As with Jule, these women's hurt, disappointment, and frustrated longing for supportive relationships come through loud and clear. These women are not cavalier about their hearts or about their treatment at the hands of the men with whom they have cast their lots.

Red also addresses the contributing factors to the physical altercation she experi-enced with her cop boyfriend. According to Red's assessment,

> The incident with her cop boyfriend happened:
> . . . due to jealousy. He was seeing some other woman, and her jealousy made her lose her temper.
> . . . because she had a hair trigger temper from both the drugs and the depression.
> . . . because he hit her, so she retaliated strongly.
> . . . because she was able to grab his weapon.
> . . . because he managed to keep the cops away by telling them to disregard the call. The police accepted his word and didn't come to help protect her.

... because he was paying the bills, which made her vulnerable.

Red's causal analysis of this critical incident includes elements of her own agency, without drifting into victim rhetoric. She also mentions factors in the relationship (her economic dependence) and the broader system of police protection (his ability to get his co-workers to disregard her call) that help the reader to comprehend Red's own retrospective understanding of her situation. In her rival perspectives section, Red talks back to the criminal justice system, welfare caseworkers, and shelter personnel she wishes would have listened to and advocated for her.

A **cop** might say: We have to disregard calls when other cops are there.
Red talks back: *The dispatcher should have realized the call was coming from his house. They should have sent somebody anyway.*
A **therapist** might say: Why is she still with the cop?
Red talks back: *He takes care of me. He's settling down and doesn't do the stuff he used to do. I'm planning to be with him until the day I die. He came into my life not knowing that I was on drugs. Now that I'm not in denial, I want to make my life good and have him in it. I don't want the relationship to stop, just the bull.*
An **advocate for battered women** might say: Red could have applied for a [civil restraining order] based on the fact that he slapped her, even if there was no police report filed. If the [restraining order] were granted, he would have been evicted from the residence. However, when the abuser is a police officer, the situation may be a great deal more complicated and is usually viewed as being a potentially lethal situation. It's also very hard to leave, because that can be very dangerous, too.
Red talks back: *No kidding. Plus I shouldn't have to leave my place, especially when he's spending most of his time with another woman at her place.*
Red's retaliation [when she held his gun to his head and put the brick through the windshield of his police car] may have gotten her charged with greater offenses than the boyfriend/police officer would have been charged with had a police report been filed.
Red talks back: *Plus it takes time to go to court and deal with everything. It's practically a full time job, with all the waiting and repeated trips and appearances downtown.*

As do many of the participants in the community literacy project, Red writes engagingly if bluntly about what she wants in heterosexual relationships. She articulates a position that feminists have to acknowledge: . . . *I want to make my life good and have him in it. I don't want the relationship to stop, just the bull.*[39] Red's narrative, her causal analysis, and her response to rival perspectives sit uneasily with the popular "victim empowerment folklore" about abuse[40]; she seems not to conform to the hegemonic notion of victim, and her turning his own gun against her police officer boyfriend is surely not the notion of empowerment the folklore envisions. Her contributions to the community literacy project also contradict the "work-first common sense" about poverty and welfare.[41] There is nothing wrong with Red's work ethic, but her mental health problems and extremely limited training and vocational options mean that there is a poor fit between what it would likely take for her to establish herself in living-wage employment and the time limits and work requirements of the restructured welfare system. As her imaginary exchange with an advocate illustrates, the law-and-order assumptions and criminological conventional wisdom about victim safety and perpetrator accountability[42] do not straightforwardly accommodate Red's account of the financial deception and subsequent problems she had with her husband or her narrative and analysis of the critical incident with her boyfriend the police officer. Most important, contrary to welfare myths about "hard living," nothing in Red's experience or her self-understanding suggests that she should have taken in stride the relationship troubles she faced or that she should be tough enough to suffer betrayal and rough treatment from the men in her life.

IT'S BEEN SAID: Women on welfare are just dependent losers. American society is based on survival of the fittest. Welfare recipients are clearly the "unfit," and there's no reason to listen to their whining.

The community literacy project provided a unique opportunity for poor and low-income women to tell their stories to unsympathetic audiences with rival perspectives—and to have a chance to still make themselves heard. But it went beyond that. The project showed these writers that with support and time, they could analyze their own situations and the broader issues of poverty, work, relationships, and welfare. They are not unfit losers; they are capable of providing reasons and responding to challenges in ways that make them important participants in deliberations over public policy. Their analyses allowed them to "talk back" in policy discussions in which they are important but generally silenced stakeholders. We distributed the booklet containing their narratives and analyses to caseworkers and welfare administrators in Allegheny County. The women presented their stories to a group of welfare and shelter staff who attended a session of the community literacy project and responded to the narratives and arguments. The process allowed them to give concrete illustrations of the challenges in their lives and the flaws and strengths of character with which they have confronted those challenges. The result is an eloquent set of stories that encompass the complexities of real life. The particulars of these women's situations—and especially the ways that relationships with controlling men obstruct not just their employment but also their realizing their life projects—do not fit very well with the categories through which the criminal justice and welfare systems try to recognize the "needs" of poor or abused women. Policies to address the social problems of poverty, addiction, mental illness, loss, and abuse will be richer if we listen carefully to what these writers have to say; personal narrative and women's analyses can enrich public deliberation about abuse, poverty, and social policy.

Conclusions

Poor people are taking a beating in this economy. Long-term unemployment, linked to the global recession and chronic corporate underinvestment and aggravated by the conservative attack on what remains of organized labor, undermines people's prospects for living-wage jobs. Misplaced concerns about government deficits, linked to conservative state bashing, further fray a miserly welfare safety net and ostensibly justify slashing social spending and abolishing collective bargaining for public sector employees. The important role of unemployment in impoverishment underscores the nugget of insight at the core of the conventional wisdom about poverty: Having a job (or two) may not get you out of poverty and debt, but *not* having a job is much, much worse. An appalling number of women are taking a beating, too, their lives shortchanged or literally cut short by the men they love, the fathers of their children, the partners to whom they have entrusted their hearts and important life decisions. Conventional wisdom identifies lack of waged work—and the earned income, mainstream values, and social connections that employment produces and reproduces—as the cause of both poverty and battering and therefore casts women's work as the best route to safety and solvency. The evidence I present in this book suggests the problems that arise from proposing women's work as the central solution to poverty and battering, especially but not exclusively for women who experience work-specific control, abuse, and sabotage. Nevertheless, current and former welfare recipients like Red and Robin resolutely put work, career options, education, and job training at the forefront of their visions of a world that would make women less vulnerable to abuse and poverty. Their focus on work opportunities as a key element in the resources they need to realize their autonomously determined life projects is not a result of their being duped by conventional wisdom, to which they freely talk back. In this concluding chapter, I use the insights I have gleaned from interviews, administrative data, and a community literacy project to continue grappling with the conventional wisdom that posits work as the panacea for poverty and battering.

I proceed in two steps. I first present the issues about life options—specifically, about the importance of employment to women's safety, solvency, and ability to pursue their life projects—that the writers in the community literacy project raise. Contrary to conventional wisdom, work is not always the best (let alone, the only) remedy for the harms of poverty and battering. However, in a capitalist society, women's equal inclusion in waged work unquestionably sustains their participating in the common life, creating equality and justice at home, and pursuing and realizing the goals they set for their own lives and the lives of their children.[1] The writers in the community literacy project make this point repeatedly, and it is central to understanding the appeal and the quandary of conventional wisdom.

Second, my empirical and interpretative exploration of the potentially paradoxical importance of waged work—especially given the challenges to the conventional wisdom I document in this book—leads me to articulate a key principle for policy, advocacy, and programs to address poverty and battering. The principle is simply that poverty and battering are both issues of human rights and social inclusion.[2] Current U.S. policy and programs address poverty and battering primarily through incentives to reform the behavior and character of the poor and victimized through personal responsibility. First and foremost in the prevailing definition of personal responsibility are the virtues and resources associated with waged work. The prevailing "'work-first' common sense"[3] has its roots in neo-liberal fantasies about the redemptive powers of employment for wayward individuals, on the one hand, paired with attacks on the ideals and efforts to privatize the institutions and programs of the welfare state, on the other. In contrast, a social justice approach includes safety and solvency among the social, civil and political, economic, and human rights that must be underwritten and guaranteed—and if necessary, the organizational means to achieve them being subsidized and provided—by democratic government.

ENVISIONING CHANGE: "WHAT IF . . .?"

An important element of the community literacy project was providing space, time, and support to current and former welfare recipients so they could imagine a counterfactual: What would have to change for the critical incidents in their lives to have turned out differently? In this part of my final chapter, I set out materials from the "What if . . .?" sections of the analyses by Red, Jule, Robin, and the other community literacy project writers. My goal is to continue putting the spotlight on the ideas and priorities of the people who are most often the targets of shame, blame, and derision; of the "politics of disgust" politicians and the media direct toward poor people and welfare recipients; of the "victim empowerment folklore" around battered women; and of the conventional wisdom regarding battering, poverty, and work.[4] As mentioned in the previous chapter, these women generally have the least opportunity to think and talk about their experiences in ways that are heard beyond their immediate circle.

Many points emerge from the writers' assessments of what might change if they lived under different rules and with different resources. They address issues of isolation and lack of support concerning addiction and mental illness. They want to be able to count on physical and mental health, drug and rehabilitation, and welfare systems and experts for information, appropriate referrals, treatment, and support rather than stigma, medication they cannot afford, and careless misdiagnoses. Over and over, Red and Jane insist on alternatives to self-medication with street drugs, and Jane and J.J. both call for a combination of counseling and drug therapies and "free services for people with mental health disorders who can only work intermittently or not at all" (J.J.). Red captures the concerns of many of the writers—including the problem of keeping up job performance while coping with addiction or mental illness—when she demands to know,

> What If. . .? We organized life so that people with depression and anxiety disorders could get the treatment and support they need instead of having to self-medicate or struggle to work when they feel terrible? THEN nobody would be stigmatized for having emotional problems or mental illness.[5]

The writers also imagine a world with more shared responsibility for raising children, a world in which, as Robin proposes, "We better educate young women and men about the realistic costs of supporting a family." They seek a supportive community for special needs children, access to child disability advocates, and less judgment and more early intervention and positive help for people whose "kids are suffering" (as Jasmine puts it). They also call for more social responsibility for gendered care.

> What If. . .? There were free home care for people with cancer, Alzheimer's, and other disabling and terminal diseases? THEN women wouldn't be torn between working and caring for their families. (Red)

> What if. . .? . . . all workplaces provided good, affordable childcare? THEN women like Jule wouldn't have to look elsewhere for help and could still be near their children. Jule may not have needed to be on welfare so long. (Jule)

On the topic of abuse, Red emphasizes the importance of rapid response from law enforcement. Red asks, "What If. . .? The police responded responsibly to distress calls? THEN women would actually be protected by the police, even if they are involved with men who are cops." Red's desire and need for protection from a man whose co-workers collude with his abuse are complicated by the fact that her boyfriend is a cop. But her plea for equal justice—she should be able to rely on police protection, no matter what the status or job of her partner—is straightforward. Red goes on to wonder how things would be different if she had found a way to disconnect from the relationship.

> What If. . .? The police could have convinced Red to kick the boyfriend out? What if Red had pursued her right to protection under the law? THEN she could have some more control over her life.

Red has a strong sense of the ways abusive and controlling men (both her ex-husband and her boyfriend) have contributed to the difficulties she has faced. She wonders whether a different approach by law enforcement might augment her capacity to set her life's path, including her ability to "pursue[] her right[s]" and take action on her own behalf. At the time, Red resorted to violence herself, holding her boyfriend's gun to his head and throwing a brick through his car window. Red responded to this self-identified crisis in her relationship with escalating physical violence. Alternatives might have led to a better outcome all the way around.

All of the writers emphasize the basic idea that women would be significantly less vulnerable to poverty and abuse if the behavioral changes demanded by the new welfare rules and provisions for obtaining protective orders were complemented by new arrangements in relationships between women and men and by shifts in the organization and practice of the institutions that structure their opportunities. The remainder of this section focuses on their writing about those two major themes.

Gender Expectations and Heterosexual Relationships

The writers in the community literacy project critically assess the damage caused by conventional notions of women's dependence on, and sacrifices in, relationships with men. Red, whose husband blew the rent money on a showy car and whose cop boyfriend cheated on her while his name was on the lease to her home, draws attention to patterns of parenting and the effects of gender socialization on women's vulnerability. She writes, "What If. . .? Parents really raised their children, encouraged their daughters to leave abusive partners, and taught their sons to respect women? THEN perhaps women wouldn't get stuck in dangerous or abusive relationships." Red also addresses the possibility that the normative expectation that women should be in heterosexual relationships might contribute to women's dependence and vulnerability to abuse. Asks Red: "What If. . .? Women didn't feel like they had to keep a man? THEN they wouldn't work so hard to keep boyfriends or even husbands who didn't treat them well."

J.J. recounts the story of the time she thought her husband was following her to work, which frightened her badly. "I went to the first house that I came to and asked the people to call the police," J.J. writes. "They did, and then they also took me down to the magistrate's office. . . . I was terrified." Partly as a result of her being late to work that morning, J.J.'s boss fired her. J.J., who left her husband after her children were grown and wound up on public assistance when she was homeless, unemployed, and newly diagnosed with bipolar disorder, speculates, "What If. . .? Women felt more comfortable challenging their husbands? THEN maybe women would get their own needs met without having to leave their relationships entirely. It might make men feel better about themselves, too." J.J. was one of the older women in the community literacy project, and the only apparently White writer; she was in her late 40s, and she had most clearly grown up with traditional expectations about marriage, motherhood, and the extent to which women were supposed to find fulfillment within the confines of feminine domesticity. She wonders, "What If. . .? Women had independent lives before marriage? THEN maybe they would have a better community of friends to turn to when times were tough, or they would develop more skills and sense of security for being on their own."

Other women echo J.J.'s comments about the importance to women's safety and solvency of combining independence and reliable social and material resources outside of marriage. Jule, who had a series of relationships with unreliable and married men, asks,

What if. . .? Jule hadn't felt so lonely when she met the men who fathered her children? Having good friends and a supportive family can help with the pain of isolation. THEN maybe she would have waited for a man ready to commit to her and the children. What if Jule found enjoyable and safe ways of meeting men?

Nikki's husband made most of the important decisions in their relationship. Despite this legacy, she did everything she could think of to establish a sense of independence for herself and her children. Nikki wonders,

> What if. . .? Women in oppressive relationships would learn to speak up for themselves and have the courage to leave and find other means of support, as Nikki did? THEN maybe fewer women would be victims of emotional abuse. Maybe more women would feel good about themselves. Maybe others in their lives would respect them.

Some of Nikki's rhetoric here sounds like the ubiquitous folklore of victim empowerment.[6] In their visions of what could be different, these women carefully balance accountability for themselves and the men in their lives, calling both for women to take action on their own behalf and for men to respond with respect.

Options for Self-determined Life Projects

The writers in the community literacy project do not just call for changes in gender socialization, the division of care work, relationships with men, and social respect. They also make a strong collective case for the transforming effects of their having more options for their life projects. When they speak and write about the importance of enhanced options for pursuing lives of their own design, the participants in the community literacy project invoke two key substantive examples. The first involves marriage, motherhood, fertility, and birth control. The second concerns education, training, and—most salient for addressing conventional wisdom and U.S. public policy about poverty and battering—work.

MARRIAGE AND MOTHERHOOD
Recall from the previous chapter that Robin is deeply skeptical of the usefulness of abstinence-only education. Talking back to a rival she casts as a sexual moralist, Robin writes: *Yes, protection is always smart. Let's make it more widely available in the schools. Let's make sex ed widely available. As for abstinence? You can suggest it as one option, but get real if you think it is the only one. Teens will be teens.* Robin also expresses grave doubts about the usefulness of the marriage promotion provisions of postrescission welfare policy. Robin asks,

> What if. . .? Bush's plan to encourage marriage is enforced? THEN low-income men and women will be enticed to marriage. . . . Low-income women who get pregnant should not have to get married. Some people are not cut out for marriage, and women may feel forced to live with men who abuse or neglect them and their children. Government-induced "shotgun" marriages are not

the answer, and marriage does not guarantee that woman and children will be better [off].

Robin takes pride in her decision to take on the challenges of motherhood before she completed her education, even as she acknowledges the high price she paid in sacrificing her ambitions so she would not have to "leave my son or become a drop-in parent." She readily holds young people accountable for the consequences of their sexual behavior. She admonishes policymakers not to leave young people without guidance, and calls for programs to "[e]ducate young women and men more about birth control. Teach young women and men that if they get pregnant they will be called mommy and daddy for the rest of their natural lives." Robin simultaneously acknowledges that inequality between women and men, moralistic insistence on sexual abstinence before marriage, and limited information about and access to birth control make sexual responsibility a challenging ideal to realize, especially for young people. Most of all, Robin rebuts the idea that the "wages of sin" should be a loveless marriage, poverty, or both.

Better information, access, and support for controlling fertility and timing and spacing births is also an important point for Jule, whose narrative in the previous chapter reveals the problems caused by the combination of her ignorance, inexperience, and wishful thinking about her body, sex, and relationships. Jule writes, "What if. . .? Young women and men were more savvy about using protection that works for them? THEN they would have more control over their finances and future." Jule makes a clear causal connection between women's control of their fertility and their ability to pursue even the most modest life projects.

Although she had better reproductive health information than Jule did, Nikki had trouble finding a birth control pill dosage that was healthy for her, and her fluctuating weight meant her diaphragm had to be refitted repeatedly. Her pregnancies were physically difficult. Recall from the previous chapter that her first baby was premature, "a miracle baby because he weighed all of three pounds." She fought with her mother and her husband over abortion during a subsequent unintended pregnancy and had misgivings about the way having more children would make her even more dependent on her controlling and unfaithful husband. Nikki wonders,

What if. . .? Nikki had other methods of birth control available and had used them? What if she alone had made the choice whether to have children or not? THEN maybe she would not have felt so trapped. Maybe she would have had one less worry in her tumultuous life.

Motherhood remains central to how women think about themselves, how the media portray women and their lives, and how politicians, policymakers, and other experts think and talk about and treat women. Marriage—a marker of heterosexual desire and desirability—remains a key component of normative femininity. As a consequence of the significance of marriage and motherhood, women's control over their sexual selves and their fertility is one important key to their leading safe and solvent lives in which they have hope of following the life paths they determine.

WORK

In addition to underscoring the importance of a more meaningful sense of control and options for marriage and motherhood, the community literacy project participants call loudly for enhanced career and training options. Based on her own experience of training for a job in nursing "because my mother was a nurse" and then finding she was not at all suited to the work to which she was assigned, Red writes about the tight constraints and unforgiving circumstances under which poor women make very limited choices.

> What If. . .? We could have more chances to figure out what we want to do in life? THEN we wouldn't be stuck if the first thing we trained to do turned out not to make us happy. If we had more options for jobs and education, we wouldn't feel so stuck.

> What If. . .? Caseworkers or job counselors could modify or adapt education, job training, and placement to help people find more agreeable jobs? What if we had better vocational training and career planning? THEN people would have more options and would be able to change later.

> What If. . .? People had more options in life? THEN we wouldn't end up in the kind of situation where one crisis can cause everything to crumble.

Red is painfully aware of the ways women's vulnerability to both poverty and abuse could be rooted in ill-informed or regrettable decisions early in life. During the community literacy project she wrote and spoke repeatedly about the importance of second chances, opportunities to change direction, and a kind of flexibility that she thought more privileged people seem to take for granted. The cramped sense of possibilities and life options contributed to Red's depression and to her vulnerability to both addiction and abuse.

Nikki voices similar concerns, although her experience as a married teen leads her to emphasize the relative timing of training, education, and marriage. In line with her vision of increased independence for young women, Nikki asks,

> What if. . .? Young women and men got the training and education necessary to support and feel good about themselves before entering into a life partnership with another person? THEN maybe each person in a serious relationship would be more empowered to make good decisions for themselves.

The way Nikki invokes the language and ideas of empowerment for good personal decision making suggests both the possibilities and the limits of this discourse. It suggests the limits, because her focus is relentlessly on individual responsibility rather than structural change. It invokes the possibilities, because she is highlighting the expansive potential of making a basic claim to personhood for poor women.

Robin, a former welfare recipient, worked during the time she participated in the community literacy project as an advocate in an organization dedicated to serving and mobilizing poor people. She considers herself incredibly fortunate to have been able to use welfare benefits—in the period before rescission brought time limits and work requirements—to finance her long-delayed college education. She points to what she sees as the three most important elements in improving outcomes for youth:

> Education, education, education. . . . Teach young men and women more about the importance of continuing their education to obtain better paying jobs. Give low-income women and men the opportunity to educate themselves via college, trade schools, and specialized training programs.

Robin is especially concerned that poor mothers be able to count higher education (as well as vocational training programs) as work-related activities that would fulfill the work requirements under the restructured welfare eligibility requirements. She reasons that pushing women directly into the low-wage labor market—the logic of work-first common sense—short-circuits women's ability to support their families, pits welfare recipients against the working poor, and drives down wages at the low end of the labor market.

Takina's experiences with the underground economy, the lure of drug trafficking, and the pain, waste, and stigma of arrest, imprisonment, and the legacy of a felony drug conviction on her record mute much of her commentary. Given the opportunity to talk back to real and imagined interlocutors, Takina mostly emphasizes the need to withstand the temptations of easy money and bad company. She volubly praises the spiritually oriented recovery program at the halfway house that was her home during the months of the community literacy project. Takina also draws from her experience to envision alternative outcomes, given a different kind of outlet and support for her social skills, tenacious drive, and desire to provide the best for herself and her children.

> What If. . .? A caseworker had arranged for Takina to take some job training classes to improve her education? Takina might have obtained a decent job and a legitimate way to get the nice things she wanted for her family. . . .

> What If. . .? There were small business loans available for welfare recipients with a work ethic and skills like Takina's? Takina might have used a loan to expand her salon to get off welfare. She might have become a "legit" entrepreneur.

It is easy to imagine Takina's running a bustling hair and nail salon that would be a social center in her community—as easy as it is to hear her pain, shame, and regret that the combination of maternal responsibilities, illegal activity, and jail time so badly derailed her early dream "to become a black history teacher." Takina's sense of promise and ambitions unrealized, options truncated, and dreams indefinitely deferred poignantly captures these writers' sense of how far a small amount of support, resources, and forgiveness might have gone toward expanding their lives. At the same time, Takina's wholesale adoption of what is essentially a neo-liberal discourse about discipline and microfinance reinforces the need to go beyond these narratives and analyses, with their emphasis on individuals' pulling themselves up by their own bootstraps.[7] In the next and final section, I integrate the community literacy project writers' visions with the insights from the interview and administrative data I have analyzed. I provide a final critique of the conventional wisdom that places work at the center of the U.S. policy response to poverty and battering and conclude by articulating a principle to inform and perhaps help motivate a progressive feminist response.

PRINCIPLED CONCLUSION

Poverty and battering are mutually reinforcing traps. A policy regime that mandates work as the foremost moral, practical, and political response to battering and poverty jeopardizes rather than guarantees the safety and solvency of battered welfare recipients. The evidence from interviews with program participants I present in Chapter 3 demonstrates that the unrecognized realities of work-related control, abuse, and sabotage give coercive and controlling men added leverage in a work-first regime. The interview and administrative data from Chapter 4 suggest that the unrecognized (and basically still unmeasured) differences between welfare recipients who do and welfare recipients who do not petition for a protective order account for the disparate impact of welfare rescission on different groups of welfare recipients and for important unintended consequences of the features of the 1996 legislation. The evidence and demands in women's writing about welfare and work and the roles each plays in crises in their lives complement the findings from the broader set of data and analyses from which I draw in this book.

The community literacy project writers' emphasis on changing gender relations and expanding their life options around motherhood, marriage, and employment makes a lot of sense. Work is central to both the rules and rhetoric of welfare and shelter systems and to poor people's and battered women's understandings of their plight. Since welfare rescission, there is more emphasis on women's work than ever before. Everywhere they turn, poor women encounter program staff, media coverage, and political talk that barrage them with "work-first common sense"[8] and "victim empowerment folklore."[9] Conventional wisdom is all the more pernicious because it generates consent by co-opting the ways ordinary people think, talk, and feel about their lives. In this case, the hegemonic explanations of poverty and battering incorporate the notion that, as Sigmund Freud is supposed to have put it, "Work and love are the cornerstones of our humanness." That life options about family and work would take pride of place in current and former welfare recipients' accounts of change is hardly surprising.

Fortunately, in spite of its being susceptible to assimilation into conventional wisdom, the demand to expand women's life options also connects issues of poverty, battering, welfare, and work to discourses of human rights that recognize women as persons and as effective characters (in both the senses I invoked in the previous chapter) in their own lives. The demand to increase women's options for fulfilling their self-determined life projects illuminates the limited and limiting ways the single-minded focus on work and protective orders draws poor and battered women into the welfare and law-and-order branches of the state. Women who are writing about welfare and work and the roles each plays in crises in their lives want a broader range of options that will expand their abilities to determine and strive toward their own life projects. Poverty, battering, *and the ill-timed and misplaced insistence on employment as the sole and universal marker of personal responsibility* make it more difficult for women to pursue this basic human right.

It is important to distinguish the notion of women's right to pursue self-determined life projects[10] from the neo-liberal language of empowerment in folklore about battered women and especially from the formulation of personal responsibility in the welfare legislation of 1996 that I critique in Chapter 2. Neo-liberal discourse devolves responsibility—and blame—for success and failure (poverty, victimization) to the individual. Policy based on conventional wisdom is neo-liberal precisely to the extent that it institutes the requirement that the individual citizen discipline herself in every realm—money, sex, work, education, motherhood, relationships.[11]

Neo-liberal attacks on welfare recipients and the institutions, programs, and people who serve them have led to a paltry and confusing patchwork of under-funded public, subsidized private for-profit, and stripped-down nonprofit legal and social services. For battered women and poor mothers, the result is frustrating, with delays and interruptions in services and benefits that they can ill afford. Welfare workers stress under increased caseloads and escalating performance criteria. Local welfare administrators espouse ideologies and implement dramatic restructuring plans with diminished resources and a controversial and sometimes contradictory mandate from state and federal legislators. Staff and administrators of organizations dedicated to battered women have to substitute professionalized fundraising and creative accounting for strategizing and mobilizing for prevention and lasting change. Advocates find themselves trying to help welfare offices and law enforcement agencies implement a welter of incongruous work requirements, time limits, exemptions, safety plans, recovery efforts, sanction schemes, and mandatory court appearances. Local workforce development boards find themselves faced with a race to the bottom that truncates their vision and squeezes them between the rock of market pressures and the hard place of political accountability. Mushrooming private program providers wind up tempted to cut corners and succumb to nepotism and profiteering.[12] Neo-liberalism and its consequences make it all the more important to conduct a progressive social diagnosis of the situation of the type that the data and analyses in this book make possible.

The challenge, then, is to articulate a principle for policy that reclaims relationships and work as the "cornerstone of our humanness" without reproducing the neo-liberal penchant for blaming the victim, reducing battering to a utility function, subverting efforts to secure decent working conditions and living wages for everyone, reinforcing compulsory heterosexuality, or obscuring the complex set of forces that impoverish and constrain women's life options. The combination of discrimination and lack of opportunity in the worlds of work and politics, on the one hand, and violence, intimidation, isolation, and control in relationships, on the other hand, undermines women's capacities for decision making and envisioning and fulfilling their self-determined life projects. Those autonomous life projects are among the basic human rights that people institute democratic governments in order to secure.[13] A social justice approach includes safety and solvency among the social, civil and political, economic, and human rights that must be underwritten and guaranteed by democratic government without regard to marital status, employment status, or immigration status.

Decoupling economic benefits and social rights from marital status is a vital step toward ensuring that men cannot hold hostage women's residency or work permits, health care, employment, housing benefits, or welfare eligibility as part of a campaign of coercive control or to keep them from reporting abuse. Similarly, decoupling economic benefits, social rights, and political personhood from employment status is central to balancing the importance of work to our humanness with the exploitative conditions of the low-wage end of the labor market. Stopping battering and helping women to exit poverty are mutually reinforcing elements in a virtuous cycle of social, economic, and political change. Making change makes sense, and developing policies and supporting practices that increase women's safety and solvency is good politics.

METHODOLOGICAL APPENDIX

The data in the three empirical chapters at the heart of this book come from a three-part multimethod study. I combine analysis of individual interviews; longitudinal administrative data about protection orders, welfare use, and earnings; and women's writing and researchers' observations and field notes from a community literacy project. These data provide the opportunity to investigate connections between welfare, abuse, and earnings, on the one hand, and how women who suffer abuse and use welfare define their own situations, on the other hand. In this appendix, I describe each of the data sources and methodological strategies in more detail.

LONGITUDINAL INTERVIEWS AND FIELD NOTES

Two graduate research assistants (now Drs. Danielle Ficco and Lisa H. Ruchti) and I collected longitudinal data from a cohort of 40 women (participants in a downtown job training, search, and placement program serving the Allegheny County welfare caseload in the summer of 2001) during the first 12 to 18 months of their transition from welfare to work. Retrospective initial and up to three quarterly follow-up interviews focused on the connections among relationships, education, work, and welfare and collected data using forced-choice measures of specifically work-related abuse[1] and women's open-ended descriptions of particular incidents. Interviewers recorded field notes during the interviews and administered the forced-choice and open-ended interview questions using a different Computer Assisted Sensitive Interview protocol for each session (retrospective, follow-up one, follow-up two, final follow-up). I conducted half of the initial interviews, and Ficco conducted the other half. We both conducted follow-up interviews, as did Ruchti, who joined the project later. We are apparently White, and were thus unable to match interviewers and respondents by apparent race-ethnicity. We conducted all interviews in English.

The initial retrospective interviews were completed between May 29 and June 27, 2001. Of the entire pool of program enrollees at the site, two were ineligible because they were pregnant. Although I was able to negotiate an agreement on the protection of human subjects that allowed us to interview women considered vulnerable because of their poverty, welfare status, and possible history of abuse, institutional review board policy at the time precluded interviewing pregnant enrollees. This unfortunate restriction—ironically designed to *protect* women from harm—in fact *conceals* harms to women; some women are at increased risk of violence and abuse from their husbands or boyfriends when they are pregnant, but arguably not any more vulnerable to exploitation or coercion by interviewers. At any rate, the interviewers recruited subjects in the first days of their enrollment in the work preparation/job search program and thus avoided selecting only those enrollees who actually stayed with the program. Only two of the 42 eligible respondents refused to participate (a response rate of 95 percent). The table in the Introduction lists the 40 interviewees by pseudonym, along with selected demographic characteristics and two useful dichotomous categories: whether or not each woman reported that she experienced abuse at work, and whether or not each woman reported that she had ever petitioned for a protective order.

The cohort of respondents is demographically similar to the caseload of welfare-to-work programs (and therefore the population of poor mothers on welfare) in Allegheny County at the time of the interviews. Allegheny County, in turn, approximates the age and education profiles of the national welfare caseload. The main demographic difference between the cohort of program enrollees who participated in the interviews and the national caseload in 2000 is the racial composition of this group of respondents. The vast majority (83 percent) self-identified as Black, compared to only 39 percent of recipients nationwide.[2] As a consequence, the examples of incidents of work-related control, abuse, and sabotage more frequently involve Black women and their partners than White women and their partners. In this book, I include race-ethnicity in my intersectional, institutional analysis. The task is somewhat easier empirically because I have sufficient numbers of self-identified Black respondents to observe similarities and differences between Black and White women as well as variability among Black women.

In order to track respondents through the first 12 to 18 months of the spell on welfare that started in May/June 2001, we conducted up to three follow-up interviews in person or by telephone at approximately quarterly intervals after the retrospective interviews. Tracking and recontacting respondents was labor intensive and not always successful; study attrition is frequently a problem in prospective longitudinal research designs, especially with low-income respondents. Fewer than half (42 percent) of the original 40 women completed the full series of three follow-up interviews. Twenty percent completed only the retrospective interview. For those eight respondents, we were unable to obtain *any* follow-up. Neither the training/placement program through which we originally recruited them nor the Department of Public Welfare had valid contact information for these respondents at any time during the 18 months we were conducting the follow-up interviews. Visits to their last-known address yielded either no forwarding information or statements from friends or relatives that the respondent was "living on the streets" or "impossible to find." For four (10 percent) of the respondents, we were able to obtain a first follow-up but no subsequent interviews. For nine (22 percent) of the respondents, the first or second follow-up (or both) is missing, but we have a final follow-up interview.

In the effort to recontact respondents for follow-up interviews, the research team sent multiple letters (using envelopes printed with the return address of the employment training program in which they had been placed, to protect their safety), made multiple calls to last-known phone numbers, used the latest information available (at 90 days postintake) from the county welfare office, and visited the last-known address. In some of the eight cases for which we were unable to obtain even a single follow-up interview, respondents had moved with no forwarding information or resident relatives reported, "She's living on the street." In other cases these addresses were vacant, condemned, or demolished by the time interviewers visited. In no case was a reinterview refused.

In the retrospective interviews, researchers asked structured questions about all "serious" relationships, starting with the relationship with the father of the woman's first child. About one half of the respondents reported being in a relationship at the time of the retrospective interview, and 28 (70 percent) had been in a relationship within three months of the retrospective interview (a period useful for comparing with the roughly quarterly intervals between follow-up interviews). Interviewers administered a physical abuse checklist and a checklist for specifically work-related control, abuse, and sabotage with reference to each of these relationships, including the current or most recent relationship. During the follow-up interviews, we administered the physical abuse and work-related control, abuse, and sabotage checklists with reference to the period since the previous interview. For subjects with gaps in the follow-up interview sequence, this means that the recall period between interviews varied considerably. In both the retrospective and follow-up interviews, for those respondents who reported that work-related sabotage or abuse included harassment or violence while they were at work, interviewers probed for details and asked open-ended questions about those events. Those incident accounts form the backbone of the data from the interviews.

As the factors associated with dropping out of the study and the factors associated with experiencing coercive control and work-related abuse and sabotage are likely to be highly correlated, we conducted an attrition analysis to compare women for whom we had follow-up interviews with those we were unable to recontact. The women who completed the full series of interviews and the women who completed only the initial retrospective interview *did not differ significantly* from each other or from the rest of the respondents on most of the measures obtained in the initial retrospective interviews. On virtually all demographic characteristics, the women did not differ significantly across interview completion categories. Women who completed the full set of interviews were significantly less likely to be never married ($p = .01$), and they less frequently reported problems with reading and writing ($p = .001$) than women who did not complete the full set of prospective interviews. Not surprisingly, women who completed the full set of interviews less frequently reported that they had trouble paying their bills in the past year ($p = .015$) than women who did not complete the full interview series. Most important, however, *there were no substantive (let alone statistically significant) differences in the rates at which women in the various interview completion categories reported any of the violence measures in their retrospective interviews.* The similarities on both demographic and abuse-related measures at the time of the retrospective interview between women who did and women who did not complete the full set of interviews suggest that subject attrition was random rather than systematic, and the results from the follow-up interviews, partial though they are, seem unlikely to be biased on the relevant work, welfare, or abuse measures. Moreover, my purpose in using the interview data is not to estimate prevalence rates for specific types of abuse but rather to describe the range of physical violence and work-related control, abuse, and sabotage the interviewees have experienced and record and analyze incidents in which abusers, abuse, and their consequences follow women to work.

The answers welfare recipients offer to inquiries about work-related control, abuse, and sabotage and to the question, "What happened that time your partner bothered you at work?" are not necessarily generalizable to all mothers or all working or battered women. Controlling, abusive partners can jeopardize any woman's ability to leave the house, work for wages, and make connections that are ostensibly beyond the abuser's control. However, work requirements (on which continued cash and other welfare benefits are contingent since Congress rescinded federal income support entitlements in 1996) give men additional leverage in campaigns of control and coercion. It is bad enough that men diminish the autonomy, dignity, integrity, and accomplishments of women through abuse; even worse, work requirements expand the purview of their threats and control. When abusers and the consequences of abuse follow welfare recipients into the workplace, women can reasonably fear that the actions of their partners will get them fired. This is a grim outcome under any circumstances, but in the context of welfare receipt, losing a job can put a woman out of compliance with work requirements. Job loss jeopardizes not just a woman's earnings, social networks, and other benefits of employment and her ability to find employment in the future, but also her eligibility for cash benefits and other services.[3] Welfare recipients thus face challenges and dilemmas that make their experiences particularly revealing of the social consequences of work-related control, abuse, and sabotage and therefore the relevance of women's employment as the site and source of partner-perpetrated coercion and violence. In sum, these data offer a unique window into an understudied form of workplace violence and an understudied from of coercive control, and therefore contribute to the empirical basis for both employers and welfare administrators to respond to partner-perpetrated abuse on the job.

LONGITUDINAL ADMINISTRATIVE DATA ON WELFARE, EARNINGS, AND PROTECTIVE ORDERS[4]

Another source of data for this book is a person-period data set that includes repeated individual-level measures of petitions for Protection From Abuse (PFA) orders, earnings, and a set of time-varying and subject-varying covariates from July 1995 to June 2000. Eileen Kopchik and I used Social Security numbers and names to match: (1) all PFA records from the Allegheny County Prothonotary,[5] (2) all AFDC/TANF recipient records from the Pennsylvania Department of Public Welfare (DPW),[6] and (3) quarterly data on earnings from the Pennsylvania Department of Labor and Industry's Bureau of Unemployment Compensation and Benefits Administration (BUCBA) for all individuals in the first two sets of data. The final data set includes

27,017 women with both wage and welfare data who are at least 16 years of age in July 1995, totaling 540,340 person-quarters of data across the five-year time span.

Measurement

Administrative data on court appearances for women seeking a civil order of protection from abuse are a problematic measure of coercive control. I obtained the population of case filings, so there is no literal sampling bias. However, petitioners in protective order cases arguably do not represent the population of battered women, either those subject to "common couple violence" or those victims of "intimate terrorism" (Johnson 2008), let alone those who suffer the combination of physical violence, intimidation, and isolation that constitutes "coercive control" (Stark 2007). Moreover, the data provide no separate measure of battering, and analysis cannot distinguish battered from nonbattered women among the welfare recipients who do not petition for a PFA. As a consequence, *these findings speak only to the effects of turning to welfare and petitioning for a PFA.* The data cannot address many interesting questions in the literature on the connections among battering, work, and welfare. For example, I cannot assess the extent to which battering obstructs work, nor can I estimate the effects of battering on welfare receipt, nor can I evaluate the effects of petitioning for a PFA on the earnings of battered welfare recipients (for example, by comparing them to the earnings of battered welfare recipients who do not petition for a PFA).

The dependent variable is quarterly earnings (logged to reduce skewness) modeled every other quarter. The analysis includes four time-invariant measures as independent variables: (1) age at the start of the study period; (2) household size, proxied using the average number of welfare recipients associated with each individual during all months on welfare; and (3, 4) two dummy variables measuring race-ethnicity, where Black individuals are the reference category. The model also includes months of welfare receipt as a time-varying covariate affecting logged earnings in that quarter. We use data on PFAs to separate the welfare recipients into two groups: 2,286 women who petition for PFAs and 24,731 women who do not. Table A.1 arrays means and standard deviations on the variables in the administrative data set for these two groups; see Chapter 4 for discussion.

Group Differences

Researchers hoping to shed light on the connections among poverty, welfare, and battering commonly face two methodological challenges. The first is how to detect and model differences between groups, especially when analyzing observational data (Rosenbaum 2002). In much research on violence against women, there are reasons to expect that there are multiple distinct groups. For example, women who petition for PFAs are different from women in abusive situations who do not; petitioners report more years of psychological and physical abuse, more negative interactions with friends and family, and more depressive symptoms than

Table A1. MEANS AND STANDARD DEVIATIONS FOR WELFARE RECIPIENTS WHO
DO AND DO NOT PETITION FOR A PROTECTION ORDER

Variable	PFA (N = 2,286)	No PFA (N = 24,731)	PFA – No PFA
(1) Initial Earnings	$635.38 (1331.20)	$488.53 (1128.70)	$146.85***
(2) Earnings Change	$1,222.22 (2436.50)	$1,394.53 (2386.00)	-$172.31**
(3) Total Months Welfare	24.45 (17.41)	17.28 (14.89)	7.17***
(4) Age	27.52 (7.54)	27.33 (7.91)	0.19
(5) Household Size	2.96 (1.13)	2.94 (1.20)	0.02
(6) White	0.54 (0.50)	0.45 (0.50)	0.09***
(7) Other Race	0.01 (0.12)	0.02 (0.14)	-0.01
(8) Logged Quarterly Earnings	3.96 (3.72)	3.71 (3.72)	0.25***
(9) Months Welfare in Quarter	1.22 (1.42)	0.86 (1.29)	0.36***

NOTE: Numbers in parentheses are standard deviations. Differences between group means are tested using two-tailed t-tests, and the results are reported as follows: **p <.01; ***p <.001 (two-tailed tests).
SOURCE: Hughes and Brush (2011, p. 329).

nonpetitioners (Duterte et al., 2008; Hutchison and Hirschel, 1998; Macy et al., 2005; Wolf et al., 2000). Thus, it is likely that PFA petitioners should be modeled as a separate group. The typical strategies for dealing with multiple groups are separate group analyses (running models independently for each group) or running fully interactive models, where interactions allow effects to vary across groups. The analysis in Chapter 4 is based on a third strategy: multigroup analysis. Multigroup analysis combines the benefits of separate analysis and interactive models; effects can be estimated independently, but statistical tests can also indicate when and how groups are different.

The problem remains of properly classifying individuals into groups. When researchers have observational rather than experimental data, we cannot be sure that we have accurately assigned people to groups, and we know they are not assigned randomly. Methodologists refer to these and similar problems as *selection effects*, and they are troublesome because selection bias can lead to errors in estimating both the differences between groups and the effects of targeted treatment or intervention (such as the effects of petitioning for a PFA on earnings that interest me for policy reasons; see Chapter 4). Although classifying individuals into groups based on stable characteristics such as sex category or race-ethnicity is often straightforward, it is harder to assign individuals to groups based on time-varying characteristics or actions, as data needed to properly classify individuals may fall outside of a study period, a problem known as censoring. In the analysis reported in Chapter 4, we use additional partial data on PFA petitions in the months directly preceding and following our study period to consider the potential effects of censoring in the context of multigroup analysis.

Intervention Effects in the Context of Policy Change

Another methodological challenge concerns tracking individual changes over time and accurately assessing outcomes for groups who do and do not participate in a program or receive a treatment, when life-course changes and targeted interventions coincide with broader institutional shifts. Are differences in outcomes due to unobserved differences between individuals, to observed or unobserved differences between groups, to policy interventions, to processes that occur predictably with the passage of time, to changes in the broader context, or to chance? The technique called piecewise latent growth curve analysis (Bollen and Curran 2006) is well suited to addressing these challenges. Latent growth curve (LGC) models analyze change over time by focusing on intraindividual change, estimating both starting positions (intercepts) and trends (slopes) for each individual's growth trajectory over time. These models employ longitudinal data, enabling comparisons of individuals to themselves over time. They also allow parameters to vary independently for PFA and non-PFA petitioning groups and (as explained above) permit exploration of the existence and nature of group differences.

Although the simplest models estimate linear change, LGC analysis is flexible enough to estimate a variety of patterns of change over time (for example, quadratic, cubic). Of particular use to us here is the *piecewise*, or spline, LGC model, which estimates more than one slope over the growth trajectory (see, for example, Paxton, Painter, and Hughes 2009). When using splines, the model estimates not only the average rate of change over each "piece" of time but also the effects of covariates (even measures that do not vary over time) separately for each period. We select July 1995 to December 1997 and December 1997 to June 2000 as two time intervals to capture earnings growth before and after Allegheny County welfare administrators implemented the provisions of the PRA, with some lag time to allow for restructuring to take effect. Figure 4.2 in the text is the unconditional,[7] two-spline model of earnings growth for Allegheny County welfare recipients who do and do not petition for a protective order. The figure is for a two-group analysis, with constrained covariances between intercepts and slopes, and constrained variance of error terms.

For a multigroup piecewise (spline) earnings model with two time periods, the individual equation is as follows:

$$y_{it}^{(g)} = \alpha_i^{(g)} + \beta_{1i}^{(g)}\lambda_{1t}^{(g)} + \beta_{2i}^{(g)}\lambda_{2t}^{(g)} + \varepsilon_{it}^{(g)}, \tag{7.1}$$

where $y_{it}^{(g)}$ represents logged quarterly earnings for the ith individual from group g at time t; $\alpha_i^{(g)}$ is the intercept for individual i from group g; $\beta_{1i}^{(g)}$ and $\beta_{2i}^{(g)}$ are the slopes for individual i from group g pre– and post–welfare rescission; $\lambda_{1t}^{(g)}$ and $\lambda_{2t}^{(g)}$ are constants manipulated to capture linear change over the two time periods, while accounting for the missing quarter of earnings data in 1996; and $\varepsilon_{it}^{(g)}$ is an error term for each individual i from group g at time t. In this model, each individual, i, has her own intercept and slope, and the superscript, g, signifies group membership, where $g = 1, 2, 3, \ldots, G$, and G is the total number of groups.

In addition to analyzing individual-level change, LGC models also estimate the mean intercept and slope for all individuals. Models estimate average initial earnings across all welfare recipients in the fourth quarter of 1995 and the average rate of change in earnings across each of the two time periods of interest. For the multigroup two-piecewise model, this leads to three additional equations:

$$\alpha_i^{(g)} = \mu_\alpha^{(g)} + \zeta_{\alpha i}^{(g)} \tag{7.2}$$

$$\beta_{1i}^{(g)} = \mu_{\beta_1}^{(g)} + \zeta_{\beta_{1i}}^{(g)} \tag{7.3}$$

$$\beta_{2i}^{(g)} = \mu_{\beta_2}^{(g)} + \zeta_{\beta_{2i}}^{(g)}, \tag{7.4}$$

where $\mu_\alpha^{(g)}$ is the mean intercept across all individuals from each group, and $\mu_{\beta_1}^{(g)}$ and $\mu_{\beta_2}^{(g)}$ are the mean slopes across all individuals from each group across each of the two time periods. The first equation represents a person's individual intercept ($\alpha_i^{(g)}$) as a function of the average intercept ($\mu_\alpha^{(g)}$) over all individuals from their group and a disturbance term ($\zeta_{\alpha i}^{(g)}$). The second two equations represent the individual slopes pre– and post–welfare rescission ($\beta_{1i}^{(g)}$ and $\beta_{2i}^{(g)}$) as a function of the average slopes ($\mu_{\beta_1}^{(g)}$ and $\mu_{\beta_2}^{(g)}$) and disturbance terms ($\zeta_{\beta_{1i}}^{(g)}$ and $\zeta_{\beta_{2i}}^{(g)}$) over the two time periods. For all models, we assume disturbances are normally distributed with unknown variances and covariances.

Figure A.1 is a path diagram of the piecewise unconditional latent growth curve model. Path diagrams such as Figure A.1 represent relations between observed (measured) and unobserved (latent) variables. Latent variables are represented with ovals, while observed variables appear as boxes. Straight arrows indicate direction of influence, while curved two-headed arrows indicate a covariance between two variables that is unexplained in the model, and measurement error is indicated by δ. In Figure A.1 (corresponding to the equations above), the factor loadings for the measures of welfare recipients' earnings on the latent intercept are fixed to 1 to represent the starting point of the growth trajectory. The loadings on the first latent slope begin at 0 in December 1995, increasing by 1 each two-quarter interval until

December 1997, indicating linear growth over the period prior to welfare rescission. The factor loadings for the second latent slope begin at 0 and do not begin to increase until June 1998, when the loadings increase by 1 each interval until the end of the period. For both of the latent slopes, the factor loadings are set to increase as if data were available for December 1996 even though they are missing. This specification of the factor loadings allows LGC models to estimate growth for each period despite unequally spaced data. The latent intercept and the slopes are freely correlated.

By employing multigroup piecewise LGC models, we are able to test whether significant differences exist between model parameters. First, we estimate a fully independent model with no cross-group constraints on model parameters. Then, we constrain model parameters of interest, for example, mean intercepts and slopes, to be the same across the two groups, and test for significant drops in model fit using a chi-square test. A significant chi-square test suggests that at least one of the constrained model parameters is significantly different across the two groups and that the parameters should be allowed to estimate freely. We also use critical ratio tests to consider whether estimates significantly vary pre– and post–welfare rescission.

In the final set of models, we incorporate predictors of welfare recipients' earnings trajectories. In these models, we introduce age, race, and household size as time-invariant covariates that affect the intercepts and slopes of welfare recipients' earnings trajectories. Months of welfare receipt also enters the model as a time-varying covariate such that the number of months an individual was on welfare during the quarter predicts individual logged earnings in that quarter. Because time on welfare is strongly associated with lower earnings, differences in welfare receipt alone could explain the difference in the earnings trajectories of the two groups. Thus, the introduction of welfare receipt is an important control when assessing the relationship between PFA petitions and earnings. Fit improves markedly once covariates are added to the model. The IFI of 0.95 and RMSEA of 0.04 both indicate optimal fit. Table A.2 arrays the results of the piecewise LGC analysis.

The first panel of Table A.2 presents the mean intercepts and slopes, net the effects of the covariates. The estimates further support our findings that petitioners have substantially different earnings trajectories from nonpetitioners. Once covariates are added to the model, petitioners continue to have higher intercepts than their nonpetitioning counterparts ($\Delta\chi^2$ = 29.14, Δdf = 1, p <.001). In fact, rather than explaining away initial differences, the covariates we add $increase$ the size of the initial gap between the two groups. Furthermore, the adjusted slopes for the two groups are quite different. Petitioners no longer experience any underlying growth in earnings over either time period, while nonpetitioners do experience wage growth. For nonpetitioners, earnings gains were more substantial during the pre-rescission period.

In the second panel of Table A.2, we are able to consider whether the time-invariant control variables have different effects on initial earnings or growth for the two groups and for the two time periods. First, comparing across groups, we find significant differences in the effects of the covariates on the intercepts and the slopes, but only for age and race. Key differences across time also emerge. For nonpetitioners, the effects of age, household size, and race vary significantly across

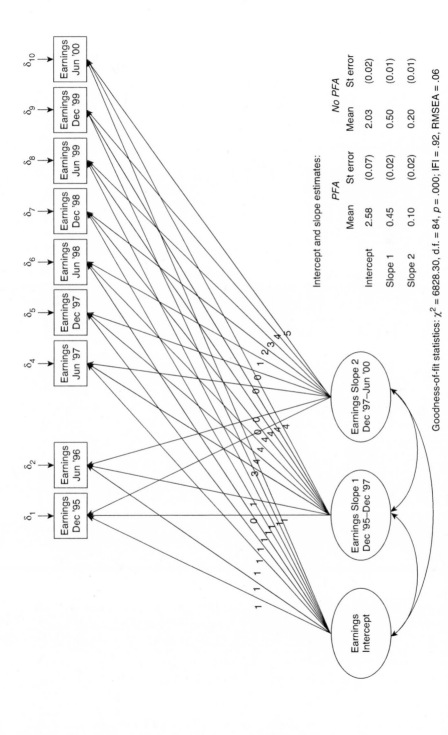

Figure A.1. Path diagram of piecewise unconditional latent growth curve model predicting second and fourth quarter logged earnings for welfare recipients who do and do not petition for a protection order, December 1995–December 1997 and December 1997–June 2000.

SOURCE: Hughes and Brush (2011, p. 331).

Intercept and slope estimates:

	PFA		*No PFA*	
	Mean	St error	Mean	St error
Intercept	2.58	(0.07)	2.03	(0.02)
Slope 1	0.45	(0.02)	0.50	(0.01)
Slope 2	0.10	(0.02)	0.20	(0.01)

Goodness-of-fit statistics: $\chi^2 = 6828.30$, d.f. $= 84$, $p = .000$; IFI $= .92$, RMSEA $= .06$

Table A2. RESULTS FROM CONDITIONAL TWO-SPLINE LATENT GROWTH CURVE MODEL COMPARING LOGGED EARNINGS OF WELFARE RECIPIENTS WHO PETITIONED FOR A PFA AND THOSE WHO DID NOT, DECEMBER 1995-DECEMBER 1997 AND DECEMBER 1997-JUNE 2000

Group Means	Intercept (α)		Slope ($\beta1$)		Slope ($\beta2$)		$\beta2 - \beta1$
	coef.	(s.e.)	coef.	(s.e.)	coef.	(s.e.)	
PFA Petitioners	4.57***	(0.32)	0.10	(0.10)	0.12	(0.08)	0.02
Nonpetitioners	2.79***	(0.08)	0.38***	(0.03)	0.27***	(0.02)	-0.11*
PFA - No PFA	1.78***		-0.28**		-0.15^t		

Effects on Intercepts and Slopes

	Intercept (α)		Slope ($\beta1$)		Slope ($\beta2$)		$\beta2 - \beta1$
Age	coef.	(s.e.)	coef.	(s.e.)	coef.	(s.e.)	
PFA Petitioners	0.03**	(0.01)	0.00	(0.00)	-0.01**	(0.00)	-0.01
Nonpetitioners	0.01***	(0.00)	0.01***	(0.00)	-0.01***	(0.00)	-0.02***
PFA - No PFA	0.02^t		-0.01*		0.00^t		
Household Size	coef.	(s.e.)	coef.	(s.e.)	coef.	(s.e.)	
PFA Petitioners	-0.37***	(0.06)	0.09***	(0.02)	0.02	(0.02)	-0.07*
Nonpetitioners	-0.28***	(0.02)	0.07***	(0.01)	0.03***	(0.00)	-0.04***
PFA - No PFA	-0.09		0.02		-0.01		

White	Dec. 1995		June 1996		June 1997		Dec. 1997	
	coef.	(s.e.)	coef.	(s.e.)	coef.	(s.e.)	coef.	(s.e.)
PFA Petitioners	-0.44***	(0.14)	0.02	(0.04)	-0.05	(0.04)	-0.07	
Nonpetitioners	0.02	(0.04)	-0.08***	(0.01)	-0.01	(0.01)	0.07*	
PFA - No PFA	-0.46***		0.10*		-0.04			
Other Race	coef.	(s.e.)	coef.	(s.e.)	coef.	(s.e.)	coef.	
PFA Petitioners	-0.13	(0.56)	-0.05	(0.18)	-0.07	(0.14)	-0.03	
Nonpetitioners	-0.74***	(0.14)	0.01	(0.05)	-0.06	(0.04)	-0.07	
PFA - No PFA	0.61		-0.06		-0.01			

Time-Varying Effects on Logged Earnings

Months Welfare	Dec. 1995		June 1996		June 1997		Dec. 1997	
	coef.	(s.e.)	coef.	(s.e.)	coef.	(s.e.)	coef.	(s.e.)
PFA Petitioners	-0.72***	(0.04)	-0.83***	(0.04)	-0.86***	(0.03)	-0.58***	(0.04)
Nonpetitioners	-0.44***	(0.07)	-1.02***	(0.02)	-0.74***	(0.01)	-0.64***	(0.01)
PFA - No PFA	-0.28***		0.19***		-0.12***		0.06	

Months Welfare	June 1998		Dec. 1998		June 1999		Dec. 1999	
	coef.	(s.e.)	coef.	(s.e.)	coef.	(s.e.)	coef.	(s.e.)
PFA Petitioners	-0.70***	(0.04)	-0.48***	(0.04)	-0.45***	(0.04)	-0.45***	(0.05)
Nonpetitioners	-0.69***	(0.01)	-0.59***	(0.01)	-0.60***	(0.01)	-0.56***	(0.01)
PFA - No PFA	-0.01		0.11***		0.15***		0.11**	

(continued)

Table A2. (continued)

| Months Welfare | June 2000 | |
	coef.	(s.e.)
PFA Petitioners	-0.55***	(0.05)
Nonpetitioners	-0.65***	(0.02)
PFA - No PFA	0.10ᵗ	

Goodness-of-fit statistics: $\chi^2 = 11237.01$, d.f. = 276, $p = .000$; IFI = .95, RMSEA = .04

NOTE: This model constrains intercept and slope covariances as well as error variances to be equal across the two groups. Earnings data for December 1996 are missing. ***$p < .001$, **$p < .01$, *$p < .05$, ᵗ$p < .10$

SOURCE: Hughes and Brush (2011, pp. 333-334).

the two time periods, while for petitioners, only household size has different effects during the pre- and postrescission time periods.

In the third panel of Table A.2, we turn to the effects of welfare receipt. The effects of welfare receipt on earnings vary significantly across the two groups during both time periods, except in two quarters—those immediately prior to and coinciding with the knot. We also find changes in the effects of welfare receipt across time. For example, for the petitioners, the first three estimated points are significantly different from the last three estimated points ($p < .001$). These results imply that welfare rescission changed the context of women's appeals to the state through both mechanisms—welfare receipt and PFA petitions—and consequently the effect of welfare receipt on earnings.

TEXTS AND FIELD NOTES FROM THE COMMUNITY LITERACY PROJECT

The writing project that provides the texts and field notes I use in this book began at a critical juncture, when, in 2002, policymakers and human service providers were reviewing the welfare rescission of 1996. Pundits, researchers, and politicians were arguing over how to interpret the outcomes of welfare reform, and they continued to debate reauthorization of welfare legislation. As they did so, they called on various stakeholders to testify to the conditions and constraints that shape the lives of poor people. My collaborator, English professor Lorraine Higgins, and I wanted to provide a venue for former and current welfare recipients to document and disseminate their stories in and beyond their communities. The project also provided an educational forum to develop and teach a set of rhetorical strategies that might steer these writers away from default hero and victim narratives and prompt them to explicate their experiences, actions, and motivations to readers not familiar with (nor sympathetic to) the details of their lives. We hoped to learn more about the obstacles subordinate groups face in producing narratives for public deliberation and more about the tools activist-rhetoricians might use to support them in the process.

Eight women—all current or former welfare recipients—participated in the eight-week writing project. Community activists in several city neighborhoods helped to identify potential participants and provided a site in a convenient community location with adequate computing and meeting facilities. Six of the participants were mothers. One was apparently White, and the other women were apparently Black. Participants ranged in age from their late 20s to their early 50s. We provided childcare, bus tickets, and a graduated system of modest compensation (in the form of grocery vouchers) to enable participation in and completion of the project. The group met twice weekly throughout March and April of 2002. To maintain confidentiality, and as a condition of approval of the project by the university's human subjects review board, the writers chose pseudonyms for themselves and the others they described in their writing.

Lorraine Higgins developed the project materials and facilitated the groups' activities. Three writing mentors joined Higgins and me in supporting the writers as they began to document their stories. The mentor's role was to listen carefully and to ask probing questions to jog the writer's memory or help her to reconstruct the chronology and context of the events she described. Mentors were careful to preserve as much of the writers' content and language as possible, and they suggested revisions only when they might (1) ensure confidentiality, (2) provide clarification and background for a reader, (3) eliminate redundancy, and (4) help the writer to adhere to standard written English rules of grammar and punctuation in those parts of the text that did not contain dialogue. The writers reviewed and approved all editing and formatting of their final texts.

Each writer produced a four-to-eight-page document for the booklet that was published at the end of the project, *Getting by, Getting ahead: Women's Stories of Welfare and Work*. Each writer's contribution contained a narrative (ranging from two to four pages in length) and four follow-up sections called "Strengths and Resources," "Contributing Factors," "Rival Perspectives," and "Taking Action." The narratives addressed a range of problems concerning the welfare system itself, employment and education, housing, family, and intimate partners. They also described impediments to mental and physical health and the effects of environmental factors, specifically neighborhood crime. Those texts, plus field notes from the sessions, along with responses to questions about the meanings of work and welfare the women in the interview study constructed for themselves and attributed to their children and partners, provide the data for the chapter on the ways welfare recipients talk back.

REFERENCES

Abramowitz, Mimi. [1988] 1996. *Regulating the Lives of Women: Social Welfare Policy From Colonial Times to the Present.* 2nd rev. ed. Boston, MA: South End Press.

Acs, Gregory and Pamela Loprest, eds. 2004. *Leaving Welfare: Employment and Well-Being of Families That Left Welfare in the Post-Entitlement Era.* Kalamazoo, MI: W.E. Upjohn Institute for Employment Research.

Adams, Adrienne E., Chris M. Sullivan, Deborah Bybee, and Megan R. Greeson. 2008. "Development of the Scale of Economic Abuse." *Violence Against Women* 14:563–588.

Adams, David. 2007. *Why Do They Kill? Men Who Murder Their Intimate Partners.* Nashville, TN: Vanderbilt University Press.

Adams, Julia and Tasleem Padamsee. 2001. "Signs and Regimes: Rereading Feminist Research on Welfare States." *Social Politics* 8:1–23.

Adkins, Kate S. and Claire M. Kamp Dush. 2010. "The Mental Health of Mothers in and After Violent and Controlling Unions." *Social Science Research* doi: 10.1016/j.ssresearch. (2010).06.013.

Alexander, Michelle. 2010. *The New Jim Crow: Mass Incarceration in the Age of Colorblindness.* New York: New Press.

Allard, M. A., R. Albelda, M. E. Colten, and C. Cosenza. 1997. *In Harm's Way? Domestic Violence, AFDC Receipt, and Welfare Reform in Massachusetts.* Boston, MA: University of Massachusetts, McCormack Institute.

Alon, Sigal and Yitchak Haberfeld. 2007. "Labor Force Attachment and the Evolving Wage Gap Between White, Black, and Hispanic Young Women." *Work and Occupations* 34: 369–398.

Amott, Theresa and Julie Matthaei. 1996. *Race, Gender, and Work: A Multi-Cultural Economic History of Women in the United States.* 2nd ed. Boston, MA: South End Press.

Anderson, Kristin. 2009. "Gendering Coercive Control." *Violence Against Women* 15: 1444–1457.

Arias, Ileana and Phaedra Corso. 2005. "Average Cost per Person Victimized by an Intimate Partner of the Opposite Gender: A Comparison of Men and Women." *Violence and Victims* 20:379–391.

Arnold, Gretchen. 2009. "A Battered Women's Movement Perspective on *Coercive Control.*" *Violence Against Women* 15:1432–1443.

Assistant Secretary for Planning and Evaluation. 2000. *Leavers and Diversion Studies: Summary of Research on Welfare Outcomes Funded by ASPE.* Washington, D.C.: DHHS.

Assistant Secretary for Planning and Evaluation. 2002. *Indicators of Welfare Dependence.* Executive summary of annual report. Washington, D.C.: DHHS.

Auerbach, Jeffrey and Kathryn Montgomery. 1986. "Babies Having Babies" (Martin Sheen, Director). In Sheen/Greenblat Productions, CBS Schoolbreak Special Season 3, Episode 3. Originally broadcast January 28, 1986. New York: CBS Schoolbreak Special Telefilm.

Babbie, Earl. 2004. *The Practice of Social Research.* 10th ed. Belmont, CA: Wadsworth/ Thomson Learning.

Bagger, Jessica, Andrew Li, and Barbara A. Gutek. 2008. "How Much Do You Value Your Family and Does It Matter? The Joint Effects of Family Identity Salience, Family-Interference-With-Work, and Gender." *Human Relations* 61:187–211.

Baker, Charlene K., Phyllis Holditch Niolon, and Hilary Oliphant. 2009. "A Descriptive Analysis of Transitional Housing Programs for Survivors of Intimate Partner Violence in the United States." *Violence Against Women* 15:460–481.

Bakker, Arnold B. and Sabine A. E. Geurts. 2004. "Toward a Dual-Process Model of Work-Home Interference." *Work and Occupations* 31: 345–366.

Bamberg, Michael G. W., ed. 1997. Special issue of *Journal of Narrative and Life History* 7.

Bangs, Ralph and J. H. Hong. 1996. *Pittsburgh Benchmarks: Black and White Quality of Life in the City of Pittsburgh and Allegheny County.* Pittsburgh, PA: University [of Pittsburgh] Center for Social and Urban Research.

Bangs, Ralph L., Cheryl Z. Kerchis, and S. Laurel Weldon. 1997. *Basic Living Cost and Living Wage Estimates for Pittsburgh and Allegheny County.* Pittsburgh, PA: University of Pittsburgh Center for Social and Urban Research.

Bangs, Ralph and S. Laurel Weldon. 1998. *Economic Benchmarks: Indices for the City of Pittsburgh and Allegheny County.* Pittsburgh, PA: University [of Pittsburgh] Center for Social and Urban Research.

Barnett, Rosalind Chait and Karen C. Gareis. 2002. "Full-Time and Reduced-Hours Work Schedules and Marital Quality: A Study of Female Physicians with Young Children." *Work and Occupations* 29: 364–379.

Bassuk, Ellen L., Angela Browne, and John C. Buckner. 1996. "Single Mothers and Welfare." *Scientific American* (October): 60–67.

Bavier, Richard. 2003. "Material Well-Being." Pp. 89–112 in *Family Well-Being After Welfare Reform,* edited by Douglas J. Besharov. New Brunswick, NJ: Transaction Publishers.

Baxter, Vern and Anthony Margavio. 1996. "Assaultive Violence in the U.S. Post Office." *Work and Occupations* 23:277–296.

Bell, Holly. 2003. "Cycles Within Cycles: Domestic Violence, Welfare, and Low-wage Work." *Violence Against Women* 9:1245–1262.

Bell, Holly, Barbara J. Lohman, and Elizabeth Votruba-Drzal. 2007. "Through a Quantitative and Qualitative Lens: Looking at the Differential Effects of Domestic Violence on Women's Welfare Receipt and Work Participation." Pp. 131–152 in *Doing Without: Women and Work After Welfare Reform,* edited by Jane Henrici. Tucson, AZ: University of Arizona Press.

Berger, Peter L. and Thomas Luckmann. 1967. *The Social Construction of Reality: A Treatise in the Sociology of Knowledge.* New York: Anchor Books.

Berns, Nancy. 2004. *Framing the Victim: Domestic Violence, Media, and Social Problems.* New York: Aldine de Gruyter.

Berns, Nancy. 2009. "Domestic Violence and Victim Empowerment Folklore in Popular Culture." Pp. 105–124 in *Violence Against Women in Families and Relationships,* vol. 4, *The Media and Cultural Attitudes,* edited by Evan Stark and Eve S. Buzawa. Santa Barbara, CA; Denver, CO; Oxford, England: Praeger/ABC-CLIO.

Besharov, Douglas J. and P. Germanis. 2003. "Introduction." Pp. 1–34 in *Family Well-Being After Welfare Reform*, edited by Douglas J. Besharov. New Brunswick, NJ: Transaction Publishers.

Blalock, H. M., Jr., ed. 1985. *Causal Models in the Social Sciences*. 2nd ed. New York: Aldine de Gruyter.

Blank, Rebecca M. 2000. "Fighting Poverty: Lessons From Recent U.S. History." Distinguished Lecture on Economics in Government delivered to a joint session of the Society of Government Economists and the American Economic Association at the annual meetings of the Allied Social Science Associations in Boston, Massachusetts, on January 8, 2000. *Journal of Economic Perspectives* 14:3–19.

Boles, James S., W. Gary Howard, and Heather Howard Donofrio. 2001. "An Investigation into the Inter-Relationships of Work-Family Conflict, Family-Work Conflict and Work Satisfaction." *Journal of Managerial Issues* 13:376–390.

Bollen, Ken and Patrick Curran. 2006. *Latent Curve Models: A Structural Equation Approach*. Hoboken, NJ: Wiley.

Bourdieu, Pierre. 1977. *Outline of a Theory of Practice,* translated by Richard Nice. Cambridge, UK: Cambridge University Press.

Boyer, Debra. 1999. "Childhood Sexual Abuse: The Forgotten Issue in Adolescent Pregnancy and Welfare Reform." Pp. 131–143 in *Battered Women, Children, and Welfare Reform: The Ties That Bind,* edited by Ruth A. Brandwein. Thousand Oaks, CA: Sage Publications.

Brandwein, Ruth A. 1999a. "Connections Between Child Abuse and Welfare." Pp. 121–130 in *Battered Women, Children, and Welfare Reform: The Ties That Bind,* edited by Ruth A. Brandwein. Thousand Oaks, CA: Sage Publications.

Brandwein, Ruth A. 1999b. "Family Violence and Welfare Use: Report From the Field." Pp. 45–58 in *Battered Women, Children, and Welfare Reform: The Ties That Bind,* edited by Ruth A. Brandwein. Thousand Oaks, CA: Sage Publications.

Brandwein, Ruth A. 1999c. "Introduction." Pp. 3–14 in *Battered Women, Children, and Welfare Reform: The Ties That Bind,* edited by Ruth A. Brandwein. Thousand Oaks, CA: Sage Publications.

Brayfield, April. 1995. "Juggling Jobs and Kid: The Impact of Employment Schedules on Fathers' Caring for Children." *Journal of Marriage and the Family* 57:321–332.

Britton, Dana. 2003. *At Work in the Iron Cage: The Prison as Gendered Organization*. New York: New York University Press.

Brooks, Margaret G. and John C. Buckner. 1996. "Work and Welfare: Job Histories, Barriers to Employment, and Predictors of Work Among Low-Income Single Mothers." *American Journal of Orthopsychiatry* 66:526–537.

Brown, Michael K. 1999. *Race, Money, and the American Welfare State*. Ithaca, NY: Cornell University Press.

Brown, Wendy. 1995. *States of Injury: Power and Freedom in Late Modernity*. Princeton, NJ: Princeton University Press.

Browne, Angela and Bassuk, Shari S. 1997. "Intimate Violence in the Lives of Homeless and Poor Housed Women: Prevalence and Patterns in an Ethnically Diverse Sample." *American Journal of Orthopsychiatry* 67:261–278.

Browne, Angela, Amy Salomon, and Shari S. Bassuk. 1999. "The Impact of Recent Partner Violence on Poor Women's Capacity to Maintain Work." *Violence Against Women* 5:393–426.

Brush, Lisa D. 1996. "Love, Toil, and Trouble: Motherhood and Feminist Politics." *Signs: A Journal of Women in Culture and Society* 21:429–454.

Brush, Lisa D. 1997. "Worthy Widows, Welfare Cheats: Proper Womanhood in Expert Needs Talk About Single Mothers in the United States, 1900-1988." *Gender & Society* 11:720–746.

Brush, Lisa D. 1999. "Woman Battering and Welfare Reform: The View From a Welfare-to-Work Program." *Journal of Sociology and Social Welfare* 26:49–60.

Brush, Lisa D. 2000. "Battering, Traumatic Stress, and Welfare-to-Work Transition." *Violence Against Women* 6:1039–1065.

Brush, Lisa D. 2001. "Poverty, Battering, Race, and Welfare Reform: Black-White Differences in Women's Welfare-to-Work Transitions." *Journal of Poverty* 5:67–89.

Brush, Lisa D. 2002a. "Changing the Subject: Gender and Welfare Regime Studies." *Social Politics* 9:161–186.

Brush, Lisa D. 2002b. "Work-Related Abuse: A Replication, New Items, and Persistent Questions." *Violence and Victims* 17:743–757.

Brush, Lisa D. 2003a. "Effects of Work on Hitting and Hurting." *Violence Against Women* 9:1213–1230.

Brush, Lisa D. 2003b. *Gender and Governance*. Lanham, MD: AltaMira Press.

Brush, Lisa D. 2003c. "Impacts of Welfare Reform." *Race, Gender and Class* 10:137–192.

Brush, Lisa D. 2003d. "'That's Why I'm on Prozac': Battered Women, Traumatic Stress, and Education in the Context of Welfare Reform." Pp. 215–239 in *Reclaiming Class: Women, Welfare, and the Promise of Higher Education in America*, edited by Sandra Dahlberg and Vivyan Adair. Philadelphia, PA: Temple University Press.

Brush, Lisa D. 2004. "Battering and the Poverty Trap." *Journal of Poverty* 8:23–43.

Brush, Lisa D. 2005a. "Philosophical and Political Issues in Research on Women's Aggression and Violence." *Sex Roles* 52:867–873.

Brush, Lisa D. 2005b. "Safety and Self-Sufficiency: Rhetoric and Reality in the Lives of Welfare Recipients." Pp. 183–192 in *The Promise of Welfare Reform: Results or Rhetoric?* edited by K. Kilty and E. Segal. Binghamton, NY: Haworth Press.

Brush, Lisa D. 2007. "Exchanges: On Violence Against Women." *Contexts* 6:5.

Brush, Lisa D. 2009a. "Guest Editor's Introduction." Special Issue on Evan Stark's *Coercive Control*. *Violence Against Women* 15:1423–1431.

Brush, Lisa D. 2009b. "Review Essay on *In an Abusive State: How Neoliberalism Appropriated the Feminist Movement against Sexual Violence*, by Kristin Bumiller; *A Typology of Domestic Violence: Intimate Terrorism, Violent Resistance, and Situational Couple Violence*, by Michael P. Johnson; *Violent Partners: A Breakthrough Plan for Ending the Cycle of Abuse*, by Linda G. Mills; *and Coercive Control: How Men Entrap Women in Personal Life*, by Evan Stark." *Gender and Society* 23:273–281.

Bufkin, J. L. and J. Bray. 1998. "Domestic Violence, Criminal Justice Responses and Homelessness: Finding the Connection and Addressing the Problem." *Journal of Social Distress and the Homeless* 7: 227–240.

Bumiller, Kristin. 2008. *In an Abusive State: How Neoliberalism Appropriated the Feminist Movements Against Sexual Violence*. Durham, NC: Duke University Press.

Bureau of Labor Statistics. 2008. "Median Weekly Earnings of Full-Time Wage and Salary Workers by Detailed Occupation and Sex." Retrieved February 18, 2010 (http://www.bls.gov/cps/cpsaat39.pdf).

Bureau of Program Evaluation. 1998. Number of Persons (Adults and Children) Receiving TANF Benefits—Allegheny County, May-June (1998). Table provided to Author. Harrisburg, PA: Department of Public Welfare.

Buzawa, Eve S. and David Hirschel. 2009. "Evolution of the Police Response to Domestic Violence." Pp. 69–90 in *Violence Against Women in Families and Relationships*, vol. 3,

Criminal Justice and the Law, edited by Evan Stark and Eve S. Buzawa. Santa Barbara, CA; Denver, CO; Oxford, England: Praeger/ABC-CLIO.

CalWORKs Project. 2002. *Impact of Alcohol and Other Drugs, Mental Health Problems and Domestic Violence on Employment and Welfare Tenure* (Policy and Practice Brief No. 2). Sacramento, CA: California Institute for Mental Health.

Cartwright, Nancy. 2007. *Hunting Causes and Using Them: Approaches in Philosophy and Economics.* Cambridge, UK: Cambridge University Press.

Center for Law and Social Policy. 2002. *New Data Show Most States Had TANF Caseload Increases in Last Year.* Washington, D.C.: CLASP.

Centers for Disease Control and Prevention. 2003. *Costs of Intimate Partner Violence Against Women in the United States.* Atlanta, GA: CDC. Retrieved March 16, 2011 (http://www.cdc.gov/ncipc/pub-res/ipv_cost/ipv.htm).

Cherry, Robert. 2007. *Welfare Transformed: Universalizing Family Work.* Oxford, UK: Oxford University Press.

Clinton, William Jefferson. 1991. "The New Covenant: Responsibility and Rebuilding the American Community." Remarks to students at Georgetown University. Retrieved March 16, 2011 (http://www.dlc.org/print.cfm?contentid=2783).

Cloward, Richard A. and Frances Fox Piven. 1974. *The Politics of Turmoil: Essays on Poverty, Race, and the Urban Crisis.* New York: Pantheon Books.

Coker, Ann L., Paige H. Smith, Lesa Bethea, Melissa R. King, and Robert E. McKeown. 2000. "Physical Health Consequences of Physical and Psychological Intimate Partner Violence." *Archives of Family Medicine* 9:451–457.

Coker, Donna. 1999a. "Enhancing Autonomy for Battered Women: Lessons From Navajo Peacemaking." *UCLA Law Review* 47:1–111.

Coker, Donna. 1999b. "Shifting Power for Battered Women: Law, Material Resources, and Poor Women of Color." *U.C. Davis Law Review* 33:1009–1055.

Collins, Jane L. and Victoria Mayer. 2010. *Both Hands Tied: Welfare Reform and the Race to the Bottom of the Low-Wage Labor Market.* Chicago, IL: University of Chicago Press.

Collins, Patricia Hill. 1994. "Shifting the Center: Race, Class, and Feminist Theorizing about Motherhood." Pp. 56–74 in *Representations of Motherhood,* edited by D. Bassin, M. Honey, and M. M. Kaplan. New Haven, CT: Yale University Press.

Collins, Patricia Hill. 1998. *Fighting Words: Black Women and the Search for Justice.* Minneapolis, MN: University of Minnesota Press.

Collins, Patricia Hill. [1990] 2000. *Black Feminist Thought: Knowledge, Consciousness, and the Politics of Empowerment.* 2nd ed. New York: Routledge.

Connell, R. W. 1995. *Masculinities.* Berkeley, CA: University of California Press.

Conrad, Peter. 2007. *The Medicalization of Society: On the Transformation of Human Conditions into Treatable Disorders.* Baltimore, MD: Johns Hopkins University Press.

Crenshaw, Kimberlé W. 1994. "Mapping the Margins: Intersectionality, Identity Politics, and Violence Against Women of Color. Pp. 93–118 in *The Public Nature of Private Violence: The Discovery of Domestic Abuse,* edited by M. A. Fineman and R. Mykitiuk. New York, NY: Routledge.

Cruikshank, Barbara. 1996. "Revolutions Within: Self-Government and Self-Esteem." Pp. 231–251 in *Foucault and Political Reason: Liberalism, Neo-Liberalism and Rationalities of Government,* edited by Andrew Barry, Thomas Osborne, and Nikolas Rose. Chicago, IL: University of Chicago Press.

Cunradi, Carol B., Raul Caetano, and John Schafer. 2002. "Socioeconomic Predictors of Intimate Partner Violence Among White, Black, and Hispanic Couples in the United States." *Journal of Family Violence* 17:377–389.

Curcio, C. 1997. *The Passaic County Study of AFDC Recipients in a Welfare-to-Work Program: A Preliminary Analysis in Trapped by Poverty, Trapped by Abuse.* Passaic County, NJ: Passaic County Board of Social Services.

Danziger, Sandra K. and Kristin S. Seefeldt. 2002. "Barriers to Employment and the 'Hard to Serve': Implications for Services, Sanctions and Time Limits." *Focus* 22: 78–81.

Danziger, Sandra K., Mary Corcoran, Sheldon Danziger, Colleen Heflin, Ariel Kalil, Judith Levine, Daniel Rosen, Kristin Seefeldt, Kristine Siefert, and Richard Tolman. 2000. "Barriers to the Employment of Welfare Recipients." Pp. 245–278 in *Prosperity for All? The Economic Boom and African Americans,* edited by Robert Cherry and William M. Rodgers, III. New York: Russell Sage Foundation.

Danziger, Sheldon. 2007. "Fighting Poverty Revisited: What Did Researchers Know 40 Years Ago? What Do We Know Today?" *Focus* 25:3–11.

Davis, Dana-Ain. 2006. *Battered Black Women and Welfare Reform: Between a Rock and a Hard Place.* Albany, NY: SUNY Press.

Davis, Joseph E., ed. 2002. *Stories of Change: Narrative and Social Movements.* Albany, NY: State University of New York Press.

Davis, Martha F. 1999. "The Economics of Abuse: How Violence Perpetuates Women's Poverty." Pp. 17–30 in *Battered Women, Children, and Welfare Reform: The Ties That Bind,* edited by Ruth A. Brandwein. Thousand Oaks, CA: Sage Publications.

DeKeseredy, Walter S. 2000. "Current Controversies on Defining Nonlethal Violence Against Women in Intimate Heterosexual Relationships: Empirical Implications." *Violence Against Women* 6:728–746.

DeKeseredy, Walter S. and Martin D. Schwartz. 1998. "Measuring the Extent of Woman Abuse in Intimate Heterosexual Relationships: A Critique of the Conflict Tactics Scales." VAWnet Applied Research Forum, National Electronic Network on Violence Against Women. Retrieved March 16, 2011 (http://www.csaj.org/documents/178.pdf).

DeKeseredy, W. S., S. Alvi, M. D. Schwartz, and E. A. Tomaszewski. 2003. *Under Siege: Poverty and Crime in a Public Housing Community.* Lanham, MD: Lexington Books.

DeParle, Jason. 2004. *American Dream: Three Women, Ten Kids, and a Nation's Drive to End Welfare.* New York: Viking.

Dryzek, John S. 2000. *Deliberative Democracy and Beyond: Liberals, Critics, Contestations.* Oxford, UK: Oxford University Press.

Duterte, E. E., Bonomi, A. E., Kernic, M. A., Schiff, M. A., Thompson, R. S., and Rivara, F. P. 2008. "Correlates of Medical and Legal Help Seeking Among Women Reporting Intimate Partner Violence." *Journal of Women's Health* 17:85–95.

Duhart, Detis T. 2001. *Violence in the Workplace, 1993-1999.* Bureau of Justice Statistics Special Report From the National Crime Victimization Survey. Washington, D.C.: U.S. Department of Justice.

Dutton, Mary Ann and Lisa A. Goodman. 2005. "Coercion in Intimate Partner Violence: Toward a New Conceptualization." *Sex Roles* 52:743–756.

Dwyer, Diane C., Paul R. Smokowski, John C. Bricout, and John S. Wodarski. 1995. "Domestic Violence Research: Theoretical and Practical Implications for Social Work." *Clinical Social Work Journal* 23:185–198.

Edin, Kathryn and Laura Lein. 1997a. *Making Ends Meet: How Single Mothers Survive Welfare and Low-Wage Work.* New York: Russell Sage Foundation.

Edin, Kathryn and Laura Lein. 1997b. "Work, Welfare, and Single Mothers' Economic Strategies." *American Sociological Review* 62:253–266.

Ehrenreich, Barbara. 2008. *Nickel and Dimed: On (Not) Getting by in America.* New York: Henry Holt and Co.

Ellwood, David T. 1996. "Welfare Reform as I Knew It: When Bad Things Happen to Good Policies." *American Prospect* 7: online version. Retrieved March 16, 2011 (http://prospect.org/cs/articles?article=welfare_reform_as_i_knew_it).

Ellwood, David T. 2000. "Anti-Poverty Policy for Families in the Next Century: From Welfare to Work—and Worries." *Journal of Economic Perspectives* 14:187–198.

Enander, Viveka. 2010. "'A Fool to Keep Staying': Battered Women Labeling Themselves Stupid as an Expression of Gendered Shame." *Violence Against Women* 16:5–31.

Engels, Friedrich. [1884] 1970. *On the Origins of the Family, Private Property, and the State,* translated by Ernest Untermann. With an introduction and notes by Eleanor Burke Leacock. New York: International Publishers.

England, Paula, Carmen Garcia-Beaulieu, and Mary Ross. 2004. "Women's Employment Among Blacks, Whites, and Three Groups of Latinas: Do More Privileged Women Have Higher Employment?" *Gender & Society* 18: 494–509.

Enke, Anne. 2007. *Finding the Movement: Sexuality, Contested Space, and Feminist Activism.* Durham, NC: Duke University Press.

Esping-Andersen, Gøsta. 1990. *The Three Worlds of Welfare Capitalism.* Princeton, NJ: Princeton University Press.

Esping-Andersen, Gøsta. 1999. *Social Foundations of Postindustrial Economies.* Oxford, UK: Oxford University Press.

Estes, Sarah Beth. 2003. "Growing Pains and Progress in the Study of Working Families." *Work and Occupations* 30: 479–493.

Falk, G. 2000. *Welfare Reform: Trends in the Number of Families Receiving AFDC and TANF.* Washington, D.C.: Congressional Research Service, Domestic Social Policy Division.

Family Support Act of 1988, Pub. L. 100-485. (1988).

Farmer, Amy and Jill Tiefenthaler. 1997. "An Economic Analysis of Domestic Violence." *Review of Social Economy* 55:337–358.

Farmer, Amy and Jill Tiefenthaler. 2004. "The Employment Effects of Domestic Violence." *Research in Labor Economics* 23:301–334.

Faulkner, Robert R. 1974. "Making Violence by Doing Work: Selves, Situations, and the World of Professional Hockey." *Sociology of Work and Occupations* 1:288–312.

Fearon, James D. 1998. "Deliberation as Discussion." Pp. 44–68 in *Deliberative Democracy,* edited by Jon Elster. Cambridge, UK: Cambridge University Press.

Felson, Richard B. 2006. "Is Violence Against Women About Women or About Violence?" *Contexts* 5:21–25.

Fine, Michelle. 1993. "The Politics of Research and Activism: Violence Against Women." Pp. 278–287 in *Violence Against Women: The Bloody Footprints,* edited by Pauline B. Bart and Eileen G. Moran. Thousand Oaks, CA: Sage.

Florida, Richard L. 2002. *The Rise of the Creative Class: And How It's Transforming Work, Leisure, Community and Everyday Life.* New York: Basic Books.

Flower, Linda, Elenore Long, and Lorraine Higgins. 2000. *Learning to Rival: A Literate Practice for Intercultural Inquiry.* Mahwa, NJ: Erlbaum.

Foucault, Michel. [1975] 1977. *Discipline and Punish: The Birth of the Prison,* translated by Alan Sheridan. New York: Pantheon Books.

Foucault, Michel. [1976] 1978. *The History of Sexuality,* vol. 1, An Introduction, translated by Robert Hurley. New York: Pantheon Books.

Foucault, Michel. [1979] 1991. Governmentality. Pp. 87–104 in *The Foucault Effect*, edited by G. Burchell, C. Gordon, and P. Miller. Hemel Hempstead, England: Harvester Wheatsheaf.

Foucault, Michel. 1980. "Two Lectures." Pp. 78–108 in *Power/Knowledge: Selected Interviews and Other Writings 1972-1977*, edited by Colin Gordon. New York: Pantheon.

Foucault, Michel. [1981] 1988. "The Political Technology of Individuals." Pp. 147–162 in *Technologies of the Self: A Seminar with Michel Foucault*, edited by L.H. Martin, H. Gutman, and P.H. Hutton. Amherst, MA: University of Massachusetts Press.

Foucault, Michel. 1984. *The Foucault Reader*, edited by Paul Rabinow. New York: Pantheon.

Fraser, Nancy. 1989. *Unruly Practices: Power, Discourse and Gender in Contemporary Social Theory*. Minneapolis, MN: University of Minnesota Press.

Fraser, Nancy and Linda Gordon. 1994. "'Dependency' Demystified: Inscriptions of Power in a Keyword of the Welfare State." *Social Politics* 1:4–31.

Frone, M. R. 2000. "Work-Family Conflict and Employee Psychiatric Disorders: The National Comorbidity Survey." *Journal of Applied Psychology* 85:888–895.

Gambles, Richena, Suzan Lewis, and Rhona Rapoport. 2006. *The Myth of Worklife Balance: The Challenge of Our Time for Men, Women and Societies*. Chichester, UK: Wiley.

Garfield, Gail. 2005. *Knowing What We Know: African-American Women's Experiences of Violence and Violations*. New Brunswick, NJ: Rutgers University Press.

Garfinkel, Irwin and Sara S. McLanahan. 1986. *Single Mothers and Their Children: A New American Dilemma*. Washington, D.C.: Urban Institute Press.

Garfinkel, Irwin, Sara S. McLanahan, and Phillip K. Robins. 1994. *Child Support and Child Well-Being*. Washington, D.C.: Urban Institute Press.

Gartner, R. and B. McCarthy. 1991. "The Social Distribution of Femicide in Urban Canada, 1921-1988." *Law and Society Review* 25:287–308.

Gelles, Richard J. and Murray R. Straus. 1989. *Intimate Violence: The Causes and Consequences of Abuse in the American Family*. New York: Simon & Schuster.

General Accounting Office. 1998. *Domestic Violence: Prevalence and Implications for Employment Among Welfare Recipients*. Report No. GAO/HEHS-99-12. Washington, D.C.: Government Printing Office.

Gennetain, L. A. 2003. "Welfare Policies and Domestic Abuse Among Single Mothers: Experimental Evidence From Minnesota." *Violence Against Women* 9: 1171–1190.

Gerson, Kathleen. 1985. *Hard Choices: How Women Decide About Work, Career, and Motherhood*. Berkeley, CA: University of California Press.

Gerson, Kathleen. 1993. *No Man's Land: Men's Changing Commitments to Family and Work*. New York: Basic Books.

Gilens, Martin. 1999. *Why Americans Hate Welfare*. Chicago, IL: University of Chicago Press.

Glass, Jennifer. 2004. "Blessing or Curse? Work-Family Policies and Mothers' Wage Growth Over Time." *Work and Occupations* 31: 367–394.

Glenn, Evelyn Nakano. 2002. *Unequal Freedom: How Race and Gender Shaped American Citizenship and Labor*. Cambridge, MA: Harvard University Press.

Goetting, Ann. 1999. *Getting Out: Life Stories of Women Who Left Abusive Men*. New York: Columbia University Press.

Goldberg, Chad Alan. 2007. *Citizens and Paupers: Relief, Rights, and Race, From the Freedmen's Bureau to Workfare*. Chicago, IL: University of Chicago Press.

Goldstein, Donna M. 2001. "Microenterprise Training Programs, Neoliberal Common Sense, and the Discourses of Self-Esteem." Pp. 236–272 in *The New Poverty Studies: The Ethnography of Power, Politics, Impoverished People in the United States*, edited by Judith Goode and Jeff Maskovsky. New York: New York University Press.

Goode, Judith and Jeff Maskovsky, eds. 2001. *The New Poverty Studies: The Ethnography of Power, Politics, and Impoverished People in the United States*. New York: New York University Press.

Goode, William J. 1969. "Violence Between Intimates." Pp. 941–977 in *Crimes of Violence*, edited by D. J. Mulvihill and M. Tumin. Washington, D.C.: U.S. Government Printing Office.

Goode, William J. 1972. "Presidential Address: The Place of Force in Human Society." *American Sociological Review* 37:507–519.

Gordon, Linda. 1994. *Pitied but not Entitled: Single Mothers and the History of Welfare*. New York: The Free Press.

Gould, Deborah B. 2009. *Moving Politics: Emotion and ACT-UP's Fight Against AIDS*. Chicago, IL: University of Chicago Press.

Gramsci, Antonio. 1971. *Selections From the Prison Notebooks*, edited and translated by Quintin Hoare and Geoffrey Nowell Smith. New York: International Publishers.

Grzywacz, Joseph G., Pamela Rao, Amanda Gentry, Antonio Marín, and Thomas A. Arcury. 2009. "Acculturation and Conflict in Mexican Immigrants' Intimate Partnerships: The Role of Women's Labor Force Participation." *Violence Against Women* 15:1194–1212.

Guttman, Amy and Dennis F. Thompson. 2004. *Why Deliberative Democracy?* Princeton, NJ: Princeton University Press.

Hagen, Jan L. and Judith Owens-Manley. 2002. "Issues in Implementing TANF in New York: The Perspective of Frontline Workers." *Social Work* 47(2):171–182.

Hammer, Rhonda. 2002. *Antifeminism and Family Terrorism: A Critical Feminist Perspective*. Lanham, MD: Rowman & Littlefield.

Hancock, Ange-Marie. 2004. *The Politics of Disgust: The Public Identity of the Welfare Queen*. New York: New York University Press.

Hancock, LynNell. 2002. *Hands to Work: Three Women Navigate the New World of Welfare Deadlines and Work Rules*. New York: William Morrow/HarperCollins.

Harrington, Michael. [1962] 1981. *The Other America: Poverty in the United States*. New York: Penguin Books.

Harris, Kathleen Mullen. 1993. "Work and Welfare Among Single Mothers in Poverty." *American Journal of Sociology* 99:317–352.

Hart, Deborah. 2008. "Trapped Within Poverty and Violence." Pp. 25–37 in *Addressing Violence, Abuse and Oppression: Debates and Challenges*, edited by Barbara Fawcett and Fran Waugh. London, New York: Routledge.

Hartley, Daniel, Elyse A. Biddle, and E. Lynn Jenkins. 2005. "Societal Cost of Workplace Homicides in the United States, 1992-2001." *American Journal of Industrial Medicine* 47:518–527.

Harway, Michèle and James M. O'Neil, eds. 1999. *What Causes Men's Violence Against Women?* Thousand Oaks, CA: Sage Publications.

Hattery, Angela. 2001. *Women, Work, and Family: Balancing and Weaving*. Thousand Oaks, CA: Sage Publications.

Hattery, Angela. 2009. *Intimate Partner Violence*. Lanham, MD: Rowman & Littlefield.

Hays, Sharon. 1996. *The Cultural Contradictions of Motherhood*. New Haven, CT: Yale University Press.

Hays, Sharon. 2003. *Flat Broke With Children: Women in the Age of Welfare Reform*. Oxford, UK; New York: Oxford University Press.

Henderson, Debra and Ann Tickamyer. 2009. "The Intersection of Poverty Discourses: Race, Class, Culture, and Gender." Pp. 50–72 in *Emerging Intersections: Race, Class, Gender in Theory, Policy, and Practice*, edited by Bonnie Thornton Dill and Ruth Enid Zambrana. New Brunswick, NJ: Rutgers University Press.

Hendricks, Scott A., E. Lynn Jenkins, and Kristi R. Anderson. 2007. "Trends in Workplace Homicides in the U.S., 1993-2002: A Decade of Decline." *American Journal of Industrial Medicine* 50:316–325.

Henrici, Jane, ed. 2007. *Doing Without: Women and Work After Welfare Reform*. Tucson, AZ: University of Arizona Press.

Henson, Kevin and Jackie Krasas Rogers. 2001. "'Why Marcia You've Changed!': Male Clerical Temporary Workers Doing Masculinity in a Feminized Occupation." *Gender & Society* 15: 218–238.

Herman, David, ed. 1999. *Narratologies: New Perspectives on Narrative Analysis*. Columbus, OH: Ohio State University Press.

Herman, David, ed. 2002. *Story Logic: Problems and Possibilities of Narrative*. Lincoln, NE: University of Nebraska Press.

Herman, David, ed. 2009. *Basic Elements of Narrative*. Malden, MA: Wiley-Blackwell.

Herman, Judith. 1992. *Trauma and Recovery*. New York: Basic Books.

Hesse-Biber, Sharlene Nagy, and Gregg Lee Carter. 2005. *Working Women in America: Split Dreams*. 2nd ed. New York; Oxford, UK: Oxford University Press.

Hetling, Andrea and Catherine E. Born. 2005. "Examining the Impact of the Family Violence Option on Women's Efforts to Leave Welfare." *Research on Social Work Practice* 15:143–153.

Hetling, Andrea and Catherine E. Born. 2006. "Specialists in Welfare Offices: Do Domestic Violence Experts Matter?" *Administration in Social Work* 30:19–36.

Hetling, Andrea, Correne Saunders, and Catherine E. Born. 2007. "'Missing' Domestic Violence Victims in Welfare Caseloads: The Discrepancy Between Administrative and Survey Disclosure Rates." *Journal of Health and Social Policy* 22:79–95.

Hetling-Wernyj, Andrea and Catherine E. Born. 2002. *Domestic Violence and Welfare Receipt in Maryland: Are Domestic Violence Victims Different From Other Welfare Recipients?* Baltimore, MD: Welfare and Child Support Research and Training Group, University of Maryland School of Social Work.

Higgins, Lorraine and Lisa D. Brush. 2006. "Personal Experience Narrative and Public Debate: Writing the Wrongs of Welfare." *College Composition and Communication* 57:694–729.

Hochschild, Arlie R. 1997. *The Time Bind: When Work Becomes Home and Home Becomes Work*. New York: Henry Holt and Company.

Hochschild, Arlie R. 2003. *The Commercialization of Intimate Life: Notes From Home and Work*. Berkeley, CA: University of California Press.

Hodson, Randy, Vincent J. Roscigno, and Steven H. Lopez. 2006. "Chaos and the Abuse of Power: Workplace Bullying in Organizational and Interactional Context." *Work and Occupations* 33: 382–416.

hooks, bell. [1994] 2006. *Outlaw Culture: Resisting Representations*. New York: Routledge.

Horsman, Jenny. 2000. *Too Scared to Learn: Women, Violence, and Education*. Mahwah, NJ: Lawrence Erlbaum Associates.

Houstoun, F. O. and S. Z. Heller. 2001. *The Maturing TANF Program: New Options for TANF Clients, Planning for the TANF Time-Limit*. Harrisburg, PA: Commonwealth of Pennsylvania Department of Public Welfare.

Hughes, Melanie and Lisa D. Brush. 2011. "Work, Welfare, and Protection Orders: Modeling Changing Earnings in the Context of Group Differences and Institutional Shifts." *Violence Against Women* 17:322–339.

Hume, David. [1777] 1975. *Enquiries Concerning Human Understanding and Concerning the Principles of Morals*. 3rd ed. with text revised and notes by P. H. Nidditch. Oxford, UK: Clarendon Press.

Hutchison, I. W. and Hirschel, J. D. 1998. "Abused Women: Help-Seeking Strategies and Police Utilization." *Violence Against Women* 4:436–445.

Hydén, Margareta. 2005. "'I Must Have Been an Idiot to Let It Go On': Agency and Positioning in Battered Women's Narratives of Leaving." *Feminism and Psychology* 15:169–188.

INCITE! Women of Color Against Violence. 2006. *The INCITE! Anthology*. Boston, MA: South End Press.

Jacobs, Jerry A., and Kathleen Gerson. 2004. *The Time Divide: Work, Family, and Gender Inequality*. Cambridge, MA: Harvard University Press.

Jencks, Christopher. 1992. *Rethinking Social Policy: Race, Poverty, and the Underclass*. Cambridge, MA: Harvard University Press.

Johnson, Michael P. 2008. *A Typology of Domestic Violence: Intimate Terrorism, Violent Resistance, and Situational Couple Violence*. Boston, MA: Northeastern University Press.

Jones-Deweever, Avis, Bonnie Thornton Dill, and Sanford Schram. 2009. "Racial, Ethnic, and Gender Disparities in the Workforce, Education, and Training under Welfare Reform." Pp. 150–179 in *Emerging Intersections: Race, Class, Gender in Theory, Policy, and Practice*, edited by Bonnie Thornton Dill and Ruth Enid Zambrana. New Brunswick, NJ: Rutgers University Press.

Jordan, Carol E. 2009. "Advancing the Study of Violence Against Women: Evolving Research Agendas Into Science." *Violence Against Women* 15:393–419.

Jurik, Nancy C. 2005. *Bootstrap Dreams: U.S. Microenterprise Development in an Era of Welfare Reform*. Ithaca, NY: ILR Press.

Katz, Michael. 1986. *In the Shadow of the Poor House*. New York: Basic Books.

Kelly, Maura. 2010. "Regulating the Reproduction and Mothering of Poor Women: The Controlling Image of the Welfare Mother in Television News Coverage of Welfare Reform." *Journal of Poverty* 14:76–96.

Kenney, C. T. and K. R. Brown. 1996. *Report From the Front Lines: The Impact of Violence on Poor Women*. New York: NOW Legal Defense and Education Fund.

Kimmel, Michael S. 2002. "'Gendered Symmetry' in Domestic Violence: A Substantive and Methodological Research Review." *Violence Against Women* 8:1332–1363.

Kingfisher, Catherine P. 1996. *Women in the American Welfare Trap*. Philadelphia, PA: University of Pennsylvania Press.

Kingfisher, Catherine P. 2001. "Producing Disunity: The Constraints and Incitements of Welfare Work." Pp. 273–292 in *The New Poverty Studies: The Ethnography of Power, Politics, and Impoverished People in the United States*, edited by Judith Goode and Jeff Maskovsky. New York: New York University Press.

Koop, C. Evans. 1985. *The Surgeon General's Workshop on Violence and the Public Health*. Washington, D.C.: U.S. Government Printing Office.

Koss, Mary P., Lisa A. Goodman, Angela Browne, Louise F. Fitzgerald, Gwendolyn Puryear Keita, and Nancy Felipe Russo. 1994. *No Safe Haven: Male Violence Against Women at Home, at Work and in the Community*. Washington, D.C.: American Psychological Association.

Kossek, Ellen Ernst, ed. 2005. *Work and Life Integration: Organizational, Cultural, and Individual Perspectives.* Mahwah, NJ: Lawrence Erlbaum Associates.

Kurz, Demie. 1995. *For Richer, for Poorer: Mothers Confront Divorce.* New York: Routledge.

Larson, Jane E. 1993. "'Imagine Her Satisfaction': The Transformative Task of Feminist Tort Work." *Washburn Law Journal* 33: 56–75.

Lehman, K. A. 2000. *"We are not home yet": Formerly homeless families define their needs and the impact of homelessness.* Doctoral dissertation (Seattle Pacific University).

Lehrner, Amy and Nicole E. Allen. 2009. "Still a Movement After All These Years? Current Tensions in the Domestic Violence Movement." *Violence Against Women* 15:656–677.

Lein, Laura, Susan E. Jacquet, Carol M. Lewis, Patricia R. Cole, and Bernice B. Williams. 2001. "With the Best of Intentions: Family Violence Option and Abused Women's Needs." *Violence Against Women* 7:193–210.

Lein, Laura, Deanna T. Schexnayder with Karen Nanges Douglas and Daniel G. Schroeder. 2007. *Life After Welfare: Reform and the Persistence of Poverty.* Austin, TX: University of Texas Press.

Lerner, Gerder. 1986. *The Creation of Patriarchy.* New York: Oxford University Press.

Levin, Rebekah. 2001. "Less Than Ideal: The Reality of Implementing a Welfare-to-Work Program for Domestic Violence Victims and Survivors in Collaboration With the TANF Department." *Violence Against Women* 7:211–221.

Libal, Kathryn and Serena Parekh. 2009. "Reframing Violence Against Women as a Human Rights Violation: Evan Stark's *Coercive Control.*" *Violence Against Women* 15:1477–1489.

Lieberman, Robert C. 1998. *Shifting the Color Line: Race and the American Welfare State.* Cambridge, MA: Harvard University Press.

Lindhorst, Taryn and Ronald J. Mancoske. 2006. "The Social and Economic Impact of Sanctions and Time Limits on Recipients of Temporary Assistance to Needy Families." *Journal of Sociology and Social Welfare* 33:93–114.

Lindhorst, Taryn, Monica Oxford, and Mary Rogers Gillmore. 2007. "Longitudinal Effects of Domestic Violence on Employment and Welfare Outcomes." *Journal of Interpersonal Violence* 22:812–828.

Lindhorst, Taryn and Julianna D. Padgett. 2005. "Disjunctures for Women and Frontline Workers: Implementation of the Family Violence Option." *Social Service Review* 3:405–429.

Lipsky, Michael. [1980] 2010. *Street-Level Bureaucracy: Dilemmas of the Individual in Public Services,* 13th anniversary expanded edition. New York: Russell Sage Foundation.

Lloyd, Susan. 1997. "The Effects of Domestic Violence on Women's Employment." *Law and Policy* 19:139–167.

Lloyd, Susan and Nina Taluc. 1999. "The Effects of Male Violence on Female Employment." *Violence Against Women* 5:370–392.

Logan, TK, Jennifer Cole, Lisa Shannon, and Robert Walker. 2006. *Partner Stalking: How Women Respond, Cope, and Survive.* New York: Springer.

Loprest, Pamela. 2001. *How Are Families That Left Welfare Doing? A Comparison of Early and Recent Welfare Leavers.* New Federalism Series B, No. B-36. Washington, D.C.: The Urban Institute.

Loseke, Donileen R. 2009. "Public and Personal Stories of Wife Abuse." Pp. 1–35 in *Violence Against Women in Families and Relationships,* vol. 4, *The Media and Cultural Attitudes,* edited by Evan Stark and Eve S. Buzawa. Santa Barbara, CA; Denver, CO; Oxford, England: Praeger/ABC-CLIO.

Loury, Glenn C. with Pamela S. Karlan, Tommie Shelby, and Loïc Wacquant. 2008. *Race, Incarceration, and American Values*. Boston, MA: Boston Review/MIT Press.

Lower-Basch, Elizabeth. 2000. *"Leavers" and Diversion Studies: Preliminary Analysis of Racial Differences in Caseload Trends and Leaver Outcomes*. Washington, D.C.: U.S. Department of Health and Human Services. Retrieved October 30, 2010 (http://aspe. hhs.gov/hsp/leavers99/race.htm).

Lown, E. Anne, Laura A. Schmidt, and James Wiley. 2006. "Interpersonal Violence Among Women Seeking Welfare: Unraveling Lives." *American Journal of Public Health* 96:1409–1415.

Lundberg-Love, Paula K. and Shelly L. Marmion, eds. 2006. *"Intimate" Violence Against Women: When Spouses, Partners, or Lovers Attack*. Westport, CT: Praeger.

Macedo, Stephen, ed. 1999. *Deliberative Politics: Essays on Democracy and Disagreement*. Oxford, UK: Oxford University Press.

MacKinnon, Catharine A. 1979. *Sexual Harassment of Working Women: A Case of Sex Discrimination*. New Haven, CT: Yale University Press.

MacKinnon, Catharine A. 1983. "Feminism, Marxism, Method, and the State: Toward a Feminist Jurisprudence." *Signs: Journal of Women in Culture and Society* 8:635–658.

MacKinnon, Catharine A. 2006. *Are Women Human? and Other International Dialogues*. Cambridge, MA: Harvard University Press.

Macy, R. J., P. S. Nurius, M. A. Kernic, and V. L. Holt. 2005. "Battered Women's Profiles Associated With Service Help-Seeking Efforts: Illuminating Opportunities for Intervention." *Social Work Research* 29:137–150.

Magnet, Myron. 1993. *The Dream and the Nightmare: The Sixties' Legacy to the Underclass*. New York: W. Morrow.

Malos, E. and G. Hague. 1997. "Women, Housing, Homelessness, and Domestic Violence." *Women's Studies International Forum* 20: 3997–3409.

Marcuse, Herbert. 1964. *One-Dimensional Man*. Boston, MA: Beacon Press.

Martin, Patrician Yancey. 2002. *Rape Work: Victims, Gender and Emotions in Organization and Community Context*. New York: Routledge.

Max, Wendy, Dorothy P. Rice, Eric Finkelstein, Robert A. Bardwell, and Steven Leadbetter. 2004. "The Economic Toll of Intimate Partner Violence Against Women in the United States." *Violence and Victims* 19:259–272.

Maxwell, Christopher D., Amanda L. Robinson, and Andrew R. Klein. 2009. "The Prosecution of Domestic Violence Across Time." Pp. 91–114 in *Violence Against Women in Families and Relationships*, vol. 3, *Criminal Justice and the Law*, edited Evan Stark and Eve S. Buzawa. Santa Barbara, CA; Denver, CO; Oxford, England: Praeger/ABC-CLIO.

Maynard-Moody, Steven and Michael C. Musheno. 2000. "State Agent or Citizen Agent: Two Narratives of Discretion." *Journal of Public Administration Research and Theory* 10:329–358.

McCauley, J., D. E. Kern, K. Kolodner, L. R. Derogatis, and E. B. Bass. 1998. "Relation of Low-Severity Violence to Women's Health." *Journal of General Internal Medicine* 13:687–691.

Mead, Lawrence. 1986. *Beyond Entitlement: The Social Obligations of Citizenship*. New York: Free Press.

Melzer, Scott A. 2002. "Gender, Work, and Intimate Violence: Men's Occupational Violence Spillover and Compensatory Violence." *Journal of Marriage and Family* 64:820–832.

Metraux, S. and D. P. Culhane. 1999. "Family Dynamics, Housing, and Recurring Homelessness Among Women in New York City Homeless Shelters." *Journal of Family Issues* 20: 371–396.

Mildorf, Jarmila. 2007. *Storying Domestic Violence: Constructions and Stereotypes of Abuse in the Discourse of General Practitioners*. Lincoln, NE; London, England: University of Nebraska Press.

Miller, Susan L. 2005. *Victims as Offenders: The Paradox of Women's Violence in Relationships*. New Brunswick, NJ: Rutgers University Press.

Miller, T., M. Cohen, and B. Wierseme. 1996. *Victim Costs and Consequences: A New Look* (NCJ 155282). Washington, D.C.: U.S. Department of Justice, National Institute of Justice.

Mills, C. Wright. 1959. *The Sociological Imagination*. New York: Oxford University Press.

Mills, Linda. 2003. *Insult to Injury: Rethinking Our Responses to Intimate Abuse*. Princeton, NJ: Princeton University Press.

Mills, Linda. 2008. *Violent Partners: A Breakthrough Plan for Ending the Cycle of Abuse*. New York: Basic Books.

Mink, Gwendolyn. 1995. *The Wages of Motherhood: Inequality in the Welfare State, 1917-1942*. Ithaca, NY: Cornell University Press.

Moe, Angela M. and Myrtle P. Bell. 2004. "Abject Economics: The Effects of Battering and Violence on Women's Work and Employability." *Violence Against Women* 10:29–55.

Moen, Phyllis, ed. 2003. *It's About Time: Couples and Careers*. Ithaca, NY: ILR Press.

Moen, Phyllis and Patricia Roehling. 2005. *The Career Mystique: Cracks in the American Dream*. Lanham, MD; Boulder, CO; New York; Toronto, Canada; Oxford, UK: Rowman & Littlefield Publishers, Inc.

Moffitt, Robert A. 2002. *From Welfare to Work: What the Evidence Shows*. Welfare Reform and Beyond Policy Brief No. 13. Washington, D.C.: The Brookings Institution.

Monson, Renee. 1997. "State-ing Sex and Gender: Collecting Information From Mothers and Fathers in Paternity Cases." *Gender and Society* 11:279–295.

Moreno, C. L., N. El Bassel, L. Gilbert, and T. Wada. 2002. "Correlates of Poverty and Partner Abuse Among Women on Methadone." *Violence Against Women* 8: 455–475.

Morgen, Sandra, Joan Acker, and Jill Weigt. 2010. *Stretched Thin: Poor Families, Welfare Work, and Welfare Reform*. Ithaca, NY: Cornell University Press.

Morgen, Sandra and Jill Weigt. 2001. "Poor Women, Fair Work, and Welfare-to-Work that Works." Pp. 152–178 in *The New Poverty Studies: The Ethnography of Power, Politics, Impoverished People in the United States*, edited by Judith Goode and Jeff Maskovsky. New York: New York University Press.

Mowery, R. 1998. *General Monthly Report*. May and June. Pittsburgh, PA: Allegheny County Assistance Office.

Murphy, Patricia A. 1993. *Making the Connections: Women, Work, and Abuse*. Orlando, FL: PMD Press.

Murphy, Patricia A. 1997. "Recovering From the Effects of Domestic Violence: Implications for Welfare Reform Policy." *Law and Policy* 19:169–182.

Naples, Nancy. 1991. "A Socialist Feminist Analysis of the Family Support Act of (1988)." *Affilia* 6:23–38.

Nelson, Julie A. 2006. *Economics for Humans*. Chicago, IL: University of Chicago Press.

Nelson, Margaret K. 2005. *The Social Economy of Single Motherhood: Raising Children in Rural America*. New York: Routledge.

Neubeck, Kenneth J. 2006. *When Welfare Disappears: The Case for Economic Human Rights*. New York: Routledge.

Neubeck, Kenneth J. and Noel A. Cazenave. 2001. *Welfare Racism: Playing the Race Card Against America's Poor*. New York: Routledge.

Neuman, Joel H. 2004. "Injustice, Stress, and Aggression in Organizations." Pp. 62–102 in *The Dark Side of Organizational Behavior,* edited Ricky W. Griffen and Anne M. O'Leary-Kelly. San Francisco, CA: Jossey-Bass.

Newman, Katherine S. 2006. *Chutes and Ladders: Navigating the Low-Wage Labor Market.* New York: Russell Sage Foundation. Cambridge, MA: Harvard University Press.

Noble, Charles. 1997. *Welfare as We Knew It: A Political History of the American Welfare State.* New York: Oxford University Press.

Noonan, Mary C., Sarah Beth Estes, and Jennifer L. Glass. 2007. "Do Workplace Flexibility Policies Influence Time Spent in Domestic Labor?" *Journal of Family Issues* 28:263–288.

Ochoa, M. and B. K. Ige, eds. 2007. *Shout Out: Women of Color Respond to Violence.* Emeryville, CA: Seal Press.

O'Connor, Julia S., Ann Shola Orloff, and Sheila Shaver. 1999. *States, Markets, Families: Gender, Liberalism and Social Policy in Australia, Canada, Great Britain and the United States.* Cambridge, UK: Cambridge University Press.

Okun, Lewis. 1986. *Woman Abuse: Facts Replacing Myths.* Albany, NY: State University of New York Press.

O'Leary-Kelly, Anne M., Emily Lean, Carol A. Reeves, and Jane Randel. 2008. "Coming Into the Light: Intimate Partner Violence and Its Effects at Work." *Academy of Management Perspectives* 22:57–72.

Olson, K. and LaDonna Pavetti. 1996. *Personal and Family Challenges to the Successful Transition From Welfare to Work.* Washington, D.C.: Urban Institute.

Omolade, Barbara. 1994. *The Rising Song of African American Women.* New York: Routledge.

Orenstein, Peggy. 2000. *Flux: Women on Sex, Work, Kids, Love and Life in a Half-Changed World.* New York: Doubleday.

Orloff, Ann Shola. 2009. "Gendering the Comparative Analysis of Welfare States: An Unfinished Agenda." *Sociological Theory* 27:317–434.

Paetzold, Ramona L. 2004. "Sexual Harassment as Dysfunctional Behavior in Organizations." Pp. 159–186 in *The Dark Side of Organizational Behavior,* edited by Ricky W. Griffen and Anne M. O'Leary-Kelly. San Francisco, CA: Jossey-Bass.

Pascale, Celine-Marie. 2007. *Making Sense of Race, Class, and Gender: Commonsense, Power, and Privilege in the United States.* New York: Routledge.

Pateman, Carole. 1988. *The Sexual Contract.* Stanford, CA: Stanford University Press.

Paxton, P., M. Painter, III, and M. M. Hughes. 2009. "Year of the Woman, Decade of the Man: Trajectories of Growth in Women's Statehouse Representation." *Social Science Research* 38:86–102.

Pearce, Diana May. 1999. "Doing the Triple Combination: Negotiating the Domestic Violence, Child Welfare, and Welfare Systems." Pp. 109–120 in *Battered Women, Children, and Welfare Reform: The Ties That Bind,* edited by Ruth A. Brandwein. Thousand Oaks, CA: Sage Publications.

Pearson, Jessica, Nancy Thoennes, and Esther Ann Griswold. 1999. "Child Support and Domestic Violence: The Victims Speak Out." *Violence Against Women* 5:427–448.

Perlow, Leslie A. 1998. "Boundary Control: The Social Ordering of Work and Family Time in a High-Tech Corporation." *Administrative Science Quarterly* 43: 328–357.

Person, Jessica, Esther Ann Griswold, and Nancy Thoennes. 2001. "Balancing Safety and Self-Sufficiency: Lessons on Serving Victims of Domestic Violence for Child Support and Public Assistance Agencies." *Violence Against Women* 7:176–192.

Peck, Wayne, Linda Flower, and Lorraine Higgins. 1995. "Community Literacy." *College Composition and Communication* 46:199–222.

Personal Responsibility and Work Opportunity Act of 1996, Pub. L. No. 104-193.

Piven, Frances Fox. 2001. "Welfare Reform and the Economic and Cultural Reconstruction of Low Wage Labor Markets." Pp. 135–151 in *The New Poverty Studies: The Ethnography of Power, Politics, Impoverished People in the United States,* edited by Judith Goode and Jeff Maskovsky. New York: New York University Press.

Piven, Frances Fox and Richard A. Cloward. [1971] 1972. *Regulating the Poor: The Functions of Public Welfare.* New York: Vintage Books.

Piven, Frances Fox and Richard A. Cloward. 1979. *Poor People's Movements: Why They Succeed, How They Fail.* New York: Vintage Books.

Platt, Melissa, Jocelyn Barton, and Jennifer J. Freyd. 2009. "A Betrayal Trauma Perspective on Domestic Violence." Pp. 185–207 in *Violence Against Women in Families and Relationships,* vol. 1, *Victimization and the Community Response,* edited by Evan Stark and Eve S. Buzawa. Santa Barbara, CA; Denver, CO; Oxford, England: Praeger/ABC-CLIO.

Plichta, Stacey B. and Marilyn Falik. 2001. "Prevalence of Violence and Its Implications for Women's Health." *Women's Health Issues* 11:244–258.

Pollack, Wendy and Davis, Martha F. 1997. "The Family Violence Option of the Personal Responsibility and Work Opportunity Reconciliation Act of (1996): Interpretation and Implementation." *Clearinghouse Review* 31:1079–1100.

Polletta, Francesca. 2009. "How to Tell a New Story About Battering." *Violence Against Women* 15:1490–1508.

Polletta, Francesca and John Lee. 2006. "Is Telling Stories Good for Democracy? Rhetoric in Public Deliberation after 9/11." *American Sociological Review* 71:699–723.

Post, Lori A., Patricia K. Smith, and Emily M. Meyer. 2009. "Media Frames of Intimate Partner Homicide." Pp. 59–80 in *Violence Against Women in Families and Relationships,* vol. 4, *The Media and Cultural Attitudes,* edited by Evan Stark and Eve S. Buzawa. Santa Barbara, CA; Denver, CO; Oxford, England: Praeger/ABC-CLIO.

Postmus, Judy L. 2004. "Battered and on Welfare: The Experiences of Women With the Family Violence Option." *Journal of Sociology and Social Welfare* 31:113–123.

Postmus, Judy L. 2009. "Domestic Violence and Children's Well-Being." Pp. 1–22 in *Violence Against Women in Families and Relationships,* vol. 2, *The Family Context,* edited by Evan Stark and Eve S. Buzawa. Santa Barbara, CA; Denver, CO; Oxford, England: Praeger/ABC-CLIO.

Potter, Hillary. 2008. *Battle Cries: Black Women and Intimate Partner Abuse.* New York: New York University Press.

Public Justice Center. 1990. *A Plea for Justice* [Video]. Easton, MD: Group Two Productions.

Purvin, Diane M. 2003. "Weaving a Tangled Safety Net: The Intergenerational Legacy of Domestic Violence and Poverty." *Violence Against Women* 9:1263–1277.

Purvin, Diane M. 2007. "At the Crossroads and in the Crosshairs: Social Welfare Policy and Low-Income Women's Vulnerability to Domestic Violence." *Social Problems* 54:188–210.

Przeworski, Adam. 1998. "Deliberation and Ideological Domination." Pp. 140–160 in *Deliberative Democracy,* edited by Jon Elster. Cambridge, UK: Cambridge University Press.

Quadagno, Jill. 1994. *The Color of Welfare: How Racism Undermined the War on Poverty.* New York: Oxford University Press.

Ragin, Charles C. 2000. *Fuzzy-Set Social Science.* Chicago, IL: University of Chicago Press.

Raphael, Jody. 1996. "Domestic Violence and Welfare Receipt: Toward a New Feminist Theory of Welfare Dependency." *Harvard Women's Law Journal* 19:201–227.

Raphael, Jody. 1997. "Welfare Reform: Prescription for Abuse? A Report on New Research Studies Documenting the Relationship of Domestic Violence and Welfare." *Law & Policy* 19: 123–137.

Raphael, Jody. 1999. "Keeping Women Poor: How Domestic Violence Prevents Women From Leaving Welfare and Entering the World of Work." Pp. 31–43 in *Battered Women, Children, and Welfare Reform: The Ties That Bind,* edited by Ruth A. Brandwein. Thousand Oaks, CA: Sage Publications.

Raphael, Jody. 2000. *Saving Bernice: Battered Women, Welfare, and Poverty.* Boston, MA: Northeastern University Press.

Raphael, Jody. 2001. "Domestic Violence as a Welfare-to-Work Barrier: Research and Theoretical Issues." Pp. 443–456 in *Sourcebook on Violence Against Women,* edited by C. M. Renzetti, J. L. Edleson, and R. K. Bergen. Thousand Oaks, CA: Sage Publications.

Raphael, Jody. 2004. *Listening to Olivia: Violence, Poverty, and Prostitution.* Boston, MA: Northeastern University press.

Raphael, Jody. 2007. *Freeing Tammy: Women, Drugs, and Incarceration.* Hanover, NH: University Press of New England.

Raphael, Jody. 2009. "The Trapping Effects of Poverty and Violence." Pp. 93–110 in *Violence Against Women in Families and Relationships,* vol. 1, *Victimization and the Community Response,* edited by Evan Stark and Eve S. Buzawa. Santa Barbara, CA; Denver, CO; Oxford, England: Praeger/ABC-CLIO.

Reese, Ellen. 2005. *Backlash Against Welfare Mothers: Past + Present.* Berkeley, CA: University of California Press.

Reeves, Carol A. 2004. "When the Dark Side of Families Enters the Workplace: The Case of Intimate Partner Violence." Pp. 103–127 in *The Dark Side of Organizational Behavior,* edited by Ricky W. Griffin and Ann O'Leary-Kelly. San Francisco, CA: Jossey-Bass.

Reeves, Carol A. and Anne M. O'Leary-Kelly. 2007. "The Effects and Costs of Intimate Partner Violence for Work Organizations." *Journal of Interpersonal Violence* 22:327–344.

Reeves, Carol A. and Anne M. O'Leary-Kelly. 2009. *A Study of the Effects of Intimate Partner Violence on the Workplace.* Unpublished Final Report of Grant 2003-RD-CX-0021. Washington, D.C.: NIJ. Copy available from author.

Renzetti, Claire M. 1992. *Violent Betrayal: Partner Abuse in Lesbian Relationships.* Newbury Park, CA: Sage Publications.

Renzetti, Claire M. 2009. "Intimate Partner Violence and Economic Disadvantage." Pp. 73–92 in *Violence Against Women in Families and Relationships,* vol. 1, *Victimization and the Community Response,* edited by Evan Stark and Eve S. Buzawa. Santa Barbara, CA; Denver, CO; Oxford, England: Praeger/ABC-CLIO.

Renzetti, Claire M. and S. L. Maier. 2002. "'Private' Crime in Public Housing: Violent Victimization, Fear of Crime and Social Isolation Among Women Public Housing Residents." *Women's Health and Urban Life* 1:46–65.

Research Forum on Children, Families, and the New Federalism. 2001. "Why Some Women Fail to Achieve Economic Security." *The Forum* 4(2): 1–3.

Richie, Beth. 1996. *Compelled to Crime: The Gender Entrapment of Battered Black Women.* New York: Routledge.

Ridzi, Frank. 2009. *Selling Welfare Reform: Work-First and the New Common Sense of Employment*. New York: New York University Press.

Riger, Stephanie, Courtney Ahrens, and Amy Blickenstaff. 2000. "Measuring Interference With Employment and Education Reported by Women With Abusive Partners: Preliminary Data." *Violence and Victims* 15:161–172.

Riger, Stephanie and Maryann Krieglstein. 2000. "The Impact of Welfare Reform on Men's Violence Against Women." *American Journal of Community Psychology* 28:631–647.

Riger, Stephanie and Susan L. Staggs. 2004. "Welfare Reform, Domestic Violence, and Employment: What Do We Know and What Do We Need to Know?" *Violence Against Women* 10:961–990.

Riger, Stephanie, Susan L. Staggs, and Paul Schewe. 2004. "Intimate Partner Violence as an Obstacle to Employment Among Mothers Affected by Welfare Reform." *Journal of Social Issues* 60:801–818.

Risman, Barbara. 1998. *Gender Vertigo: American Families in Transition*. New Haven, CT; London, England: Yale University Press.

Rivara, R., M. Anderson, P. Fishman, A. Bonomi, R. Reid, D. Carrell, and R. Thompson. 2007. "Healthcare Utilization and Costs for Women With a History of Intimate Partner Violence." *American Journal of Preventive Medicine* 32:89–96.

Roberts, Dorothy. 1997. *Killing the Black Body: Race, Reproduction and the Meaning of Liberty*. New York: Pantheon Books.

Roberts, Paula. 1999. "Pursuing Child Support for Victims of Domestic Violence." Pp. 59–78 in *Battered Women, Children, and Welfare Reform: The Ties That Bind*, edited by Ruth A. Brandwein. Thousand Oaks, CA: Sage Publications.

Rollins, J. H., R. N. Saris, and I. Johnston-Robledo. 2001. "Low-Income Women Speak Out About Housing: A High-Stakes Game of Musical Chairs." *Journal of Social Issues* 57: 277–298.

Romero, Diana, Wendy Chavkin, Paul H. Wise, and Lauren A. Smith. 2003. "Low-Income Mothers' Experience With Poor Health, Hardship, Work and Violence: Implications for Policy." *Violence Against Women* 9:1231–1244.

Romero, Diana, Wendy Chavkin, Paul H. Wise, Lauren A. Smith, and Pamela R. Wood. 2002. "Welfare to Work? Impact of Maternal Health on Employment." *American Journal of Public Health* 92:1462–1468.

Roofless Women with M. Kennedy. 1996. "A Hole in My Soul: Experiences of Homeless Women." Pp. 41–56 in *For Crying out Loud: Women's Poverty in the United States*, edited by Diane Dujon and Ann Withorn. Boston, MA: South End Press.

Rose, Jacqueline. 1988. "Margaret Thatcher and Ruth Ellis." *New Formations* 6:3–29.

Rose, Nikolas. 1993. "Government, Authority and Expertise in Advanced Liberalism." *Economy and Society* 22:283–299.

Rose, Nikolas. 1996. "Governing 'Advanced' Liberal Democracies." Pp. 37–64 in *Foucault and Political Reason: Liberalism, Neo-Liberalism and Rationalities of Government*, edited by Andrew Barry, Thomas Osborne, and Nikolas Rose. Chicago: University of Chicago Press.

Rosenbaum, Paul. 2002. *Observational Studies*. 2nd ed. New York: Springer.

Rothman, Emily F. and Phaedra S. Corso. 2008. "Propensity for Intimate Partner Abuse and Workplace Productivity: Why Employers Should Care." *Violence Against Women* 14:1054–1064.

Salcido, Lillian M. 2007. "Looking for Home: Welfare Reform and the Illusion of Prosperity." Pp. 83–98 in *Doing Without: Women and Work After Welfare Reform*, edited by Jane Henrici. Tucson, AZ: University of Arizona Press.

Salmon, Wesley C. 1998. *Causality and Explanation*. New York; Oxford, UK: Oxford University Press.

Salomon, Amy, Shari Bassuk, and Margaret Brooks. 1996. "Patterns of Welfare Use Among Poor and Homeless Women." *American Journal of Orthopsychiatry* 66:510–525.

Sassen, Saskia. 2001. *The Global City: New York, London, Tokyo*. 2nd ed. Princeton, NJ, and Oxford: Princeton University Press.

Saunders, Daniel G., Mark C. Holter, Lisa C. Pahl, Richard M. Tolman, and Colleen E. Kenna. 2005. "TANF Workers' Responses to Battered Women and the Impact of Brief Worker Training: What Survivors Report." *Violence Against Women* 11:227–254.

Saunders, Hilary. 2009. "Securing Safety for Abused Women and Children in the Family Courts." Pp. 41–65 in *Violence Against Women in Families and Relationships*, vol. 2, *The Family Context*, edited by Evan Stark and Eve S. Buzawa. Santa Barbara, CA; Denver, CO; Oxford, England: Praeger/ABC-CLIO.

Schneider, Joseph W. 1985. "Social Problems Theory: The Constructionist View." *Annual Review of Sociology* 11:209–229.

Schneiderhan, Erik and Shamus Khan. 2008. "Reasons and Inclusion: The Foundation of Deliberation." *Sociological Theory* 26:1–24.

Schram, Sanford F. 2006. *Welfare Discipline: Discourse, Governance, and Globalization*. Philadelphia, PA: Temple University Press.

Scott, Ellen K. 2010. "'I Feel as if I Am the One Who Is Disabled': The Emotional Impact of Changed Employment Trajectories of Mothers Caring for Children with Disabilities." *Gender and Society* 24:672–696.

Scott, Ellen K., Andrew S. London, and Nancy A. Myers. 2002. "Dangerous Dependencies: The Intersection of Welfare Reform and Domestic Violence." *Gender and Society* 16:878–897.

Seccombe, Karen. 2010. *"So You Think I Drive a Cadillac?" Welfare Recipients' Perspectives on the System and Its Reform*. 3rd ed. Boston, MA: Pearson Allyn and Bacon.

Sen, Amartya. 1985. *Commodities and Capabilities*. New York: Elsevier Science.

Sen, Amartya. 2009. *The Idea of Justice*. Cambridge, MA: Belknap Press of Harvard University Press.

Sev'er, Aysan. 2002. *Fleeing the House of Horrors: Women Who Have Left Abusive Partners*. Toronto, Canada: University of Toronto Press.

Sharp, Shane. 2009. "Escaping Symbolic Entrapment, Maintaining Social Identities." *Social Problems* 56: 267–284.

Shepard, Melanie F. and Ellen L. Pence, eds. 1999. *Coordinating Community Responses to Domestic Violence: Lessons From Duluth and Beyond*. Thousand Oaks, CA: Sage.

Sherman, Lawrence and Richard Berk. 1984. "Police Response to Domestic Violence Incidents." *American Sociology Review* 49: 261–271.

Sherman, Lawrence W., Douglas A. Smith, Janell D. Schmidt, and Dennis P. Rogan. 1992. "Crime, Punishment, and Stake in Conformity: Legal and Informal Control of Domestic Violence." *American Sociological Review* 57: 680–690.

Shipler, David K. 2004. *The Working Poor: Invisible in America*. New York: A. Knopf.

Shulman, Beth. 2003. *The Betrayal of Work: How Low-Wage Jobs Fail 30 Million Americans and Their Families*. New York: New Press.

Skocpol, Theda. 1992. *Protecting Soldiers and Mothers: The Political Origins of Social Policy in the United States*. Cambridge, MA: Harvard University Press.

Small, S. A. and D. Riley. 1990. "Toward a Multidimensional Assessment of Work Spillover." *Journal of Marriage and the Family* 52:51–61.

Smith, Anna Marie. 2007. *Welfare Reform and Sexual Regulation*. Cambridge, UK: Cambridge University Press.

Smith, Dorothy E. [1974] 1987. "Women's Perspective as a Radical Critique of Sociology." Pp. 84–96 in *Feminism and Methodology: Social Science Issues*, edited by Sandra Harding. Bloomington and Indianapolis, IN: Indiana University Press.

Smith, Dorothy E. 1987. *The Everyday World as Problematic: A Feminist Sociology*. Boston, MA: Northeastern University Press.

Smith, Erica L. and Donald J. Farole, Jr. 2009. "State Court Processing Statistics: Profile of Intimate Partner Violence Cases in Large Urban Counties." Bureau of Justice Statistics Special Report, NCJ 228193. October. Washington, D.C.: U.S. Department of Justice, Office of Justice Programs.

Smith, Lauren A., Diana Romero, Pamela R. Wood, Nina S. Wampler, Wendy Chavkin, and Paul H. Wise. 2002. "Employment Barriers Among Welfare Recipients and Applicants With Chronically Ill Children." *American Journal of Public Health* 92:1453–1457.

Snow, David A. and Robert D. Benford. 1988. "Ideology, Frame Resonance, and Participant Mobilization." *International Social Movement Research* 1:197–217.

Snow, David A., E. Burke Rochford, Jr., Steven K. Worden, and Robert D. Benford. 1986. "Frame Alignment Process, Micromobilization, and Movement Participation." *American Sociological Review* 51:464–481.

Snyder, Karrie Ann and Adam Isaiah Green. 2008. "Revisiting the Glass Escalator: The Case of Gender Segregation in a Female Dominated Occupation." *Social Problems* 55: 271–299.

Solinger, Rickie. 2001. *Beggars and Choosers: How the Politics of Choice Shapes Adoption, Abortion, and Welfare in the United States*. New York: Hill and Wang.

Soss, Joe, Sanford F. Schram, T. P. Vartanian, and E. O'Brien. 2001. "The Hard Line and the Color Line: Race, Welfare, and the Roots of Get-Tough Reform." Pp. 225–249 in *Race and the Politics of Welfare Reform*, edited by Sanford F. Schram, Joe Soss, and Richard C. Fording. Ann Arbor, MI: University of Michigan Press.

Stack, Carol. 2001. "Coming of Age in Oakland." Pp. 179–198 in *The New Poverty Studies: The Ethnography of Power, Politics, Impoverished People in the United States*, edited by Judith Goode and Jeff Maskovsky. New York: New York University Press.

Staggs, Susan L. and Stephanie Riger. 2005. "Effects of Intimate Partner Violence on Low-Income Women's Health and Employment." *American Journal of Community Psychology* 36:133–145.

Stanko, Elizabeth A., D. Crisp, C. Hale, and H. Lucraft. 1998. *Counting the Costs: Estimating the Impact of Domestic Violence in the London Borough of Hackney*. Swindon, UK: Crime Concern.

Stanton, Elizabeth Cady. 1981. "The Solitude of the Self." Pp. 246–254 in *Elizabeth Cady Stanton and Susan B. Anthony: Correspondence, Writings, Speeches*, edited by Ellen C. Dubois. New York: Schocken Books.

Stark, Evan. 2006. "Commentary on Johnson's 'Conflict and Control: Gender Symmetry and Asymmetry in Domestic Violence.'" *Violence Against Women* 12:1019–1025.

Stark, Evan. 2007. *Coercive Control: How Men Entrap Women in Personal Life*. New York: Oxford University Press.

Stark, Evan. 2009. "Rethinking Coercive Control." *Violence Against Women* 15: 1509–1525.

Stark, Evan and Eve S. Buzawa, eds. 2009. *Violence Against Women in Families and Relationships*. Santa Barbara, CA; Denver, CO; Oxford, England: Praeger/ABC-CLIO.

Stark, Evan and Ann Flitcraft. 1996. *Women at Risk: Domestic Violence and Women's Health.* Thousand Oaks, CA: Sage Publications.

Stein, Laura W. 1999. *Sexual Harassment in America: A Documentary History.* Westport, CT: Greenwood Press.

Steiner, Jürg, André Bähtiger, Markus Spöndli, and Marco R. Steenbergen. 2004. *Deliberative Politics in Action: Analysing Parliamentary Discourse.* Cambridge, UK: Cambridge University Press.

Steinmetz, George. 2005. *The Politics of Method in the Human Sciences: Positivism and Its Epistemological Others.* Durham, NC: Duke University Press.

Stets, Jan E. and Stacy A. Hammons. 2002. "Gender, Control, and Marital Commitment." *Journal of Family Issues* 23:3–25.

Strevens, Michael. 2008. *Depth: An Account of Scientific Explanation.* Cambridge, MA: Harvard University Press.

Stone, Katherine V. W. 2004. *From Widgets to Digits: Employment Regulation for the Changing Workplace.* Cambridge, UK: Cambridge University Press.

Swanberg, Jennifer and TK Logan. 2005. "The Effects of Intimate Partner Violence on Women's Labor Force Attachment: Experiences of Women Living in Rural and Urban Kentucky." *Journal of Occupational Health Psychology* 10:3–17.

Swanberg, Jennifer, TK Logan, and Carol Macke. 2005. "Partner Violence, Employment and the Workplace: Consequences and Future Directions." *Trauma, Violence, and Abuse* 6:286–312.

Swanberg, Jennifer, Carol Macke, and TK Logan. 2006. "Intimate Partner Violence, Women and Work: A Descriptive Look at Work Interference Tactics, Coping with Violence on the Job, and Informal Workplace Support." *Violence and Victims* 21:561–578.

Thapar-Björkert, Suruchi and Karen J. Morgan. 2010. "'But Sometimes I Think . . . They Put Themselves in the Situation': Exploring Blame and Responsibility in Interpersonal Violence." *Violence Against Women* 16:32–59.

Thill, Kathryn Phillips and Karen E. Dill. 2009. "Domestic Violence in American Magazines." Pp. 81–104 in *Violence Against Women in Families and Relationships,* vol. 4, *The Media and Cultural Attitudes,* edited by Evan Stark and Eve S. Buzawa. Santa Barbara, CA; Denver, CO; Oxford, England: Praeger/ABC-CLIO.

Thompson, J. A. and J. S. Bunderson. 2001. "Work-Nonwork Conflict and the Phenomenology of Time." Work and Occupations 28: 17–39.

Tjaden, Patricia and Nancy Thoennes. 1998. *Prevalence, Incidence, and Consequences of Violence Against Women: Findings From the National Violence Against Women Survey.* Washington, D.C.: National Institute of Justice and Centers for Disease Control and Prevention.

Tolman, Richard. 1999. "Guest Editor's Introduction." *Violence Against Women* 5:355–369.

Tolman, Richard, Sheldon K. Danziger, and Daniel Rosen. 2002. *Domestic Violence and Economic Well-Being of Current and Former Welfare Recipients.* Joint Center for Poverty Research Working Paper 304. Evanston and Chicago, IL: Northwestern University/ University of Chicago.

Tolman, Richard and Jody Raphael. 2000. "A Review of Research on Welfare and Domestic Violence." *Journal of Social Issues* 56:655–682.

Toro, P. A., C. W. Bellavia, C. V. Daeschler, B. J. Owens, D. D. Wall, J. M. Passero, and D. M. Thomas. 1995. "Distinguishing Homelessness From Poverty: A Comparative Study." *Journal of Consulting and Clinical Psychology* 63: 280–289.

Townsend, N. W. 2002. *The Package Deal: Marriage, Work, and Fatherhood in Men's Lives.* Philadelphia, PA: Temple University Press.

Turner, Lesley, Sheldon Danziger, and Kristin S. Seefeldt. 2006. "Failing the Transition From Welfare to Work: Women Chronically Disconnected From Employment and Cash Welfare." *Social Science Quarterly* 87:227–249.

U.S. Census Bureau. 2010. "MS-1. Marital Status of the Population 15 Years Old and Over, by Sex and Race: (1950) to Present." *Historical Time Series*. Retrieved October 29, 2010 (http://www.census.gov/population/socdemo/hh-fam/ms1.xls).

Valenti, Jessica. 2009. *The Purity Myth: How America's Obsession with Virginity Is Hurting Young Women*. Berkeley, CA: Seal Press.

Van Echtelt, Patricia, Arie Glebbeek, Suzan Lewis, and Siegwart Lindenberg. 2009. "Post-Fordist Work: A Man's World? Gender and Working Overtime in the Netherlands." *Gender and Society* 23:188–214.

Venkatesh, Sudhir Alladi. 2009. *Off the Books: The Underground Economy of the Urban Poor*. Cambridge, MA: Harvard University Press.

Violence Against Women Act of 1994, Pub. L. No. 103-322. (1994).

Violence Against Women and Department of Justice Reauthorization Act of (2005), Pub. L. No. 109-162, 119 Stat. 2960. 2005. Retrieved March 16, 2011 (http://frwebgate.access. gpo.gov/cgi-bin/getdoc.cgi?dbname=109_cong_bills&docid=f:h3402enr.txt.pdf).

Vostanis, P., S. Cumella, J. Briscoe, and F. Oyebode. 1996. "A Survey of the Psychosocial Characteristics of Homeless Families." *European Journal of Psychiatry* 10: 108–117.

Wacquant, Loïc. 2008. *Urban Outcasts: A Comparative Sociology of Advanced Marginality*. Malden, MA: Polity Press.

Wacquant, Loïc. 2009. *Punishing the Poor: The Neoliberal Government of Social Insecurity*. Durham, NC, and London: Duke University Press.

Walby, Sylvia. 2004. Counting the Costs. London: Equalities Unit. Retrieved March 16, 2011 (http://www.equalities.gov.uk/pdf/cost%20of%20domestic%20violence%20su mm%20sep%2004.pdf).

Walker, S., C. Spohn, and M. DeLone. 2000. *The Color of Justice: Race, Ethnicity, and Crime in America*. 2nd ed. Belmont, CA: Wadsworth Thomson Learning.

Weir, Margaret, Ann S. Orloff, and Theda Skocpol, eds. 1988. *The Politics of Social Policy in the United States*. Princeton, NJ: Princeton University Press.

Weiss, Elaine. 2000. *Surviving Domestic Violence: Voices of Women Who Broke Free*. Scottsdale, AZ: Agreka Books.

West, Candace and Don H. Zimmerman. 1987. "Doing Gender." *Gender and Society* 1:125–151.

Western, Bruce. 2006. *Punishment and Inequality in America*. New York: Russell Sage Foundation.

White, Lucie E. 1990. "Subordination, Rhetorical Survival Skills, and Sunday Shoes: Notes on the Hearing of Mrs. G." *Buffalo Law Review* 38:1–58.

Williams, Christine. 1992. "The Glass Escalator: Hidden Advantages for Men in the 'Female' Professions." *Social Problems* 39:253–267.

Wilson, William J. 1997. *When Work Disappears: The World of the New Urban Poor*. New York: Knopf.

Winkelmann, Cecilia I. 2004. *The Language of Battered Women: A Rhetorical Analysis of Personal Theologies*. Albany, NY: State University of New York Press.

Wisner, Catherine L., Todd P. Gilmer, Linda E. Saltzman, and Therese M. Zink. 1999. "Intimate Partner Violence Against Women: Do Victims Cost Health Plans More"? *Journal of Family Practice* 48:439–443.

Wolf, M. E., V. L. Holt, M. A. Kernic, and F. P. Rivara. 2000. "Who Gets Protection Orders for Intimate Partner Violence." *American Journal of Preventive Medicine* 9:286–291.

Woodward, James. 2003. *Making Things Happen: A Theory of Causal Explanation.* New York: Oxford University Press.

Wright, P. and T. Herivel, eds. 2003. *Prison Nation: The Warehousing of America's Poor.* New York, London: Routledge.

Young, Iris Marion. 2000. *Inclusion and Democracy.* Oxford, UK: Oxford University Press.

Zippel, Kathrin S. 2006. *The Politics of Sexual Harassment: A Comparative Study of the United States, the European Union, and Germany.* Cambridge, UK: Cambridge University Press.

CHAPTER 1: INTRODUCTION

1. The names of all women and the people mentioned in the interviews and community literacy project reported in this book are pseudonyms.
2. Pub. L. No. 104-193. On "work-first," see Collins and Mayer (2010); Hancock (2002); Morgen, Acker, and Weigt (2010); Ridzi (2009).
3. Demographers and others who study populations through time refer to people who share a start date—for school, for training, or even simply for birth—as a cohort. Because all 40 women started in the program at the same time, I refer to them this way.
4. On the reauthorization debate and outcomes, see Cherry (2007) and DeParle (2004). On "sexual regulation," see Smith (2007) and Abramovitz ([1988] 1996). On the contemporary purity movement and the effects of abstinence-only education and campaigns against access to abortion and reproductive health services and information, especially on poor women and women and girls of color, see Valenti (2009).
5. The declining caseloads and other changes leading up to and following welfare repeal are clearly set out in Assistant Secretary for Planning and Evaluation (ASPE; 2000, 2002), Cherry (2007), and DeParle (2004). The good news: Caseload numbers went down, and employment rates, earnings, and even wages rose. Nationally, child poverty fell from 21.8 percent in 1994 to 16.2 percent in 2000 (Acs and Loprest 2004; ASPE 2000; Besharov and Germanis 2003; Falk 2000; Loprest 2001; Moffitt 2002). The bad news: About a third of the welfare caseload decline between 1995 and 2000 (and more of the decline in food stamp rolls) was due to lower program participation by people eligible for benefits. That is, a substantial share of the steep decline in the number of people on welfare was not due to decreased need or increased income from work. Rather, many poor people were deterred from seeking or receiving income assistance by complex eligibility rules and increased shame and stigma (Hancock 2002; Ridzi 2009), as well as the declining value of benefits. See studies of how these dynamics played out in seven counties in Texas (Lein and Schexnayder with Douglas and Schroeder 2007); Milwaukee and Racine, Wisconsin (Collins and Mayer 2010); and three sites in Oregon (Morgen, Acker, and Weigt 2010).
6. Center for Law and Social Policy (2002).
7. See DeParle (2004); Morgen, Acker, and Weigt (2010); Ridzi (2009).
8. DeParle (2004). See also Ridzi (2009). Bill Clinton (1991) delivered the "end welfare as we know it" line in a campaign speech at Georgetown University.

9. A few critical words about definitions: *Battering* and *abuse* are the force and force-threats with which batterers shape the dynamics of relationships when they attack, coerce, and control their spouses, dates, or lovers. As feminist legal scholar Catharine MacKinnon (2006) notes, the modifiers *domestic, intimate partner, spousal,* and *family* emphasize the private and therefore putatively apolitical character of violence, abuse, and battering. I follow Evan Stark (2007) and Paula Lundberg-Love and Shelly Marmion (2006) in placing "domestic" in quotation marks to mark this problem. As with *domestic,* the modifiers *family, spousal,* and *intimate partner* also leave unmarked the gender dynamics of perpetration and victimization. The current term of art is *intimate partner violence* (IPV; on the widespread use of IPV as a keyword and concept in research on violence against women, see Jordan 2009). Like *violence, battering* implies a level of physical action and harm but can also convey the more psychologically oriented *control* or *abuse. Conflict* implies specific motive, context, and mutuality, all of which feminist researchers have long recommended viewing as empirically variable rather than definitional. I use *battering* and *abuse* interchangeably. Where necessary, I refer to *partner-perpetrated* violence and other abuse; where possible, I refer specifically to the fact that it is overwhelmingly men who seek to control and sabotage the labor force participation, domestic labor, motherhood, and sexuality of their current and former wives and girlfriends (Stark 2007). I use *IPV* when that is the term used by the researchers, policymakers, activists, or others whose work I am discussing, or when I refer to what Gail Garfield critically calls "the government-sponsored discourse on violence against women" (2005:1).

10. For similar accounts of men who control women's access to toilet and bath/shower facilities in their own homes, see Stark (2007).

11. See the Methodological Appendix for details of this longitudinal cohort study.

12. See, e.g., Cherry (2007); Danziger et al. (2000); Davis (2006); DeParle (2004); Harris (1993); Hays (2003); Nelson (2005); Romero et al. (2003); Smith (2007); Smith et al. (2002); Turner, Danziger, and Seefeldt (2006).

13. As is true of the national welfare caseload, although the majority of women in this cohort had their first child by the time they were 20, very young mothers were by no means the largest age group among welfare recipients. In 1995–1996, when the debate over repealing welfare was at its peak, teen mothers made up a mere one half of 1 percent of the national welfare caseload (Hancock 2004). The age distribution of the cohort of work-first program participants is not just an artifact of the agreement with the institutional review board that precluded our interviewing minors.

14. Only one woman disclosed being in a lesbian relationship.

15. It is impossible to tell from this research if a large proportion of those leaving welfare are doing so by getting married (one of the stated goals of the 1996 legislation). Welfare may well be the income source of last resort for women who were poor while they were married and continue to be poor (and have sole custody of minor children) after they are divorced. We cannot tell from these demographic data the likely effects of welfare reforms on relationships in general, but it would appear that the "mandate for marriage" included in the 1996 welfare reforms is having only minimal influence on the partnering decisions of this group of welfare recipients.

16. It is significant that a sizable minority of these welfare recipients had petitioned for protective orders. Because I was interested in the connections among work, battering, poverty, and welfare, I did not want to study just battered women (by using a shelter sample, for example). Preliminary research indicated that even without targeting battered women, by studying welfare recipients, even in a small cohort of just 40 women,

there would be ample data on battering in general and work-related control, abuse, and sabotage in particular. See Chapter 3 and the Methodological Appendix.

17. See, e.g., Bell, Lohman, and Votruba-Drzal (2007); Brush (2002b, 2003a); Lindhorst and Mancoske (2006); Lown, Schmidt, and Wiley (2006); Salcido (2007); Stark (2007); Tolman, Danziger, and Rosen (2002); Turner, Danziger, and Seefeldt (2006).
18. Mowery (1998).
19. Bangs and Weldon (1998:15).
20. DeParle (2004:215). See also Jones-Deweever, Dill, and Schram (2009); Lower-Basch (2000).
21. Bureau of Program Evaluation (1998).
22. Pittsburgh was the 10th most residentially segregated of the 49 largest cities in the nation (Bangs and Hong 1996:25).
23. Bangs and Weldon (1998:15).
24. See, e.g., Davis (2006); Hancock (2004); Kingfisher (1996, 2001); Morgen, Acker, and Weigt (2010); Smith (2007).
25. Ridzi (2009).
26. From our interview data, we know that very few of the women enrolled in this work-first program were sanctioned during the period of the retrospective and follow-up interviews. We did not ask specifically about enrollment and cannot compare welfare applicants who did and did not enroll in the program, so these reasons for the skewed racial-ethnic composition of the cohort of enrollees we interviewed are based in informed speculation rather than empirical evidence. See especially Brush (2001); Davis (2006); Henderson and Tickamyer (2009); Jones-Deweever, Dill, and Schram (2010); Morgen and Weigt (2001); Potter (2008). I am also grateful for conversations with Gail Garfield for insights into the racial composition of the welfare rolls.
27. Berns (2009).
28. Morgen, Acker, and Weigt (2010); Ridzi (2009); Smith (2007).
29. See, e.g., Edin and Lein (1997a, 1997b); Ehrenreich (2008); Harris (1993); Shulman (2003).
30. See, e.g., Abramovitz ([1988] 1996); Brush (1997); Katz (1986); Foucault (1984).
31. Danziger (2007). It is a matter of folk wisdom among poverty researchers that Michael Harrington's moving account of poverty and inequality in *The Other America* helped to create a climate for relatively effective antipoverty policy and practice.
32. See, e.g., Riger, Staggs, and Schewe (2004); Smith et al. (2002).
33. See, e.g., Hochschild (1997, 2003); Jacobs and Gerson (2004); Kossek (2005); Moen (2003); Moen and Roehling (2005).
34. Brush (2002b). See also Riger, Ahrens, and Blickenstaff (2000).
35. Brush (2003a). See also Riger, Staggs, and Schewe (2004), whose longitudinal study of 965 Illinois mothers who had received public assistance found that "recent (but not past) intimate partner violence is associated with women's working fewer months" (p. 801).
36. Stark (2007).
37. Raphael (1996, 2000); Tolman and Raphael (2000).
38. Raphael (1996:205–206).
39. Brandwein (1999a).
40. Raphael (1996).
41. Murphy (1993, 1997). Issues of control (over self, circumstances, and others), connection (with self and others), and meaning (in both language and life) are central to

the violation of battering and can make learning in general and literacy-oriented learning in particular a challenge (Horsman 2000).

42. For summaries and analyses of early findings from local and state prevalence studies of violence and abuse in the welfare caseload and among low-income women, see Brush (2002b); Raphael (2000, 2001, 2009); Research Forum on Children, Families, and the New Federalism (2001:1); Riger and Krieglstein (2000); Riger and Staggs (2004); Tolman (1999: Table 1, pp. 357–361).

43. Allard et al. (1997). Not surprisingly, the more items there are in the interview index, the higher is the prevalence rate.

44. Curcio (1997).

45. Lloyd (1997); Lloyd and Taluc (1999).

46. Browne and Bassuk (1997). See also Browne, Salomon, and Bassuk (1999); Salomon, Bassuk, and Brooks (1996).

47. Pearson, Thoennes, and Griswald (1999).

48. Tolman, Danziger, and Rosen (2002).

49. Brandwein (1999a, 1999b).

50. Roberts (1999); Scott, London, and Myers (2002).

51. Lein and Schexnayder (2007); Morgen, Acker, and Weigt (2010); Ridzi (2009).

52. Scott, London, and Myers (2002).

53. Boyer (1999); Cherry (2007).

54. Hattery (2009); Raphael (1996, 2000).

55. Davis (2006); Hancock (2002); Monson (1997); Morgen, Acker, and Weigt (2010); Ridzi (2009); Smith (2007); Valenti (2009).

56. Chapter 4 of this book deals systematically with this research and the arguments and frameworks on which it is based. For reviews, see Brush (2002b); Farmer and Tiefenthaler (2004); and Riger and Staggs (2004).

57. See review and evidence in Riger, Staggs, and Schewe (2004).

58. Pollack and Davis (1997).

59. Danziger and Seefeldt (2002:76).

60. Houstoun and Heller (2001).

61. Allegheny County is not exceptional in this regard. Everywhere researchers have studied FVO implementation, it is spotty at best. For example, Lindhorst and Padgett find in an exploratory study in Louisiana that very few welfare workers "screen for domestic violence, refer identified victims to community resources, and waive program requirements that would endanger the women or with which they are unable to comply" (2005:405), and welfare recipients consequently seldom receive supportive services. A combination of welfare applicants' hesitations about disclosing that they are abused (e.g., Person, Griswold, and Thoennes 2001; Saunders et al. 2005) and welfare workers' discretionary powers (e.g., Hagen and Owens-Manley 2002; Maynard-Moody and Musheno 2000) contributes to low rates of screening and waivers for battered welfare recipients. See also Lein et al. (2001) on Texas, Levin (2001) on Chicago, Postmus (2004) on New York State, and Hetling, Saunders, and Born (2007) on Maryland.

62. The conflicts that Tonya experienced were acute. They also raise more general issues of research ethics in the three data collection efforts that are the empirical foundation for this book. The researchers had no access to the intake and referral process by which the 40 women in the cohort wound up in this work-first program. Moreover, the protocol that the University of Pittsburgh Institutional Review Board approved for protecting the confidentiality, dignity, and safety of research subjects stipulated

that we could not share results from specific interviews with the program staff; for example, we could not mention Tonya in particular. However, we were able to distribute palm cards with resources and phone numbers that the Women's Center and Shelter donated and talk about safety planning and resources at any time during the interviews. Because this research was with welfare recipients and not targeted at battered women, we faced different issues in research ethics than those that frequently arise in research with what institutional review boards typically consider "vulnerable populations." We made every effort to protect the identities and privacy of the women who participated in the interview and to promote their safety and dignity, and we had permission to refer them directly to the Women's Center and Shelter for counseling if they were upset by the interview process. The institutional review board further granted an exemption from obtaining signed, informed consent from the women whose administrative records form the basis for the analysis at the end of Chapter 4; I argued that contacting more than 20,000 women who had applied for protective orders, whose filings were publicly available on the county website, would be more likely to put them at risk than would using their data, stripped of individual identifiers, in an aggregate analysis. For both the 40 women who participated in the retrospective and prospective interview studies and the eight women who participated in the community literacy project, we had funding to purchase gift cards from a regional supermarket that enabled us to "give back" to them without having to collect the Social Security numbers that the university would have required if we paid them by check. We also paid for bus fare and provided childcare during sessions of the literacy project. Finally, many participants in the interviews and community literacy project mentioned that it was important to them that their information and experiences be used to help people understand poverty, abuse, welfare, and the complex ways they connected in their lives. As Nikki wrote in a journal entry that became the epigraph for the booklet Lorraine Higgins and I produced from the community literacy project:

> At the end of our project, I sit watching each and every woman around the table as she reads her story. I notice how different we seem—different lifestyles and backgrounds—all kinds of shapes, sizes, and colors. And yet somehow, we all are still the same. I may not agree with the way others are handling their problems, but I see that they do handle them in the best ways they know how. We are strong-willed women, beautiful, powerful, able to endure all things. In this we are the same. Maybe someday some of us will be speakers, helping others learn about welfare, helping other women get ahead. I don't know what the future may hold. No one can really know until it unfolds. But I look at these faces and hear these stories and imagine the possibilities.

63. For additional details on data sources and analysis, see Brush (2000, 2002b); Higgins and Brush (2006); Hughes and Brush (2011); and the Methodological Appendix.

64. For critiques, see Brush (2001, 2004); Davis (2006); DeKeseredy and Schwartz (1998); General Accounting Office (1998); Miller (2005).

CHAPTER 2: CONVENTIONAL WISDOM AND ITS DISCONTENTS

1. The Earned Income Tax Credit is "the most important antipoverty program since the Great Society" (DeParle 2004:110; DeParle describes the program and the rhetoric and politics around it on pp. 109–111).

2. Gramsci (1971).

3. Bourdieu (1977:164).

4. Moreover, people's everyday interactions produce and reproduce hegemony as we hold one another accountable (on accountability in how people "do" gender in particular, see West and Zimmerman 1987 and the sources cited therein). The classic U.S. sociological source on the "social construction of reality" is Berger and Luckman (1967). For compelling contemporary critical treatments of what they call "common sense"—that is, the understandings of their situations and prospects that ordinary people develop that incorporate, inform, and occasionally oppose cultural values and ideas in broad circulation—see Goldstein (2001); Pascale (2007); Ridzi (2009).

5. Berns (2009).

6. See, e.g., Bumiller (2008); Buzawa and Hirschel (2009); Maxwell, Robinson, and Klein (2009); Mills (2003, 2008); Stark (2007).

7. Ridzi (2009). See also Hancock (2002).

8. Hancock (2004). See also Smith (2007).

9. On moral entrepreneurs in social movements and social problems theory, see Schneider (1985).

10. Woodward (2003) emphasizes the importance of "making things happen" as the foundation for causal analysis. See Salmon (1998) for a historical review and Cartwright (2007) and Strevens (2008) for current debates about causality among philosophers of science. For radical critique, see Marcuse (1964) and, more recently, Steinmetz (2005).

11. I describe and analyze some key aspects of VAWA later in this chapter.

12. See, e.g., Cloward and Piven (1974); Piven and Cloward ([1971] 1972, 1979).

13. See, e.g., Gordon (1994); Skocpol (1992).

14. See, e.g., Abramowitz ([1988] 1996); Brown (1999); Glenn (2002); Goldberg (2007); Jencks (1992); Lieberman (1998); Weir, Orloff, and Skocpol (1988).

15. Family Support Act of 1988. Pub. L. 100-485.

16. I describe and analyze some key aspects of this legislation later in this chapter.

17. The financial crisis, severe recession, and "jobless recovery" of 2008–2011 prompted economic stimulus and recovery provisions that stopped far short of a full employment policy and the programs of public works, "green" energy and construction, investment in education, public health, etc., that would make such a policy realizable and politically, ecologically, and economically sustainable.

18. See, among others, Abramowitz ([1988] 1996); Collins and Mayer (2010); Gordon (1994); Lein and Schexnayder (2007); Morgen, Acker, and Weigt (2010); Skocpol (1992); Solinger (2001).

19. For the past three decades in the United States, neoliberals have been augmenting the law-and-order state and dismantling the welfare state. Neoliberal tools include legislation (e.g., the Violence Against Women Act of 1994; the Personal Responsibility Act of 1996), budget priorities, constraints and incentives designed to shape the practices of front-line law-and-order and welfare offices, and a sustained media campaign about the public disorders represented by batterers and welfare recipients. The safety net offered by the law-and-order state was bolstered by federal legislation in the 1990s as the feminist social movement to stop violence against women percolated up to national politicians, local law enforcement agencies responded to activists' demands for coordinated community responses to battering, and the penal strategy of neoliberal local, statewide, and national politicians expanded systems for surveillance, incarceration, and probation (Shepard and Pence 1999; Stark 2007; Wacquant 2009). In addition, the attacks on the World Trade Center and the Pentagon on September 11, 2001, led to the creation of a national Department of Homeland Security and justified

heightened militarization, securitization, and surveillance in response to international terrorist threats. In contrast, the safety net offered by the welfare state was increasingly frayed and under widespread political attack as neoliberals neglected continuing threats to women's security in the context of "intimate terrorism" (Johnson 2008; see also Hammer 2002), rescinded entitlements, privatized social services, disciplined labor, ignored the gendered effects of deindustrialization and other economic restructuring, and incarcerated marginalized populations (see, e.g., Collins and Mayer 2010; Morgen, Acker, and Weigt 2010; Piven 2001; Schram 2006; Wacquant 2009). National investment in militarization and securitization of everyday life, especially since 9/11, has meant fewer resources for unemployment, pensions, social services, battered women's shelters, and progressive responses to globalization and economic crises. In the cases of both the law-and-order state and the social security state, legislators, news and opinion makers, street-level bureaucrats, and taxpayers invoked moralism, budget crisis and economic rationality, and national security to justify intense surveillance and stigma of marginalized men and women in the interests of behavioral modification and social control.

20. For reviews and critiques from a variety of perspectives, see Buzawa and Hirschel (2009); Maxwell, Robinson, and Klein (2009); Mills (2003, 2008). Coker (1999a, 1999b) and INCITE! Women of Color Against Violence (2006) focus especially on alternative community reconciliation as a viable alternative to criminological logic and mass incarceration.

21. Berns (2009:106). See also Berns (2004).

22. Berns (2009:106).

23. See also Loseke (2009) on narratives of battering in public and private storytelling contexts.

24. Berns (2009:106).

25. Berns (2009:108).

26. See also Enander (2010); Thapar-Björkert and Morgan (2010).

27. See generally Gramsci (1971).

28. As Berns puts it, "... the stories we tell about domestic violence focus on, or frame, victims of domestic violence while leaving out offenders and structural, cultural, and institutional factors that contribute to violence" (2009:107; see also 2004).

29. See Richie (1996) on what she calls "gender entrapment."

30. On "framing" in social movement theory, see Snow and Benford (1988); Snow et al. (1986). Stark (2007) analyzes how excluding broader dynamics, material analyses, and political critiques of male dominance from theory, political mobilization, and legislation and policy has contributed to the "stalled revolution" in the movement to end men's abuse of their current and former girlfriends and wives.

31. Empowerment discourse complements the discourse of "codependency" from popular psychology movements such as Alcoholics Anonymous, where the sufferer is instructed to distinguish between the things she can change (her own feelings, behaviors, responses, and attitudes) and the things she cannot (anyone else's feelings, behaviors, reactions, etc.). See, e.g., Brown (1995).

32. See, e.g., Felson (2006). Both the violence of normal masculinity and the specifically racialized rhetoric of the law-and-order logic rely on notions of the "natural" that direct attention, surveillance, law enforcement, sentences, and punishment selectively and disproportionately toward poor and racial-ethnic minority men. Racist stereotypes cast Black men in particular as sexual predators or as simultaneously disdained, frustrated, and bent on exercising what little masculine privilege they can by picking

on someone even lower in the social hierarchy (usually assumed to be "their" women and children). See generally Harway and O'Neil (1999). For critical analyses from a feminist "intersectional" perspective, see, e.g., Crenshaw (1994); Hattery (2009). For more critical approaches to criminology, see, e.g., DeKeseredy (2000); Richie (1996).

33. Goode (1969, 1972). See Chapter 4 for a discussion of the specifically economic rationality of men's battering.

34. See, e.g., Crenshaw (1994); Richie (1996).

35. Hancock (2004).

36. Hancock (2004). See also Kelly (2010); Seccombe (2010); Solinger (2001).

37. Rose (1988); Brush (2003b).

38. The labels for the political position implicit in the politics of disgust can be confusing, especially when translating between U.S. and European contexts. The political stance that generates the politics of disgust is considered *conservative* in the United States, but could also accurately be classified as a form of the market fundamentalism and welfare state bashing congruent with the laissez-faire rhetoric of *neo-liberalism*. Some of the same debates have played out in the context of European welfare states in the past three decades. On the one hand, Margaret Thatcher pioneered the Conservative Party's focus on business climate with neo-liberal experiments in market fundamentalism and welfare state bashing. Thatcher's political campaign against the postwar welfare state consensus included militant repression of organized labor (e.g., using police powers to break the miners' strike), privatization of welfare state services and public utilities (for instance, competitive contracting and sell-off of transportation infrastructure), rollbacks of democratic participation (such as abolition of the Greater London Council), and foreign military adventurism (e.g., in Islas Malvinas/Falkland Islands). On the other hand, social democrats across Europe have focused on poverty and inequality (including gender and race inequality) in terms of the causes and remedies for *social exclusion* and have tried to maintain corporatist arrangements for governing capitalism, including tripartite capital-labor-state bargaining over economy-wide wage-and-benefits packages. See, e.g., Brush (2003b); Esping-Andersen (1990, 1999); O'Connor, Orloff, and Shaver (1999).

39. Ridzi (2009).

40. On the historical roots of the work, family, and sexual ethics in the American welfare state, see, among others, Abramovitz ([1988] 1996).

41. On the apocryphal Reagan "welfare queen" story, see DeParle (2004:72); see also Gilens (1999). For specifically feminist analyses and critiques, see, e.g., Solinger (2001) and Reese (2005). Hancock (2004) shows how both media representations and legislative debates contributed to the formation of the racist, sexist image of the welfare queen.

42. Thill and Dill (2009). See also Berns (2004, 2009); Kelly (2010); Post, Smith, and Meyer (2009).

43. See Higgins and Brush (2006); Schneiderhan and Khan (2008). I deal explicitly with these issues in Chapter 5.

44. See Abramowitz ([1988] 1996); Roberts (1997); Smith (2007).

45. See, e.g., Anderson (2009); Risman (1998).

46. See, e.g., Bumiller (2008); Coker (1999a, 1999b); Garfield (2004); INCITE! Women of Color Against Violence (2006).

47. Collins (1998, [1990] 2000). See also Brush (1997, 2001, 2003c); Davis (2006); Garfield (2004); hooks ([1994] 2006); Kelly (2010); Neubeck and Cazenave (2001); Omolade (1994); Potter (2008); Roberts (1997); Smith (2007).

48. Goetting (1999). Goetting's proposed notion that battering "takes two" contrasts sharply with notions of "mutuality" or "reciprocity" in battering. See, e.g., the debate between Felson (2006) and his critics (including myself, Angela Hattery and Earl Smith, and Walter DeKeseredy, all in the *exchanges* section of the Winter 2007 issue of *Contexts*).
49. Stark (2007).
50. Davis (2006); Garfield (2005); Hattery (2009).
51. Libal and Parekh (2009); MacKinnon (2006); Stark (2007, 2009).
52. Collins and Mayer (2010:162–163). See also Neubeck (2006); Piven (2001).
53. Raphael (1999, 2009). See also Hart (2008).
54. Stark (2007). The following paragraphs draw liberally, and with the kind permission of Sage Publications, from Brush (2009a).
55. Stark (2007:10).
56. Stark (2007:5). See also Dutton and Goodman (2005); Stets and Hammons (2002).
57. Stark (2007:13).
58. Again, I mean hegemonic in the sense alluded to by Italian neo-Marxist Antonio Gramsci in his *Prison Notebooks* (1971): hegemonic power organizes relations of domination and subordination and generates a modicum of consent by articulating elements of people's interests and common sense understandings to those of rulers and government rather than relying exclusively on repression, force, and police powers.
59. Adams and Padamsee (2001). See also Brush (2002a, 2003b).
60. Collins (1998; [1990] 2000). See also Brush (1996, 1997, 2001, 2003c); Davis (2006); Garfield (2005); hooks ([1994] 2006); Kelly (2010); Neubeck and Cazenave (2001); Potter (2008); Roberts (1997); Smith (2007).
61. See, e.g., Hancock (2004); Solinger (2001).
62. See, e.g., Brush (2003c).
63. See, e.g., Alexander (2010); INCITE! Women of Color Against Violence (2006); Wacquant (2009).
64. Collins and Mayer (2010); Morgen, Acker, and Weigt (2010); Piven (2001); Schram (2006).
65. PRA, Title 1, Part A, Sec. 401(a).
66. Author's calculations from Current Population Survey Historical Time Series (U.S. Census Bureau 2010: Table MS-1).
67. For extensive summaries and analyses of the demographic and political shifts behind welfare rescission, see, e.g., Cherry (2007); DeParle (2004); Hancock (2004); Shipler (2004); Smith (2007). For analysis of changes in measures, assessments, and policies on poverty, see, e.g., Danziger (2007); Blank (2000); Ellwood (2000).
68. This version of the conservative mantra for avoiding poverty comes from Magnet (1993).
69. For an analysis of the intersecting race, class, and gender politics of this legislation, see Brush (2003c). On the historic role of labor discipline and the combination of economic and moralistic motivations in state provision for "the unemployed, the idle, and vagabonds," see Foucault (1984:131–135). For extensive studies of how these dynamics played out at various sites in the United States, see Lein and Schexnayder (2007); Morgen, Acker, and Weigt (2010); and Collins and Mayer (2010).
70. See Cherry (2007); DeParle (2004); Ellwood (1996); Hancock (2002); Ridzi (2009); Shipler (2004).

71. For accounts of change and continuity in the interactions between caseworkers and other "street-level bureaucrats" (Lipsky [1980] 2010) in welfare offices and the welfare applicants and recipients into whose lives they increasingly peer and prod, see, e.g., Kingfisher (2001); Morgen, Acker, and Weigt (2010). For research that is especially applicable to the issue of battered welfare recipients, whose eligibility for exemptions from work requirements and time limits caseworkers assess, see, e.g., Lein et al. (2001); Lindhorst and Padgett (2005).

72. See especially Hancock (2004); Hays (2003); Reese (2005).

73. Although they come from a wide variety of political positions, many researchers and commentators nevertheless focus on the importance of employment: see, e.g., Bane and Ellwood (1996); Cherry (2007); DeParle (2004); Jencks (1992); Wilson (1997). On sexual restraint or paternal responsibility or both, see in addition Garfinkel and McLanahan (1986); Garfinkel, McLanahan, and Robins (1994); Magnet (1993); Mead (1986). For assessments and critiques, see, e.g., Goldstein (2001); Raphael (1996).

74. For assessments and critiques, see, e.g., Hancock (2002); Morgen, Acker, and Weigt (2010); Ridzi (2009).

75. For assessments and critiques, see, e.g., Neubeck (2006); Piven (2001); Schram (2006).

76. Subtitle A.

77. Subtitle B.

78. Subtitle C.

79. Subtitle D.

80. Subtitle F.

81. Subtitle G.

82. Sub. B, Chap. 1. Authorized appropriations totaled $2 million for the first five years of the original legislation.

83. Sub. A, Chap. 2. Chapter 2 defines a protection order as "any injunction or other order issued for the purpose of preventing violent or threatening acts or harassment against, or contact or communication with or physical proximity to, another person," and defines a spouse or intimate partner to include "(A) a spouse, a former spouse, a person who shares a child in common with the abuser, and a person who cohabits or has cohabited with the abuser as a spouse; and (B) any other person similarly situated to a spouse who is protected by the domestic or family violence laws of the State in which the injury occurred or where the victim resides" (§2266). Chapter 2 also includes what is known as the "full faith and credit" provision of VAWA (§2265). "Full faith and credit" means that local officials are required to enforce the terms of protection orders issued in any court in any jurisdiction, even if the provisions for protection orders in the enforcing jurisdiction are different from the provisions in the jurisdiction where the order originated.

84. Sub. B, Chap. 3. For some of the debate on "mandatory arrest" and overviews of police and prosecutorial response, see Buzawa and Hirschel (2009); Maxwell, Robinson, and Klein (2009); Mills (2008).

85. Sub. B, Chap. 4.

86. Sub. B, Chap. 9.

87. Sub. B, Chap. 5.

88. Sub. B, Chap. 6.

89. Sub. B, Chap. 8.

90. Sub. B, Chap. 10.

91. Sub. A, Chap. 3.
92. Sub. A, Chap. 1.
93. Sub. A, Chap. 2.
94. Sub. A, Chap. 4. "Rape shield" laws shield women from questions that impugn their sexual morals, dress, comportment, past relationships, and consent to sex with the defendant or other partners, or that might otherwise suggest to a jury that they "asked for it."
95. Sub. A, Chap. 5.
96. For extended critiques of the public/private distinction in hegemonic approaches to violence against women in general and partner-perpetrated abuse in particular, see especially MacKinnon (1983) and Stark (2007).
97. Brush (2003b).
98. In Chapter 4 of this book, I assess some of the research behind this and other estimates of the costs of violence against women.
99. Title II, Sec. 201. In this section, Congress also set out findings on nonreporting of sexual assault in rural areas, geographic isolation, elder abuse and barriers for older victims leaving abusive relationships, specific vulnerabilities of women with disabilities and immigrant women, and evidence of heavy use and consequent underfunding of the National Domestic Violence Hotline service.
100. Arnold (2009); Lehrner and Allen (2009).
101. Stark (2007).
102. "Initiatives… directed toward making the police more sensitive, prosecutors more responsive, judges more receptive, and the law, in words, less sexist… fail[] to address, as part of the strategy for state intervention, the conditions that produce men who systematically express themselves violently toward women, women whose resistance is disabled, and the role of the state in this dynamic. Criminal enforcement in these areas, while suggesting that rape and battery are deviant, punishes men for expressing the images of masculinity that mean their identity, for which they are otherwise trained, elevated, venerated, and paid" (MacKinnon 1983:643).
103. Garfield (2005:2).
104. Ibid., 3.
105. Stark (2007). See also for various perspectives Bumiller (2008); Davis (2006); Enke (2007); Martin (2005); Mills (2008).
106. See, e.g., Buzawa and Hirschel (2009); Sherman and Berk (1984); Sherman et al. (1992).
107. See, e.g., Coker (1999a, 1999b); Mills (2003, 2008).
108. Maxwell, Robinson, and Klein (2009).
109. Stark (2007:10).
110. This section is my gloss on the somewhat contradictory accounts of these changes in Florida (2002); Moen and Roehling (2005); Stone (2004); Van Echtelt et al. (2009).
111. Florida (2002); Gambles, Lewis, and Rapoport (2006); Perlow (1998).
112. Collins and Mayer (2010); Piven (2001); Shipler (2004); Shulman (2003).
113. See Brush (2003c) and the sources cited therein.
114. Skocpol (1992).
115. Brush (1997).
116. Moen and Roehling (2005).
117. MacKinnon (1983); Pateman (1988).
118. Collins and Mayer (2010); Schram (2006).

119. Collins and Mayer (2010).

120. Collins and Mayer (2010:xiii).

121. Hetling and Born (2005) find that although the work and welfare-use patterns of waiver recipients do not differ from those of nonvictims, battered women whose situations were undocumented in the welfare office and therefore did not receive waivers "received fewer months of welfare and earned less income" (p. 143).

122. Hetling and Born (2006) find that establishing experts trained in both battering and welfare policy in welfare offices has no effect on women's disclosures or administrative documentation of those disclosures and has a negative effect on waivers through the FVO.

123. Brandwein (1999c).

124. See, e.g., Baker, Niolon, and Oliphant (2009). The issue of work-related control, abuse, and sabotage is central to the next chapter.

125. I say "strategically" rather than "cynically" because in the absence of other evidence, I believe advocates were working in good faith. Despite desperate misgivings about Clinton's plan to end welfare, and despite evidence of extensive problems with FVO implementation documented by Rebekah Levin (2001), Andrea Hetling and her colleagues (2005, 2006, 2007), and others, I do not think the advocates and sponsors of the FVO *merely* wanted to slow down the welfare legislation (see also DeParle 2004). There is an interesting oral history yet to be done to shed empirical light on these issues.

Chapter 3: What Happens When Abusers Follow Women to Work?

1. For easy reference, readers can find in the Introduction a table of pseudonyms and basic characteristics of the 40 women we interviewed.

2. Since Congress rescinded federal entitlements to income support for poor mothers and their children, women who refuse to cooperate with paternity establishment and child support enforcement efforts by the state can fail to qualify or lose their benefits. See the previous two chapters for more elaborate accounts of the requirements imposed by Congress's rescission of welfare entitlements. On welfare recipients' accounts of the relative importance of mandatory paternity establishment, child support as debt collection, and their own and their children's safety, see Pearce (1999); Pearson, Thoennes, and Griswold (1999); Roberts (1999).

3. Some women explained a driver's license was "not a priority" or "I haven't had time to get one." Others said, "I don't like to drive," "I never had a learner's permit," or "It was stolen and I never renewed it." Several acknowledged that they had lost their licenses because of drunk driving charges. Of the women with no license, 7 percent said it was because they had no car. Not having a car is not necessarily an insurmountable barrier to work in Pittsburgh; for example, I have never owned a car, and have commuted for over 15 years on my bicycle, by Port Authority bus, or on foot. However, some women in this study reported that not having a car or license was an obstacle to employment. For instance, Harriet, 30, had found a job as a mechanic's apprentice at the first follow-up interview. She noted that she needed a driver's license for that position. By the final follow-up, more than a year after the initial retrospective interview, Harriet still did not have a license, had no car, and had lost the apprenticeship opportunity. See Turner, Danziger, and Seefeldt (2006) on having no car or driver's license as a correlate of women's chronic disconnection from employment and cash welfare. Perhaps most interesting is that one in five of the women with no driver's

license (including Harriet) had never learned to drive at all. For example, Edna, 22, confessed that she was scared to drive. In addition to being a requirement for some jobs and training opportunities, such as Harriet's apprenticeship, passing the driver's license exam is a mainstream marker of passage into early adulthood, represents a certain potential for physical independence, and provides state-issued identification important for day-to-day transactions as well as other travel. In states with "motor voter" laws, Departments of Motor Vehicles are an important site of voter registration. Moreover, never learning to drive and never passing the license exam can signal problems with literacy or learning disabilities. For instance, Karen, 18, explained forthrightly that she has no license because she is dyslexic and cannot read well enough to pass the exam.

4. See, e.g., Newman (2006: chap. 4); Ridzi (2009: chap. 6); Stack (2001).
5. "Ignorant" is a common critical epithet for disdained people or institutions. Black students in my classes often refer to racists and racism by saying, "That's just ignorant." The label distances the speaker from the disdained object or person, while giving the benefit of the doubt; in contrast to the unacknowledged prejudice of the pitiful racist, the speaker understands the social dynamics of difference and knows what is appropriate in social interaction. Larnice's ex is expressing his disdain both for her and her dependence on public assistance and for an institution that supports "people like her." See also Newman (2006), who notes in a similar context that one of her respondents "says that she has run into some 'ignorant' people before, but she maintains that she's never personally experienced racism" (p. 178).
6. See previous and following chapters for details on restraining orders.
7. See, e.g., DeParle (2004); Ridzi (2009).
8. Gelles and Straus (1989).
9. Recall from the Introduction that demographers and others who study populations through time call the group of people who share a start date—for school, for job training, or even simply for birth—a *cohort*. I frequently refer to the 40 women who started their work-first program together as a cohort.
10. See, e.g., Goode (1969, 1972); Gelles and Straus (1989). I explore in detail a specific version of exchange theory, a game theoretic approach, in the next chapter. Note the echoes, in exchange theory, of the victim empowerment folklore, which asserts that women can and should stop being battered by exercising their powers of "voice" and "exit" (see previous chapter and Berns 2009).
11. Cost sharing and income sharing are the two main accounting methods in financial child support calculations (see Garfinkel and McLanahan 1986; Garfinkel, McLanahan, and Robins 1994). Cost-sharing methods conceive of fair ways for non-custodial parents to share the costs of raising children and emphasize the politics of parental responsibility; parents should bear and share the costs of having children. Income-sharing methods conceive of fair ways for noncustodial parents to share their income with their children and emphasize the politics of poverty prevention; the state should "fill the gap" between parental contributions and the poverty line. In both cases, the state holds even noncustodial parents financially responsible for at least some of the costs of raising the next generation. In the *financial* sense, cost-sharing and income-sharing plans are often about as effective at reducing child poverty as trying to squeeze blood from a turnip, but Senator Daniel Patrick Moynihan made the *moralistic* point succinctly when he insisted society must "make the daddies pay" (see DeParle 2004).

12. Researchers distinguish carefully between work-interference-with-family or work-to-family conflict (problems or stressors from work that "spill over" into family life, decreasing the time, patience, and energy that workers have for tasks and people at home) and family-interference-with-work or family-to-work conflict (problems or stress from family that "spill over" into work, reducing productivity and increasing absenteeism, health care costs, and other organizational problems). See, e.g., Bagger, Li, and Gutek (2008); Boles, Howard, and Donofrio (2001); Estes (2003); Frone (2000); Moen and Roehling (2005); Small and Riley (1990); Thompson and Bunderson (2001). Reeves (2004) synthesizes research findings on work–family conflict specific to issues of battering and employment.

13. For example, Gerson (1985, 1993) conveys the difficult choices both women and men face as they seek to balance changing expectations for work and family (see also Townsend [2002] on men's work/family choices and Brayfield [1995] on men's "juggling jobs and kids"). Hochschild (1997, see also 2003) eloquently describes the "time bind" that results from women's increased work hours and the ironies of workplaces that feel like oases of productivity, personal growth, and appreciation compared to homes fraught with stress, drudgery, and discord. Orenstein (2000) analyzes the sensation of "flux" caused by trying to operate as both parent and worker in a "half-changed world." Hattery (2001) documents the impact of women's ideologies about mothering on their employment choices and therefore the degree to which they experience work and family as interwoven. Jacobs and Gerson (2004) place the long-running debate over interpreting changes in work, family, and gender in the context of variation in the divides between work and family, ideal and actual working time, parents and other workers, the underemployed and the overworked, and women and men. Van Echtelt et al. (2009) find that the "post-Fordist" organization of work—emphasizing autonomy, flexibility, and performance for workers in "knowledge"-based firms—is less "woman-friendly" than organizational analysts might have hoped. Bagger, Li, and Gutek (2008) provide a concise review of much of this research and find that the salience of family identities buffers the predicted deleterious effects of high family interference with work on job satisfaction, at least for women. In one of the most comprehensive treatments, on which I rely for much of the discussion about regime change in the previous chapter, Moen and Roehling (2005) place "work–family conflict" in a broad structural and cultural frame, observing the ways the class and gender bargains of America at midcentury formed a "career mystique" and a "feminine mystique." These complementary—indeed, mutually dependent—arrangements presuppose a lock-step trajectory of full-time school, breadwinning employment, and retirement for men, and a lifetime of mother-and-housewife support and part-time or interrupted labor force participation by women. In an era of increasing job insecurity, changing family and household formation and fertility patterns, and growing numbers of dual-earner households, both gendered "mystiques" have broken down. At the same time, couples can no longer rely on the traditional bargain between employers and workers in which job security and incrementally increasing returns to seniority and firm-specific skills gave male breadwinners incentives to work full time and more during women's prime reproductive years. The death throes of the old bargain—in which employers continue to expect employees to contribute to profits through extensive work effort, without accommodating the family responsibilities of their workers or providing the employment stability or steady, incremental increases in pay and benefits that formerly characterized

primary-sector employment—reproduce the gendered division of labor and neo-traditional, male breadwinner/female homemaker solutions to the dilemmas individual couples face. Moreover, the persistence of the career mystique as a set of ideas that organize expectations that are out of step with actual needs and practices intensifies contradictions and conflict.

14. See, e.g., Cunradi, Caetano, and Schafer (2002); Davis (2006); Garfield (2005); Kurz (1995). On the contradictory predictions of these models, see Riger and Krieglstein (2000).

15. Reeves (2004:115–117).

16. Reeves observes: "Despite its obvious relevance, there has been almost no research on family violence that enters the workplace" (2004:117; see also p. 120).

17. I explore this issue more fully in the next chapter.

18. See, e.g., Newman (2006); Wilson (1997). For contrasting views that focus on exploitation and alienation as characteristic properties of low-waged work in particular, see Ridzi (2009); Wacquant (2008).

19. Risman (1998). See also Bagger, Li, and Gutek (2008); Bakker and Geurts (2004); Barnett and Gareis (2002); Estes (2003); Glass (2004); Jacobs and Gerson (2004); Moen and Roehling (2005); Noonan, Estes, and Glass (2007); Thompson and Bunderson (2001).

20. Grzywacz et al. (2009).

21. See, e.g., Johnson (2008); Larson (1993)Stark (2007).

22. See, e.g., Goetting (1999); Sev'er (2002); Weiss (2000).

23. See, e.g., Davis (2006); Riger, Ahrens, and Blickenstaff (2000); Sharp (2009); Winkelmann (2004).

24. Jody Raphael's (2000) interviews with Bernice similarly show that poor men sometimes apparently perceive women's employment as threatening to sexual possessiveness and breadwinner status. She argues persuasively that threats to masculinity can motivate men's efforts to disrupt or sabotage women's work (see also Hattery 2009; Kimmel 2002). On the centrality of heterosexuality and breadwinning in projecting an appearance of hegemonic masculinity, see Connell (1995); Henson and Rogers (2001); Snyder and Green (2008).

25. For reviews, see, e.g., Brush (2000); Raphael (1999, 2001); Riger, Ahrens, and Blickenstaff (2000); Riger and Krieglstein (2000); Riger and Staggs (2004). Workplace-based surveys of the prevalence of workers' experiences with partner-perpetrated violence and abuse include research conducted by Carol Reeves, Anne O'Leary-Kelly, and their collaborators; see, e.g., O'Leary-Kelly et al. (2008); Reeves and O'Leary-Kelly (2007, 2009). More generally, on differences in and consequences of labor force attachment patterns, see Alon and Haberfeld (2007); England, Garcia-Beaulieu, and Ross (2004).

26. See, e.g., Brush (2002b); Davis (1999); Raphael (1999, 2000); Sev'er (2002); Stark (2007); Weiss (2000).

27. Stark (2007) reports a case in which an abuser coerced his partner to steal from her employer and conceal the evidence through her bookkeeping skills. Richie (1996) analyzes the ways Black women are especially vulnerable to being coerced into being accomplices in their abusers' criminal activities, with devastating consequences.

28. Examples include Bell (2003); Bell, Lohman, and Votruba-Drzal (2007); Browne, Salomon, and Bassuk (1999); Henrici (2007); Lloyd and Taluc (1999); Purvin (2003); Scott, London, and Myer (2002).

29. DeKeseredy et al. (2003); Renzetti and Maier (2002).

30. See, e.g., Brandwein (1999); Brush (1999, 2000, 2003a); CalWORKs Project (2002); Gennetain (2003); Lloyd and Taluc (1999); Purvin (2007); Tolman, Danziger, and Rosen (2002); Tolman and Raphael (2000).

31. See, e.g., Davis (1999); Kenney and Brown (1996); Murphy (1993); Olsen and Pavetti (1996); Raphael (1996).

32. Examples include Bell, Lohman, and Votruba-Drzal (2007); Browne, Salomon, and Bassuk (1999); Brush (2004); DeKeseredy et al. (2003); Koop (1985); Lown, Schmidt, and Wiley (2006); McCauley et al. (1998); Plichta and Falik (2001); Salcido (2007); Stark and Flitcraft (1996).

33. See, e.g., Bell, Lohman, and Votruba-Drzal (2007); Brush (2002b, 2003a); Lindhorst and Mancoske (2006); Lown, Schmidt, and Wiley (2006); Salcido (2007); Stark (2007); Tolman, Danziger, and Rosen (2002); Turner, Danziger, and Seefeldt (2006).

34. Reported rates of physical violence vary enormously across studies of women on public assistance, ranging from 10 to 77 percent for current or recent physical abuse (compared to a rate of less than 2 percent for women in the general population) and from 22 to 83 percent for lifetime abuse among women on public assistance (compared to 22 percent in the general population; Riger, Staggs, and Shewe 2004:802). See also Tjaden and Thoennes (1998); Tolman and Raphael (2000). The differences across studies are attributable to many factors; see Brush (2002b). Cross-study differences in reported rates and estimates of the prevalence, incidence, or severity of battering reveal much more about methods and measures for data collection in a particular study than they reveal about the specific sample or population from which it is drawn. The rates I report in this chapter are all from a cohort study. See the Methodological Appendix.

35. Barbara experienced work-specific control, abuse, and sabotage (see below). But the timing of her partner's abuse did not seem to her to be related to her working per se.

36. See Brush (2003a) for additional empirical evidence and interpretation.

37. To interfere with women's employment is one important means of men's exercising coercive control over women's everyday activities, such as housework and waged work (Stark 2007:5, 228–229).

38. See, e.g., Goetting (1999); Sev'er (2002).

39. Riger, Ahrens, and Blickenstaff (2000).

40. Brush (2000, 2002b).

41. See, e.g., Bell (2003); Purvin (2003); Raphael (2000); Scott, London, and Myers (2002).

42. Brush (1999).

43. See, e.g., Brush (2003a).

44. Brush (2003a). "Jealousy" is of course an emotion, and in the many cases where women attribute abuse to men's protecting their breadwinner status or enforcing sexual fidelity, the abuse and violence could be both expressive and instrumental.

45. See, e.g., Davis (2006); Mink (1995); Neubeck and Cazenave (2001); Quadagno (1994); Roberts (1997).

46. See, e.g., Henderson and Tickamyer (2009); Morgen, Acker, and Weigt (2010); Soss et al. (2001).

47. Henderson and Tickamyer (2009:54, references omitted). See also Brush (2001); Davis (2006); Jones-Deweever, Dill, and Schram (2009).

48. We assumed that most of these relationships were racially homogeneous. On the racial dynamics of imprisonment, probation, and sentencing, see Alexander (2010);

Loury (2008); Walker, Spohn, and DeLone (2000) Wacquant (2009); Western (2006); Wright and Herivel (2003); see also Ochoa and Ige (2007). See the next chapter for consideration of the effects of men's incarceration on women's transitions from welfare to work.

49. Raphael (2000).
50. Logan et al. (2006).
51. See, e.g., Reeves and O'Leary-Kelly (2007, 2009); O'Leary-Kelly et al. (2008).
52. On hockey players, see Faulkner (1974). On prison guards, see Britton (2003).
53. On bullying in the workplace, see Hodson, Roscigno, and Lopez (2006). On workplace sexual harassment, see MacKinnon (1979); Paetzold (2004); Stein (1999); Zippel (2006). On aggression in the workplace more generally, see Neuman (2004).
54. Baxter and Margavio (1996).
55. Duhart (2001:1).
56. Duhart (2001:2–3); Hendricks, Jenkins, and Anderson (2007:320).
57. Duhart (2001:8).
58. Duhart (2001:10); Hartley, Biddle, and Jenkins (2005); Hendricks, Jenkins, and Anderson (2007).
59. Unfortunately, Bureau of Justice Statistics data on the location of incidents in "intimate partner violence" cases do not include a specific category for the workplace. It is possible that many of the incidents involved in the 6.9 percent of IPV cases in 16 large counties in May 2002 that took place in a "public place" or "other location" were in fact incidents that occurred at the woman's workplace (Smith and Farole 2009:3), but the research evidence is extremely limited.
60. Jody Raphael (1999, 2000) reported extensively on this phenomenon in a Chicago job training program; her early observations inspired many activist-researchers, including me.
61. For examples of "beeper games" and other strategies their husbands and boyfriends use to control and frighten women, at home and beyond, see Stark (2007: chap. 8). See also Logan et al. (2006) on men's extension of stalking to work settings.
62. Hancock (2002); Ridzi (2009).
63. See previous chapter and Murphy (1993); Raphael (1996).
64. Winkelmann (2004).
65. Stark (2007:257–258).
66. Brush (2003c); Fraser and Gordon (1994); Hattery (2009); Stark (2007).
67. Public Justice Center (1990), cited in Polletta (2009).
68. Brush (2005b). See next chapter for more on estimating the work-related costs of battering for welfare recipients in Allegheny County.
69. Amott and Matthaei (1996); Hesse-Biber and Carter (2005).
70. See, e.g., Adkins and Dush (2010); Brush (2000); Danziger et al. (2000); Koop (1985); Lown, Schmidt, and Wiley (2006); McCauley et al. (1998); Plichta and Falik (2001); Romero et al. (2003); Staggs and Riger (2005); Stark and Flitcraft (1996).
71. Brush (2003d). At the time of the retrospective interviews, treating posttraumatic stress symptoms with Prozac was an "off-label" or unofficial use of the prescription antidepressant, which has since become a standard treatment. Psychopharmacological consensus notwithstanding, the question of using drugs to treat the symptoms of trauma in battered women remains vexed. On the one hand, drugs can enable women in physical and emotional pain to contain their emotions, shore up damaged self-esteem and depressed will to live, avoid collapse, and thus meet the minimalist demands of everyday life and conform to the expectations of employers, customers,

and caseworkers. On the other hand, as critics of the medicalization of social problems have pointed out more generally, "the expert 'discovery' and medical model of battering and trauma generates more intrusive interviews, bureaucratic red tape, and prescription pill-popping instead of more talking back and fighting back by welfare recipients" (Brush 2003d; see also Conrad 2007). The shattering physical and emotional pain of being abused by a current or former partner and the stress, distress, vulnerabilities, and indignities of low-wage work, poverty, welfare dependency, and social exclusion are real. They are probably best met with a combination of every means at our disposal for alleviating both painful symptoms and their probable causes. Drugs may well relieve pain, and social movement organizing for justice can be a method of pain management as well as a method for addressing root causes.

72. Brush (2000).
73. Dutton and Goodman (2005); Stets and Hammons (2002).
74. Adams (2007); Connell (1995); Kimmel (2002); Melzer (2002).
75. West and Zimmerman (1987).
76. A classic empirical rebuttal of gender-neutral theories of work organizations—in this case, specific to discrimination and tokenism rather than exchange theory, but providing a wonderfully analogous example—is sociologist Christine Williams's article proposing to complement the concept of the "glass ceiling" with the notion of the "glass escalator" (1992; see also Snyder and Green 2008).
77. Hancock (2002) and DeParle (2004) both observe the connections among a history of abuse and neglect, addiction issues, and women's ability to obtain and maintain employment or participate in activities required to maintain welfare eligibility. See also comments by Red, Takina, Jane, and other participants in the community literacy project in Chapter 5.
78. Nationally, see Shipler (2004); Shulman (2003).
79. See, e.g., Edin and Lein (1997a, 1997b).
80. Newman (2006); Stack (2001).
81. See, e.g., Hesse-Biber and Carter (2005).
82. In Allegheny County, basic living costs in 1996 were $24,376/year after taxes or $29,976/year before taxes; a living wage for a single parent with two children younger than 6 years of age was estimated at $14.84/hour in 1997. Adding 40 cents per hour per year to adjust for inflation and other increases in the cost of living, in 2001 (when these data were collected), the "self-sufficiency standard" for a single parent with two children younger than 6 years of age was $16.40/hour. These estimates are from Bangs, Kerchis, and Weldon (1997) and conversations on updates with Ralph Bangs in September 2001.
83. Mary went back to high school after she had her first child, but did not finish 10th grade. She later managed to complete a two-year associate's degree program in electronics at a local training school, but because of childcare problems, it took her four years.
84. West and Zimmerman (1987).
85. Stark (2007); West and Zimmerman (1987). The dynamics of coercive control explain both the ineffectiveness of measures such as protective orders in guaranteeing women's human rights, and why the *hitting is wrong* rhetoric and strategy of law enforcement and antiviolence programming alike has led to a "stalled revolution" in feminist efforts to end battering (Stark 2007). See Chapter 2.
86. On employers' responses to battering more generally, see Reeves (2004).
87. See Chapter 2 and the references therein, especially Moen and Roehling (2005).

88. Brush (2000, 2002b).
89. Brush (2003a, 2003b, 2003c); Collins and Mayer (2010); Morgen, Acker, and Weigt (2010).
90. See Magnet (1993) and Chapter 2.

CHAPTER 4: CALCULATING THE COSTS OF TAKING A BEATING

1. Recent overviews of the connections between poverty and battering include Renzetti (2009), who reviews the evidence from numerous large-scale studies, and Raphael (2009), who summarizes the findings from three extensive life-history interviews with women facing abuse in the context of welfare, stripping and prostitution, and addiction and imprisonment.
2. Readers who recall the sketch of the economic situations of the women in the cohort of work-first program participants we studied that I presented at the end of the previous chapter will realize that Reena's hourly earnings were at the high end of the wage distribution, well above the mean. Full-time and even part-time work at the post office has historically been very desirable for women, men of color, and especially women of color. At the post office, internal labor markets and pay scales operate according to strict qualification and seniority regulations, and hiring and promotion practices follow antidiscrimination and affirmative action principles. The occupations associated with the post office consequently have among the smallest wage gaps between female and male employees in the U.S. economy (e.g., the median weekly earnings of postal service clerks who are women is 94 percent of the median weekly earnings of postal service clerks who are men), and hourly wages are relatively high (Bureau of Labor Statistics 2008). See also Newman (2006) on housing authority and other city or civil service positions as desirable "high road" jobs that have historically offered men and women of color—even those with minimal formal education—the realistic opportunity to earn a living wage and eventually to exit poverty.
3. On the wages and efforts to make ends meet of poor single mothers and others, see also DeParle (2004); Edin and Lein (1997a, 1997b); Goode and Maskovsky (2001); Hancock (2002); Newman (2006); Shulman (2003).
4. Bangs and Weldon (1998).
5. See General Accounting Office (1998); Olson and Pavetti (1996).
6. Recall from the Introduction that the age distribution of the women at the time of the interview was *bimodal*, with most of the women falling into either the 18-to-21-year range (relatively new mothers, recently on welfare), or the 30-to-35-year range (mothers of older children, often longer-term welfare recipients). The age distribution matters because the stigmatized image of welfare recipients is utterly contradictory: *By definition, it is impossible simultaneously to be a teenager and a long-term welfare recipient.* It is also important to understand both the rate of teen childbearing and the age distribution of recipients in order to avoid what Hancock calls "correspondence bias" (2004:7)—in this instance, the assumption that welfare recipients are all teen mothers, a common error in media coverage, political rhetoric, and even some policy analyses (p. 132). Cherry (2007) exhibits this particular form of correspondence bias, especially in his Chapter 4. Reena, 38, more clearly fit the image of the long-term welfare recipient than she did the teen mother stereotype.
7. For a review of feminist conceptions of the ways contradictory expectations about earning and caring contribute to gender inequality in general and the gendered character of welfare state policies and practices, see Orloff (2009). See also Brush (2003b); Nelson (2006).

8. See especially the longitudinal Women's Employment Study (e.g., Danziger and Seefeldt 2002; Danziger et al. 2000).

9. VAWA 2005 Title II, Sec. 201(3).

10. Max et al. (2004:259).

11. Economic costs can be an important part of what sociologist Donileen Loseke calls "the public story of wife abuse" (2009:6; see also p. 2).

12. Miller, Cohen, and Wierseme (1996).

13. For the CDC report, see www.cdc.gov/ncipc/pub-res/ipv_cost/ipv.htm. See also Stanko et al. (1998); Walby (2004).

14. Farmer and Tiefenthaler (2004:313). See also the conceptual discussion of the costs of work disruption, work-related stalking, and absenteeism, tardiness, and work distraction caused by partner-perpetrated abuse in O'Leary-Kelly et al. (2008) and Logan et al. (2006).

15. See, e.g., Henrici (2006); Koop (1985); Koss et al. (1994); Lown, Schmidt, and Wiley (2006); McCauley et al. (1998); Plichta and Falik (2001); Stark and Flitcraft (1996); Tjaden and Thoennes (1998).

16. Dwyer et al. (1995).

17. Murphy (1993, 1997). See also Raphael (2000, 2004, 2007, 2009).

18. Dissociation is a cognitive and emotional process of separation. Unconsciously or deliberately, people dissociate by separating themselves from a source or experience of pain or trauma. For example, people may experience themselves as separate from their bodies or imagine a traumatic event as though it were happening to someone else or even to them but at a "safe" distance.

19. Someone with a flat affect is difficult for observers to "read" emotionally, because his or her emotional states, responses, or feelings do not seem to register in facial expression or posture. Trauma is not the only reason for flattened affect; facial expressions are socially constructed and culturally specific, and observers can have trouble perceiving emotional cues across cultural differences (e.g., when eye contact protocols vary from one culture to another) or due to perception, cognition, and expression patterns associated with autism spectrum disorders.

20. See, e.g., Herman (1992).

21. Coker et al. (2000).

22. For a summary, see O'Leary-Kelly et al. (2008).

23. Rivara et al. (2007).

24. Wisner et al. (1999).

25. Arias and Corso (2005:386).

26. Rothman and Corso (2008).

27. Readers may hear in this aspect of game theory an echo of the language and logic of the victim empowerment folklore (Berns 2009) and the exchange theory (Goode 1969) I set out in Chapters 2 and 3.

28. Farmer and Tiefenthaler (1997:338).

29. Ibid., 342.

30. Ibid., 351.

31. For feminist arguments about why this is basically the wrong question, see Goetting (1999); Weiss (2000).

32. Perhaps the least victim-blaming of these individual, psychological approaches comes from betrayal trauma theory (see, e.g., Platt, Barton, and Freyd 2009). See also Evan Stark's (2007) analysis of the "special reasonableness of battered women."

33. Farmer and Tiefenthaler (1997:339).

34. Farmer and Tiefenthaler (1997:339).
35. Farmer and Tiefenthaler (1997:346, citing Okun 1986). See also the various models of poverty and battering and the centrality of work in addressing them that I set out in Chapter 2.
36. Ū(I^W(V), X). Farmer and Tiefenthaler (2004:308).
37. Farmer and Tiefenthaler (2004:308–309).
38. Brush (2009a); Harway and O'Neil (1999); Stark (2007).
39. Farmer and Tiefenthaler (2004).
40. Brown, Salomon, and Bassuk (1999); Lloyd and Taluc (1999).
41. Brush (2004); Tolman, Danziger, and Rosen (2002).
42. Bell (2003); Purvin (2003).
43. Raphael (1996); Scott, London, and Myers (2002).
44. See, e.g., Adkins and Dush (2010); Bassuk, Browne, and Buckner (1996); Brooks and Buckner (1996); Brush (2000).
45. Raphael (1996, 1997).
46. See, e.g., Moreno et al. (2002).
47. Lehman (2000); see also Metraux and Culhane (1999); Roofless Women with Kennedy (1996).
48. See, e.g., DeKeseredy et al. (2003); Malos and Hague (1997); Rollins, Saris, and Johnston-Robledo (2001); Vostanis et al. (1996).
49. Browne, Salomon, and Bassuk (1999). See also Bufkin and Bray (1998); Toro et al. (1995).
50. See, e.g., Davis (1999); Goetting (1999); Raphael (2000); Weiss (2000).
51. Browne, Salomon, and Bassuk (1999); Brush (2000); Horsman (2000); Lloyd and Taluc (1999); Riger, Ahrens, and Blickenstaff (2000); for a summary and discussion of measurement issues, see Brush (2002b).
52. Hetling-Wernyj and Born (2002:iii).
53. See, e.g., Duterte et al. (2008); Hutchison and Hirschel (1998); Macy et al. (2005); Wolf et al. (2000).
54. Danziger et al. (2000).
55. Tolman, Danziger, and Rosen (2002:11).
56. See, e.g., Bell, Lohman, and Votruba-Drzal (2007); Brooks and Buckner, (1996); Browne, Salomon, and Bassuk (1999); Brush (2000, 2002b); General Accounting Office (1998); Lloyd and Taluc (1999); Moe and Bell (2004); Olson and Pavetti (1996); Raphael (1999, 2000, 2001); Riger, Ahrens, and Blickenstaff (2000); Riger and Staggs (2004); Shepard and Pence (1988); Swanberg and Logan (2005); Swanberg, Logan, and Macke (2005).
57. Farmer and Tiefenthaler (2004:301).
58. Ibid., 316–317.
59. Logan et al. (2006). See also Swanberg, Logan, and Macke (2005); Swanberg, Macke, and Logan (2006).
60. Farmer and Tiefenthaler (2004:313). Their rough estimate of the earnings lost by battered women who work starts with the assumption that there are approximately 1.5 million battered women in the United States, 65 percent of whom work for pay. Therefore, 975,000 women lose earnings as a result of "domestic violence." Cost per incident is approximately $20/month, and the average woman reported four incidents in the past 12 months. The cost per woman is $960/year multiplied by 975,000 battered women who work for pay = total yearly earnings lost at $936 million (p. 324).

61. Arias and Corso (2005:386). Given the wage gap (and therefore the significant difference in the market value of women's and men's labor) and the fact that Arias and Corso found *no* significant differences between women and men in mean days of productivity loss, the difference in productivity loss is especially interesting. Also, although 69.5 percent of men were employed full time and only 45.8 percent of women were employed full time, Arias and Corso did not control for days worked per year or for part-time versus full-time employment.

62. Walker, Spohn, and DeLone (2000); Western (2006); Wright and Herivel (2003).

63. Hattery (2009).

64. Hattery (2009:73). For additional examples, see Goetting (1999), Sev'er (2002), and Weiss (2000).

65. Stark (2007). See also Richie (1996) on the ways women of color may be especially vulnerable to their partners' coercing them into crime; gender and race dynamics "entrap" them into cooperating with their partners' fencing stolen goods or distributing drugs, for example.

66. Adams (2007).

67. Brush (2003d).

68. Riger, Ahrens, and Blickenstaff (2000:161).

69. Adams et al. (2008). From their description of their research procedures and findings, it is not clear if the items represent different and cumulative degrees of a phenomenon (for instance, escalating levels of work interference or severity of abuse) and therefore are associated with different points on an underlying continuum, so that their aggregation actually has the properties of a scale (Babbie 2004).

70. Farmer and Tiefenthaler (2004).

71. Another possibility is that they are both subject to some unobserved factor, in which case the model is poorly specified. See Blalock (1985).

72. Bavier (2003); Moffitt (2002).

73. Brandwein (1999b).

74. See, e.g., Brush (2001, 2003c); Stark (2007).

75. Brush (2003a).

76. I discuss attrition, or the analytical problems caused by individuals' dropping out of a longitudinal study over the course of time, in the Methodological Appendix.

77. Western (2006) summarizes many of the problems associated with the gross overrepresentation of Black men in U.S. prisons. See also Alexander (2010); Loury (2008); Wacquant (2009).

78. On protective orders as a tool for protecting battered women through the courts, see Saunders (2009).

79. See the Methodological Appendix for details on data sources and analyses, for tables and figures, and for a more technical exposition of the findings of this research.

80. Davis (1999:18).

81. Brandwein (1999b:49). The variation that Brandwein reports is the range in yearly percentages over the entire period of her study. The absolute numbers vary as well; see her Table 4.1, p. 50.

82. See Methodological Appendix for details.

83. Recall from Chapters 1 and 2 that Pennsylvania passed the Family Violence Option of the Personal Responsibility Act, allowing local welfare administrators to grant battered women temporary waivers from time limits in particular, without counting battered women against the "hardship exemptions" the states are allowed as they restructure welfare. On the rates at which local welfare offices consult experts on

battering, screen welfare applicants, and grant exemptions to time limits and work requirements through the FVO, see, e.g., Hetling and Born (2005, 2006).

84. Brandwein (1999b:49, my emphasis).
85. Brandwein (1999b:58, my emphasis).
86. Brandwein (1999b:51).
87. Hume ([1777] 1975).
88. See, e.g., Ragin (2000).
89. Logically, precedence is necessary but not sufficient for causality. Just because I smoked a pack of unfiltered Camels every day *before* I developed lung cancer doesn't guarantee that it was prolonged and intense exposure to the carcinogens in tobacco smoke that *caused* my lung cancer, but the causal relation is logically plausible. However, if I didn't start smoking cigarettes until *after* I developed lung cancer, the carcinogens in the cigarettes I smoked could not have *caused* my lung cancer.
90. See the Methodological Appendix for details.
91. Brandwein (1999b:47).
92. That is, the initial earnings difference is not exclusively attributable to the racial gap in earnings. See the Methodological Appendix, especially Tables A1 and A2.
93. Brandwein does not have data from both before and after welfare rescission, which is part of why she does not ask or answer this question.
94. See the Methodological Appendix and Hughes and Brush (2011).
95. For details, see the Methodological Appendix and Hughes and Brush (2011).
96. Bavier (2003); Moffitt (2002).

CHAPTER 5: WELFARE RECIPIENTS TALK BACK

1. See Fraser (1989) on "expert needs talk." See also Higgins and Brush (2006); Hydén (2005).
2. See the moving account of this difficulty in White (1990).
3. Higgins and Brush (2006). See also Dryzek (2000); Fearon (1998); Guttman and Thompson (2004); Macedo (1999); Poletta (2009); Polletta and Lee (2006); Przeworski (1998); Schneiderhan and Khan (2008); Steiner et al. (2004); Young (2000).
4. This notion is from Mills (1959).
5. Throughout this chapter and the next, I present materials from the community literacy project as the writers produced and approved them in the booklet they collectively created. Spelling, grammar, and formatting (bullet points, italics, etc.) are reproduced as the writers presented them. In a few instances, as I did in the interview excerpts in the chapter on work-specific control, abuse, and sabotage, I have removed institutional identifiers.
6. Red and the other writers in the community literacy project chose their own pseudonyms. The women called themselves Red, Jane, Nikki, Takina, J.J., Jule, Jasmine, and Robin. They also chose pseudonyms or omitted names for other people featured in their writing. For details, see the Methodological Appendix.
7. On the elements of narrative, see Loseke (2009:2). See also Davis (2002); Herman (1999, 2002, 2009).
8. Peck, Flower, and Higgins (1995).
9. For details on the community literacy project, see the Methodological Appendix and Higgins and Brush (2006). On rivaling, see Flower, Long, and Higgins (2000).
10. The writers met face-to-face with local caseworkers and job developers from the welfare office who had read their narratives. Equipped with their polished narratives,

the writers engaged the caseworkers on the relatively neutral territory of the community literacy project. In addition to the narratives, in this chapter I draw from field notes and transcripts of the collective conversation that ensued.

11. Hancock (2004). See Chapter 2 for an extensive discussion of the politics of disgust and the "'work-first' common sense" (Ridzi 2009) that accompanied those politics during the period I conducted the interviews and literacy project. See also Higgins and Brush (2006).

12. Fine (1993:286).

13. For a historical review through the Family Support Act of 1988, see Brush (1997); Mink (1995); Naples (1991). See also Nelson (2005).

14. Institutional ethnographer Dorothy Smith theorizes the everyday world as problematic ([1974] 1987, 1987). See also Gould (2009).

15. Higgins and Brush (2006). See also Mildorf (2007); Polletta (2009); Stark (2007).

16. See Chapter 2 and Berns (2009).

17. To the extent possible, I have included lengthy excerpts and maintained formatting such as bullet points in order to preserve the integrity of the writers' contributions to the community literacy project.

18. Higgins and Brush (2006).

19. See Abramovitz ([1988] 1996).

20. In addition to the narratives, lists of contributing factors, and discussions of rival perspectives the participants in the community literacy project produced, what follows also draws from field notes and transcripts from group discussions with the writers about the project and each other's written work and from a face-to-face meeting between the writers and a group of caseworkers and job developers from a local welfare office. See the Methodological Appendix for details.

21. These section headings are from the conversations we had with the writers and capture their sense of the rhetoric they face. This chapter does not exhaust the set of myths and stereotypes the writers enumerated and addressed, which included the following:
    - Welfare recipients are too lazy to undertake the difficult preparations necessary for a better life.
    - Welfare recipients have multiple kids by multiple fathers to get welfare checks. Welfare encourages promiscuity and women having children they cannot afford.
    - Welfare recipients don't want to work. People on welfare act as though the government owes them a living.
    - These welfare people are buying shrimp and lobster, and ordinary taxpayers, working people, can't afford to buy such things. Living on welfare is living in luxury.

22. See, e.g., Hesse-Biber and Carter (2005); Moen (2003); Moen and Roehling (2005).

23. When she mentioned having watched "after-school specials" about teen pregnancy, Robin could have been referring to a CBS Schoolbreak Special titled "Babies Having Babies" (Auerbach and Montgomery 1986). The phrase was a common one in political and popular culture at the time, when Robin was finishing high school.

24. On political, emotional, and practical obstacles these writers faced to participating in the community literacy project, see Higgins and Brush (2006).

25. Ridzi (2009). See also Chapter 2.

26. See, e.g., Collins (1994); Garfield (2005); Omolade (1994); Roberts (1997).

27. For analyses, see, e.g., Gilens (1999); Solinger (2001); Soss et al. (2001).

28. See, e.g., Scott (2010) on mothers of children with disabilities.

29. On some of the contradictions of these desires and the rhetoric and expectations of intensive mothering that go along with them, see Hays (1996, 2003).
30. The interviews and the community literacy project materials also make clear the importance of their children's disabilities or health problems in poor women's lives. Their responsibilities for caring for ill or disabled children contribute to these women's vulnerability to poverty and dependency on men.
31. Sassen (2001).
32. For example, Newman (2006) and Stack (2001) document instances of parents and their teen children who are competing for jobs at the same fast-food establishments.
33. See Newman (2006). On the widespread problem of low-wage work in the United States in the 1990s and 2000s, see especially Shulman (2003).
34. See, e.g., Collins and Mayer (2010); Edin and Lein (1997a); Hesse-Biber and Carter (2005); Moen and Roehling (2005); Newman (2006).
35. Vankatesh (2009).
36. Ridzi (2009).
37. Magnet (1993).
38. On hard living, see Kurz (1995). On the ways this formidable combination can result in the man's exercising coercive control without physical violence, see Stark (2007).
39. See especially Mills (2003).
40. Berns (2009).
41. Ridzi (2009).
42. See, e.g., Crenshaw (1994); Davis (2006); Garfield (2005); Potter (2008); Richie (1996); Stark and Buzawa (2009).

CHAPTER 6: CONCLUSIONS

1. In *The Origins of the Family, Private Property, and the State,* Marx's collaborator Friedrich Engels ([1884] 1970) famously argues that the twin pillars of women's subordination are women's domestication and monogamous marriage. Monogamy and the gendered sexual double standard regulate women's fertility and fidelity in the interests of private property, rules of inheritance, and certainty about paternity. More important for our present concerns with the conventional wisdom about work, Engels asserts that the material basis for women's domestication is a combination of men's economic supremacy and, above all, women's exclusion from social production (in a capitalist mode of production, waged labor). For feminist elaboration, see, e.g., Lerner (1986), and for feminist critique, see, e.g., MacKinnon (1983).
2. MacKinnon (2006); Sen (1985, 2009); Stark (2007). See also Libal and Parekh (2009).
3. Ridzi (2009). See Chapter 2.
4. See Chapters 2 and 5.
5. As in the previous chapter, these materials are verbatim excerpts from the writers' contributions to the community literacy project.
6. See Chapter 2.
7. See, e.g., Goldstein (2001); Jurik (2005); Kingfisher (2001); Rose (1993, 1996).
8. Ridzi (2009). See Chapter 2.
9. Berns (2009). See Chapter 2.
10. For this concept, I am drawing most directly from Stark (2007), but there is a long and distinguished feminist tradition in this vein. My personal favorite is Elizabeth Cady Stanton's 1892 speech (delivered when she resigned from the National American

Woman Suffrage Association at the age of 77) contemplating the fundamental "solitude of the self" and the consequent importance of preparing every woman to serve as captain of her own vessel (1981).

11. Foucault ([1979] 1991, 1980, [1981] 1988). See also Brush (2003b); Cruikshank (1996); Kingfisher (2001); Rose (1993, 1996).

12. See, e.g., Arnold (2009); Collins and Mayer (2010); Levin (2001); Lindhorst and Padgett (2005); Morgen, Acker, and Weigt (2010); Piven (2001); Pollack and Davis (1997); Ridzi (2009); Schram (2006).

13. To quote the unanimous declaration of the 13 United States of America: "… life, liberty and the pursuit of happiness. That to secure these rights, governments are instituted…."

METHODOLOGICAL APPENDIX

1. Brush (2002b); Riger, Ahrens, and Blickenstaff (2000).

2. Davis (2006); Neubeck and Cazenave (2001).

3. See, e.g., Brush (1999, 2000); Bell, Lohman, and Votruba-Drzal (2007); Browne, Salomon, and Bassuk (1999); Lloyd and Taluc (1999); Lown, Schmidt, and Wiley (2006).

4. The material in this section of the appendix closely follows Hughes and Brush (2011), which is also the source for all of the tables and figures in the appendix.

5. In addition to subject identifiers, protective order records include the dates of preliminary hearings (for a temporary, one-week injunction), dates of follow-up hearings (at which the family court judge could grant a 12-month restraining order), and dates of repeat filings (with the same defendant or a different defendant).

6. Cash assistance for low-income mothers was called Aid to Families with Dependent Children (AFDC) before the PRA and Temporary Assistance to Needy Families (TANF) after Congress rescinded entitlements in 1996. The welfare records include time-varying monthly data on welfare receipt and the number of individuals in the household on welfare as well as subject-varying measures of race-ethnicity, age, and sex.

7. An unconditional model shows how one variable changes over time, without any other predictors ("conditions") included.